HOW TO RENOVATE
A HOUSE IN FRANCE

How to Renovate a House in France

By David Ackers, Jérôme Aumont, & Paul Carslake

Published by Ascent Publishing Ltd
2 Sugar Brook Court
Aston Road, Bromsgrove
Worcestershire
B60 3EX

ISBN 0-9544669-3-4

First published in the United Kingdom by Ascent Publishing Limited, 2004

Colour reproduction by Wyndeham Argent
Printed in the United Kingdom by Wyndeham Grange
Paper supplied by McNaughton Publishing Papers Ltd

www.renovationfrance.net
Email us! renovation@centaur.co.uk

HOW TO RENOVATE A HOUSE IN FRANCE

THE ESSENTIAL GUIDE TO CREATING YOUR DREAM HOME IN FRANCE

BY DAVID ACKERS, JÉRÔME AUMONT & PAUL CARSLAKE

Contents

Chapter 1
THE RIGHT HOUSE

What kind of house do you really want in France? We discuss the options, from the tiny holiday cottage to the eventual retirement home. And is it ever possible to make a killing on French property?

Chapter 2
WHAT'S THE DAMAGE?

A run through of all the trouble-spots to look out for when buying a house. Plus an introduction on how to get the building work going.

Chapter 3
THE APPROACH

How good a job do you really need to do? We compare the 'purist' approach to restoring old property with the more down-to-earth, quicker, and cheaper route. Take your pick!

Chapter 4
RECLAIMED MATERIALS

If you want to add a bit more authenticity and beauty to your project, you can go out and buy it. A guide to what's around.

Chapter 5
ROOFS & WALLS

The heavy duty work needed to get your house weatherproof. We look at the various roof styles across France, and how to make your stone walls look good.

Chapter 6
SORTING OUT THE INSIDE

More serious building work here, with a guide to damp-proof courses, new upper floors, and options for how to deal with walls inside your house.

Contents

Chapter 7
**MAKING
WOOD GOOD**

The charm of flaking paint and 19th century fittings on windows, doors and shutters can quickly wear off if they start to fall apart. How to renew without ruining the look.

Chapter 8
**LOFTY
AMBITION**

Creating a room in the roof can add value to your home, as well as giving you extra space. A guide to what's involved.

Chapter 9
THE CAVE

If you have a spare basement or outbuilding on your property, you could turn it into a French-style cave, or wine cellar. It's also a place where blokes hang out together. Helps bonding with your neighbours.

Chapter 10
**KITCHENS &
BATHROOMS**

Creating an individual kitchen or bathroom, with a bit of French style to it, is not as difficult as you may think!

Chapter 11
FIREPLACES

It's not just a large part of the French population that is addicted to smoking. Many big fireplaces are too! We try to find out why. Plus some tips on using wood-burning stoves.

Chapter 12
**GARDENS &
TERRACES**

If you are renovating inside, you could renovate outdoors too. An introduction to some of the ways of using space outside the house.

Chapter 13
**SWIMMING
POOLS**

A look at what's on the market, how they are put together, and what they can cost.

The Basics

Acknowledgements

Apologies in advance to anyone we have forgotten on this long list. Our warmest thanks to: Catherine and Martin Gamble for providing the inspiration for this project; the international team at Coté-Maison in Paris for work on our earlier ventures in this area; Peter Harris and the Ascent and Centaur teams for support and ideas; Estelle Kalp for designing the book; Charlotte Saint-Arroman and Nan Maokhamphiou for keeping it all together in London; for comments on drafts, thanks to Ian and Mary Roberts, Surveyors en France (with special thanks to Pierre Weingaertner and James Latter), Derek Rogers, and Oliver Cockell. For technical expertise, thanks to Olivier Bermond, Architecte dplg; Hélène Benault, Architecte de Bâtiments de France; Alain Mainhagu, 'taille de pierre' teacher extraordinaire; colleagues at UNAID; Bruno, Pascal & Alain at BCA Matériaux Anciens. For sound technical advice, thanks to Sébastien and Emmanuel, and for their tireless support, 'merci' to Stéphanie and Mireille; for further technical comment on drafts, thanks to Philippe Piédon-Lavaux, Craig Hutchinson, Ray Fletton, Imogen Barneaud, and Marc-Henri Hermann (contact details on page 220). And in production, thanks to Ray Granger for additional words, and to Jacqui Canham and David Fowler for the thorough proof-reading, and to sub-editors John Dunn and Lee Johnson. Thanks finally to all the photographers and agencies for some brilliant work.

Welcome to How to Renovate a House in France!

This book has been created with the simple aim of helping you out with your renovation projects in France, whatever the size of your property, and whatever your budget.

Doing up an old place ought to be a fun, pleasurable and very rewarding experience. That's how it should be. But we have all heard stories where projects go horribly wrong. The large number of partly-renovated old properties on the market in France suggests that many of these renovation projects are not as easy as people think.

In this book, we want to get your creative juices flowing, to help you decide what is best for your house, and to show you what kind of work will be involved in making your dream become a reality.

We also hope to help you dodge potential problems, and complete your renovation project with a smile on your face, as the proud owner of a beautiful property in France.

And to avoid hunting around on the internet for English guides to the French way of doing things, we have included a whole chunk of heavy-duty administrative stuff about buying a property, planning permission, builders, project planning, septic tanks and more, in the back section of this book. There's even a short piece about kissing your new neighbours!

So enjoy the book – and good luck with your projects.

Or, as our French friends would say: 'Bonne lecture et bon courage!'

FOR SALE:
Desirable single-story
holiday home to renovate.
Peaceful location with
open views across
lavender fields. Traditional
design, lots of original
features, chimney, porch.
Accommodation comprises
one room, with the possi-
bility to extend, subject to
a change in the planning
laws, if you're lucky.
Water and electricity in the
local village. Nearest
access road 300m.
Ideal for those seeking
to downshift from a busy
urban lifestyle, and
who enjoy a challenge.

THE RIGHT HOUSE

Only you can know if you have found the right house in France. Like many people, you may have started your house hunting without a clear idea of what kind of house you really wanted, and relied simply on luck and gut feeling to guide your choice. Eventually though, you begin to picture yourself living in the place, spending holidays there, inviting friends around, and enjoying it. And once you know exactly why you have bought the house, you start to get a much clearer idea about how you want to renovate it.

Plenty of room for your friends Vast houses can look like good value for money, but often the price is low because the expense of the renovation work needed puts off many buyers. Of course, a big place is great for family gatherings, but if you decide to run part of your house as a gîte to help pay the bills, what will you do if your friends and relatives expect to come and stay with you for free, right in the middle of your peak letting season?

'In the summer, you could get your younger guests to sleep in tents, creating a mini-Glastonbury festival.'

Wherever you choose to go house hunting in France, the odds are that you will already have done a fair bit of research into the logistics of getting there, the local property prices, climate, hours of sunshine, nearest major towns, attractions, beaches, mountains and so on. You may also have thought about what kind of place would suit your friends and family who might come to stay with you: whether they are kids who want somewhere safe and fun to play, elderly relatives who want to avoid steep steps, or just groups of friends who'd like somewhere comfortable to stay when they make the journey across to France to visit you.

And there is quite a difference between what goes into making a successful holiday home and a place where you may eventually move permanently to start a new life in France, or simply to retire.

The right house for the right reason

The occasional holiday home It would be a safe guess that most of the current wave of British people (and many other non-French Europeans too) who are buying a place in France are doing so with the aim of creating a holiday home. Affordability and location are the top priorities for most house hunters. The first obviously depends on your budget, while location will, of course, be influenced by regional airports and budget airlines, and by motorway or ferry links, not to mention the climate, proximity to the sea, mountains, or beautiful countryside. And when considering a holiday home, don't ignore the 'holiday' part of the deal. In terms of simple bricks and mortar, it is easy to find an ideal second home in France. But quite a few are in a place where you might only want to go on holiday once or twice.

A third important factor, which is often overlooked, is size: how big a house do you actually need?

If the plan is to entertain family, friends, children or grandchildren with the possibility of everyone turning up at Christmas or in the summer, you may be tempted to get a large place with the potential of loft conversion or outbuildings to turn into guest rooms. However, these kind of conversion projects can be expensive, and there are much cheaper alternatives. In the summer, for example, if you have a bit of space in the garden, you could get some of your younger guests to sleep in tents, creating a kind of mini-Glastonbury rock festival on your own doorstep. In the winter, if you are near enough to a decent guesthouse or B&B, you could put up your guests there. Even if you paid for rooms and hired a car for your guests every time they came to visit, and bought them each a bottle of champagne to drink on arrival, this could still work out a lot cheaper and less troublesome than converting a barn into guest rooms.

'If your house is miles from the nearest large supermarket, you will need plenty of space to store food.'

Pools winner
The gîte business is a tough one, and with more renovated barns and out-houses coming into the market every year, competition is fierce. A swimming pool will boost your chances of getting bookings, though it is worth working out what your profit will be on the rentals you charge, and how many weeks it will take for the pool to pay for itself.

Alternatively, if there are other second homes in your local area, you could get to know the owners and rent or even simply borrow one of these for your guests.

However, even if you decide not to create a lot of additional guest sleeping space, you may still want to consider the size of your dining area and reception room. Do you have a dining area large enough to get a table of, say, a dozen people sitting down at the same time, and a reception room where people can circulate easily over an aperitif?

Then there are practical factors like the kitchen. If your house is some distance from a town, you will need plenty of space to store food to avoid making endless trips to the supermarket during your holidays. Enough space for two large fridges, for example, and a freezer, can be extremely useful.

If you are lucky enough to afford a spacious house with plenty of guest space, consider how many bathrooms you need, and make sure the plumbing system can cope. Your guests in the winter months will thank you for a good heating system. Note that if you are planning to install oil-fired central heating, the boilers can be pretty big and quite noisy when they fire up overnight, so need a room all of their own. And be generous with sound insulation.

The second home to rent out If you plan to make some money by renting out your home, it is worth knowing how much you can expect to make before starting out on expensive renovation work. If you look at the market for holiday rentals in your chosen area, via web-sites, private ads or brochures, you will find out what is the 'going rate' for various kinds of rentals. But take a pessimistic view of rental income. Bear in mind that the weekly rental charged in brochures

Planning restrictions get stricter

If you find a property that appears to be full of potential for expansion, you will need to get up to speed on the relevant planning restrictions. It is impossible to generalise on what would or would not be acceptable. But here are two situations where you could easily run into trouble. One is when your property is within a few hundred metres of some kind of listed building – such as a chateau, a church, or even a historic ruin. The other is if your property is quite spacious in relation to the amount of land that it sits on. In these circumstances, converting a barn or even just a loft space could tip you into the danger zone in terms of the maximum living space allowed on a given plot size.

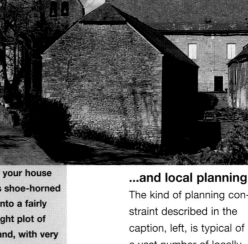

A fine old listed building dominates not only the village, but the local planning rules too. If your house is within five hundred metres of a listed building (un monument historique), your freedom to alter the external appearance of your property will be limited.

Listed buildings...
Looking out of your upper windows at a 15th century chateau across the valley may provide you with a great view, but it could also lead to some planning headaches. Under the current ruling, if your house is within 500m of a 'monument historique' (the equivalent of a listed building in the UK) then any new building, demolition or renovation work will need approval from the official, national French planning authority: the *Architecte des Bâtiments de France* (the ABF). Even if the property is outside this zone, but within line of sight of the listed building, then you will still need to get special permission for exterior work to your property. This rule cuts both ways. On the one hand, it can seem a tough constraint on what you can do with your property. However, it is also the driving force that keeps some of France's villages so stunningly beautiful.
For more on planning, see p193, and for protection zones, p203.

If your house is shoe-horned onto a fairly tight plot of land, with very little to spare, then you could find that converting one of your barns is ruled out by local planning laws. This is designed to avoid overcrowding, especially in villages.

...and local planning
The kind of planning constraint described in the caption, left, is typical of a vast number of locally-based measures drawn up by local communes in France, and which are to be found in the local planning document. This is either the *Plan d'Occupation des Sols* (POS) or the newer, PLU, or *Plan Local d'Urbanisme*, which is gradually replacing the POS. These plans carve up the local area into zones where you can or cannot build, and include a host of rules and regulations. If you have a project in mind (such as a change-of-use from a barn to a gîte, for example), then to be on the safe side, you can apply for outline planning permission (the *Certificat d'Urbanisme*) during the three-month gap between signing the *Compromis de Vente* and the final *Acte de Vente* when the sale is completed. You will then know for sure that you can make that vital barn conversion once you own the house.

does not reflect what the owners get: agencies typically take 15%, and sometimes 30%, and some holiday companies and websites that spend big money on marketing could take a 50% cut of what your guests are paying per week. The other crucial factor is how much time the property is left unrented, earning you no money. One simple way to assess this risk is to find holiday rentals in the area you are interested in, ring up during peak season and ask about availability in a fortnight's time. If properties are generally available, it suggests there could be a bit of a glut in the market. That is not the end of the world, but it could mean that starting up your rental business could be slow, at least before 'word-of-mouth' helps you out.

If you want to get bookings where others don't, you may need to invest in a good swimming pool, choose a good-looking house in a popular location, and put aside a marketing budget. Your renovation project will have to look great too, right down to the last detail of home decoration.

Letting a home is something of a 'people business' and the welcome your guests receive needs to be carefully judged according to what they want. Do they want to be your best friends for the week, or would they prefer to do their own thing? If they come back again, you will be getting customers next year for no extra marketing spend. Trying to get such repeat business can be elusive, and depends partly on the holiday potential of your location, but also on the care, attention and money you have spent on the accommodation.

The most important thing to remember is there are lots of new gîtes opening in France all the time, so competition is fierce. The best approach is to create a very good gîte, but don't start off in a position where you rely on the rental income to live on.

'Ring up holiday home rentals in peak season and ask about availability in two weeks' time. If properties are

The school run
Small rural schools in France are becoming an endangered species as pupil numbers fall and budget cuts start to force closures or mergers, not without vigorous protests from outraged parents. For many British families moving to France to live there permanently, the education system is a major attraction, despite the linguistic challenge. But it is worth checking to see if the local school in your area will still be there in five years' time.

'enerally free, it suggests there is a glut in the market.'

Hedging your bets over crime

Rural crime in France exists, of course, and the most sensible way to get peace of mind is to invest in good quality doors, windows, and shutters. Don't leave anything really valuable in your house, and buy a good insurance policy. Beyond this though, buying a house that is not too isolated, or which can be seen by passers-by, will help. Ideally, get to know the neighbours, let them know when you are expecting visitors, or even pay someone to visit the property regularly. It will all add to your peace of mind.

Network operators Gîtes de France is the biggest and best-known network of gîtes, and runs a five-level quality ranking system taking account of the outside space, the quality of the building, and its internal decor. There are currently around 42,000 rural gîtes in its network, with some 2,000 being added each year. According to its own figures, the average gîte will be rented for around 17 weeks per year. One in four clients are non-French.

The B&B business As with the casual rental of your second home, you will need to look closely at the B&B market, or *chambres d'hôtes* as this is known in French. Living in France and running a B&B business (for example, in your converted barn or outhouses) is hard work. But as it is a relatively easy business to get into, there will be plenty of rivals out there, all seeking a slice of the same market. Getting passing trade would be a bonus, but for that you will have to think about the nearest main road and what kind of holiday traffic it carries before you even buy your property.

The longer term second home If you are planning on living in your second home for months at a time, certain elements of the location, such as proximity to decent shops, become much more important. Equally, the level of finish required will become higher, especially in terms of your central heating, insulation, kitchens and bathrooms.

You will probably want covered parking for your car, and a high level of security against burglary, as you will be leaving more valuable possessions in the house. If the place is eventually to become a permanent home, when you retire, for example, then the amenities of a local town will become essential.

'The trick now is to get in at the start of the next wave: to discover which département will become 'th

new Dordogne'. It's a gamble, easy to get wrong.'

The permanent home for emigrating families OK, it's obvious. Schools, shops, a nearby town centre, and jobs. If you led an urban lifestyle in Britain, consider the double impact of not only emigrating and having to learn a new language, but shifting into a rural lifestyle as well. Talk to people who have done it, and find out about the downside of downshifting as well as all the advantages.

Village schools are great for young children, but class sizes are dropping and some face being axed or merged, meaning a bus ride or a school run every day. Rural property that is close to motorway links is always more expensive, but you are in effect paying for the convenience.

Some people are considering the possibilities of living in France and working 'freelance' for overseas companies via the internet. Eventually, everyone will have a broadband link, though for the time being, in some communes, you will not get broadband unless a minimum number of subscribers are prepared to pay for it. So choosing a village with a large number of non-French settlers, or one popular with a new generation of younger French people, could turn out to be a sound move.

The investment property A real gamble this one, as the property market in France moves only sluggishly and making big gains on the property ladder is hard to do. That said, in certain rural second home hotspots people who got in early have made a killing, with prices doubling for some kinds of properties over the last five years. The trick now is to get on at the start of the next new wave: to discover which *département* will become 'the new Dordogne.'

If you buy a property with the idea of doing it up and then selling it for a profit, keep in mind the people who will buy the property from you. A cheap house needing a bit of work, in a nice village, will usually sell quickly. But if you renovate the house rather too lavishly,

'At first glance, it looks like an incredibly ambitious project: you live as a resident in one country, and try to

someone to handle: you live as a resident in one country, and try to get a new house built in another. However, a new house project can be a good deal more straightforward than a renovation project, which can be hard to plan and manage from a distance because of unseen problems that only appear once the job has started.

With a new-build, you will spend a great deal of time on the initial planning with your architect or building company, but after that, once the site starts, it should run to a predictable time-frame and budget. Less lying awake at night worrying, then, and a more reliable project all round.

Fun with timber OK, we admit it: this fits in with nobody's image of that charming little place in France. But a newly-built home can be economical and very stylish, as this timber-framed home shows only too well. Costs compare well with buying and renovating a farmhouse.

and put it on the market for a higher price to cover your costs, you could be a long time looking for buyers. A study carried out in the early 1990s by London University researchers found that many British buyers preferred to buy their French second home from French owners, as if buying a house from other Brits somehow spoiled the dream!

Above all, you will need to make sure that your renovation work is appreciated by the future buyers, and not ripped out because they don't share your sense of style.

It sounds obvious, but the smaller the house you buy, the cheaper and quicker will be the renovation work required. Even if it needs a new roof, it will only be a small roof. If you are stripping beams, there will not be that many to strip. And so on. In fact, you can work wonders on a pocket-sized place, and sell it on as a charming and affordable little holiday home, for a modest profit if you are lucky.

Building a new house

With pressure on prices starting to show in some of the most popular regions of France for second home ownership, it is little wonder that some people seeking holiday homes are looking instead at building plots and thinking about constructing a new home.

At first glance, this looks like an incredibly ambitious project for

The downside, in many people's eyes, of the new build is the kind of knee-jerk feeling that the house will either lack charm, or else look like a tacky copy of an 'authentic' older French house. It is certainly possible to commission an architect or house-builder to design you a house lacking in charm, and you don't have to go far in France to find them. You will also find a few tacky lookalike rustic houses, though this is quite rare because local planning restrictions tend to discourage this. However, there are some truly brilliant examples of new houses throughout France, built either in a completely contemporary style, or in a style that makes a close and faithful copy of a traditional local house. Timber-framed homes are relatively quick to erect, and can be exciting architecturally. Some people have copied New England-style clapper-board houses, and built them in the middle of the pine forests bordering the Atlantic.

All this does not have to be expensive or time-consuming. If you imagine a new build taking about a year to complete from start to finish, it compares well with an averagely complicated renovation job. The value of land is, of course, directly linked with the location, but for an individual, good quality new property you could end up paying less than for a similar sized old house plus all the renovation costs. So it's worth thinking about. (For more on the ins and outs of getting a new house built, see pp198-201.)

et a new house built in another. But it can be a good deal more straightforward than a renovation project.'

New for old
New builds do not have to be ultra-modern, of course. This house on Ile d'Yeu, off the west coast of France, takes all its style from traditional architecture, and will quickly weather itself into a house that looks much older than it really is, thanks to careful use of traditional materials (the roman tiles, the exposed stone, the natural lime renders). Inside, though, expect all the conveniences of a modern house.

Chapter 2

WHAT'S THE DAMAGE?

ASSESSING THE WORK REQUIRED

'I've bought a stone barn in Normandy to renovate. It's just the stone walls and a roof. All it needs now is the insides. Can anyone help?' This plea for advice, seen on a website chat forum, shows the scale of the problem facing some people embarking on a project in France. 'All it needs now is the insides' suggests that in this person's mind, it is a simple job. Buy a barn or ruin that has been unoccupied for fifty years. Then, get a builder in for a week or so, install those 'insides', and let that lazy holiday idyll begin. If only!

Room to expand
A typical farmhouse configuration, with the adjoining stone barn which could be converted into additional living space. Despite the flaking render on the low wall running in front of the buildings, the walls of the house and barn have been looked after, and the shutters and windows are in good condition. Converting the barn raises the question of where to create window openings without ruining its character. The tiny vents just below the eaves of the barn should not be enlarged. However, the barn door could be glazed, and one or more tall, narrow windows could also look good. Rooflights may be less effective where ceilings are very high.

If only it were as simple as that. But unfortunately, as anyone who has ever tried to renovate anything knows, the only certainty at the start of any project is that there is bound to be uncertainty just around the corner. Buying an old building to renovate is no different. You don't know what you're getting yourself into. Which is all part of the excitement.

When looking at an older property, it is probably better to think about it as you would if you were buying a second-hand classic sports car, rather than a romantic dream home. Rusty bodywork, or sagging suspension, don't make an old car more beautiful. But for the more romantic buyers of French property, a peeling wall or sagging roof just adds to the charm. Yes, the existing patina of flaking paint, or mould, or moss, or just dirt, can get some house buyers pretty excited. But at the same time, it can hide some very nasty defects.

However much estate agents will charm you with their lovely French accents and hospitable glasses of *apéritif maison* at the end of

'Imagine the estate agents are selling you a used car, and kick the proverbial tyres. Be sharp, and be savvy.'

a hot afternoon's house hunting, you will need to keep things in perspective. Why not imagine they are selling you a used car, and kick the proverbial tyres. In short, be sharp, and be savvy.

The problem for most people, though, is to know how much the potential renovation work will cost relative to the cost of the house. The authors' project records show the most dramatic ratio of 'purchase price to restoration costs' to date as 1:10, which is exceptional. A typical DIY renovation with a bit of artisan input could cost as little as one tenth of the purchase price. However, there is a vast spec-

Nature trail
Check for damage from roots, or damp, if a house is hidden by foliage. Drain runs can be badly affected by roots, while thick foliage prevents walls drying out properly. Uprooting is the answer.

'Seek out trusted locals, and ask them to recommend a good builder.'

trum between these two extremes – representing tens of thousands of pounds of expense. A great many renovators spend between one quarter and three-quarters of the cost of the house on building works. If you just buy a shell of a house (the walls, roof, windows and doors) then the renovation works will probably equal the purchase price of the house.

Surveys of the kind carried out for mortgage lenders in the UK are not required in France. However, most buyers would benefit from expert advice before committing to buy, and you can find English-speaking surveyors (some are actually British surveyors who have moved to France) who will give your potential purchase a thorough examination. You will also usually get a detailed document describing the building and its faults, and giving a priority hit-list of what building jobs are required to put it right.

In terms of the buying process, the time to do this is once you have found the house you think you want to buy. At this stage, you include the so-called *clauses suspensives* which are basically get-out clauses that you can have inserted into the contract, provided the vendor agrees. This means you could, for example, agree to buy the house subject to the structure being assessed as sound by an independent expert, or subject to outline planning permission being granted for a barn conversion. (For more on the buying process, see pp168-176.)

Your estate agent may offer to find you a builder to assess the property. Whether you take them up on this (and it is the easiest path), or try to find a builder yourself, comes down to the level of trust you feel you have established with your agent. If you do try to find a builder independently, seek out trusted locals and ask them if they can recommend someone.

We will return to the question of builders and running the project at the end of this chapter, and again on pp190-193. First, we aim to run through the various things you should be thinking about when you are viewing an old rural house. It's not quite the same as having a builder right alongside you, but it's a start.

The roof

The first thing most French people look at when buying a house is the roof. However, many British people seeking their rural dream home in France will try not to look too closely – on the basis that the older and more uneven the roof, the more charming the house. In reality, though, drafts, leaks, termites or woodworm are not so appealing, and have to be dealt with, particularly

ALL ABOUT EAVES
This undulating roof will probably leak, as the canal tiles no longer fit together properly. But the roofing job could be limited to replacing a section of the roofing timbers, and re-using most of the existing tiles.

if the first phase of the work will involve any loft conversions. If the roof is not sound, the rest of your renovation works will suffer.

Carpentry is key. The condition of the timbers is crucial, and they could have been weakened by woodworm or the effects of rain and damp. You will need a professional to assess this for you, and it is vital information. A new roof cover with new timbers could be double the price of a new roof cover alone.

Looking for trouble

Thatched roofs if looked after, can last for up to 40 years. So if you are buying a thatched house, it is essential to find out when the roof was last replaced or substantially repaired, and which local thatchers you can turn to. They are a rare breed. One renovation project in Haute Normandie involved a wait of a year before the chosen thatcher could start. He then juggled several sites simultaneously and finished the job a year later. Only then could interior refurbishment work really get going.

When you look at slate and tiled roofs (take binoculars, and get inside the roof space if you can) watch out for any tiles that are slipping – usually caused by the nails, slate hooks or pegs that fixed them failing. If some are already failing, then it's likely that they are all heading that way, and the problem will just get worse. What's more, the French slates (*ardoises*) originally from the Angers region and which are found on much housing in France, are not as durable as those used in Britain, and are thus more prone to crack or split if you try to re-use them.

As well as the visible gutters and downspouts, the flashing work is largely unseen, often in zinc, and may need renewal too.

If you are planning to convert the loft space into rooms, and will install skylights or dormer windows of some kind, then there is even more reason to carefully repair or renew the roof at the outset. For one thing, you should start with a sound roof cover (at least checked over by a roofer) if you are to convert the loft space. And if you are chopping out large swathes of roof to make space for Velux or other windows, it could be worth renewing the whole roof at the same time.

You may be surprised at the size of the holes needed to create skylights. And so renewing rusted slate hooks (for example) on the remaining areas of roof may be an affordable task once the scaffolding (for the skylights) is already in place.

On canal tiled roofs the roof slope is less steep, and the tiles sit one on top of the other. Here it is more likely to be bad weather, or more seriously, the deterioration of the wooden roofing structure itself, that will cause tiles to slip, or gaps to open up between them. (More on this in Chapter 5.)

If a roof 'sags' this may not necessarily be a bad thing. Some buildings with slated or tiled

HOW FAR DO YOU GO?
One of the problems you could face is working out how to stop renovation work from ruining the character of your property. Strip the moss from the roof, and the greenery from the walls of this fairy-tale cottage, and its unique charm is dramatically reduced. However, if the work is essential, you will have no choice.

NEW TILES REQUIRED, BUT GREAT OLD TIMBER STRUCTURE RETAINED
This roof on this house was covered with the basic kind of *tuiles mécaniques* which interlock (*simple emboîtement*) but which are eventually prone to frost damage and deterioration. They need to be laid over waterproof roofing felt if you want to avoid leaks as the roof ages. Vegetation growing out of the flashing around the chimney stack is a sure sign of a lack of maintenance. In fact, this roof needed replacing, though the timber structure turned out to be sound, and was retained. The owner eventually added insulation and renovated the already converted loft-space.

Looking for trouble

roofs had a curve designed into the structure at verges and eaves from the start. This is because a slightly concave surface from ridge to eaves allowed the overlapping tiles to form a better weatherproof seal, and could direct water run-off away from more leaky masonry areas such as the base of chimney stacks and gable ends. Such features may still be seen on outbuildings, for example, which may have never been re-roofed, or on your region's *Monuments Historiques*.

Inside the roof space, take a look at the roofing timbers. The biggest load-bearing timbers are, of course, the most expensive to replace, but unless they have been attacked by parasites, they are likely to be reasonably sound. Sticking a knife into the timber is a basic test, but the best bet is to seek a professional opinion.

If the wood is OK, you may still need to get it checked for ter-mites (though the vendors may have a certificate to show it is termite-free), or have a preventative treatment applied. If the loft has been converted, with timbers hidden behind plasterboard, you could ask the vendor for invoices to prove that wood treatment (if required) has been carried out properly.

Roof insulation will be important if you are in the warmer regions of France, as well as the colder areas, and above all if you plan to turn your roof space into bedrooms.

There are some highly efficient insulating technologies on the market today, some of which replace the rafters, sitting directly on the side timbers. Alternatively, even if the existing timbers are extremely uneven, you will still be able to insulate the loft and make it habitable, for example by use of plasterboard or other types of panels, suspended from metal rails. (For more on this, see Chapter 8.)

The walls

When house hunting, look at the walls with four common problems in mind: cracks, damp, leaning and bulging, and failing render or pointing. To a degree, these are

all interconnected. Assessing whether a crack is of structural significance needs expert advice, as does specifying the appropriate remedies. Try to find out about prevailing or potential subsidence, flooding, future road schemes etc. (the latter can permanently alter drainage patterns). And look for changes outside the house (such as a new terrace, or drive-way, or tennis court, or a large tree that has been removed) that may have affected the drainage or humidity of the ground around the house or other buildings.

When ground movements do occur, cracks are often found in the area between, for example, the original house and a newer extension, as they are each built on separate foundations. When it comes to subsidence, a notaire or estate agent may be familiar enough with that property or vicinity to give advice, but they don't have to.

A wall that is leaning or bulging can be dangerous, as if it goes out too far the building's upper floors and roof could collapse. Again, it will take expert advice to assess the causes (often relating to cross-tie beams having been removed in the past), how far the damage has gone, and what will be the solution (whether it needs a complete re-build or the installation of tie-rods to hold it all together, for example).

If the walls are in exposed stone, the next thing to look for is the condition of the pointing. In many areas, the stone walls of a traditional rural building may actually have neatly built exterior facings in stone (which are visible), but will have been infilled with loose stone rubble, clay or even débris behind.

This means that loose or cracked joints between the stones on the outside will allow water into the central more loosely built zone. This will show itself as damp patches inside the house, or as localised swelling of the wall, perhaps caused by clay contained in the inner skin becoming damp and expanding. The more cracks and water ingress there is, the

SUBSIDENCE CRACKS
The cracked wall on the side of this house was caused by subsidence of the soil, causing the front wall of the house to move out slightly. The solution was to install steel tie-bars under the first floor and at roof height, literally holding the house together.

Learn to love lime

Limewash render, known as 'chaux' in French, makes an excellent protective skin for your house, as it keeps damp and moisture out of your walls, while its 'breathable' qualities allow any moisture that is in the walls to escape – rather like high-tech wet-weather gear for hiking.

more trouble you get, as during frosts the damp cracks are enlarged.

So if you see defective pointing on the outside of the wall, have a look inside the house on the other side of that wall and look for the tell-tale signs of damp.

If the stonework is not visible, and has not been covered in modern cement-based renders, or even paintwork, then it is probably covered with a lime render (known as *enduit à la chaux)*. This is an excellent, natural, breathable

STRAIGHT UP
You can gain confidence about the structure of a property just by looking at the straightness of the walls. This superb renovated bâtisse has immaculately jointed stonework and plumbline-straight walls down four storeys. The roof is in good nick too.

render that usually takes its colour from natural pigments or the local sand colour. Pigmented limewashes may also have been brushed over. Very often, most of the buildings will take on a local hue, depending on the local sands available.

While limewash allows a wall to 'breathe', sections of wall that are particularly thin, such as exposed chimney stacks and below window ledges, can breathe too much, and allow damp to penetrate. Another point to look out for.

If the render is old and badly cracked, you will need to repair or replace it, which is a job for professionals or

well-practised DIYers. If it is cracked across a large area, the wall behind may be moving, and again you will need expert advice. If, however, it is intact, but discoloured, you can refresh it with a limewash coating (called *badigeon)* which is much cheaper and highly effective, but can look messy if you just slap it on.

Removing the render and exposing the stones is also a possibility, but depends on how the stone wall has been built. If the stones are quite small or have been built in a style clearly not intended to be seen, you could end up with more pointing than actual visi-

A word of warning. These figures will vary greatly (double or half, if not more) depending on what your house is like, where it is, and how the jobs fit in with other work at the time. Figures don't include VAT (see p190), but assume you use professional builders. Painting and decorating is not included.

- **Renovate a derelict house to a standard fit for a high quality B&B business: €600 to €2,000 per sq m.**
- Renovate a 'lived in' house that needs modernising (including new roof): €400 to €2,000 per sq m.
- **A new two-pitched roof of 150 sq m (remove and dispose of old roof, then install new slates, battens, underfelt, flashing, guttering): €70 per sq m (€120 per sq m with dormers/skylights).**
- Re-render a wall with lime render (including hacking off the old render and raking out joints, and scaffolding hire): €40-€60 per sq m. Repointing the wall would cost roughly the same amount.
- **Lay a new concrete floor, with reinforcement and damp-proof course (includes removing old floor in concrete, clay etc): €45-€80 per sq m.**
- Plasterboard partition walling (supply and fit, metal rail system with insulation): €30 per sq m.
- **Knock through a wall to create a new window, including limestone surround: €500 for small window, €1,500 for a doorway.**
- Build a new upstairs floor for a building 10m by 5m (using concrete 'pot and beam' system): €4,000, not including finished ceiling or flooring.
- **A new window, double glazed, made to measure by a joiner: €300-€1,500, depends on complexity.**
- Septic tank and soakaway system (supply and installation) for a 3-bedroom house: €3,000-€6,000.
- **Rewire a 3-bedroom house: €5,000.**
- Install a 10m by 5m swimming pool (unheated): €15,000 upwards.
- **Install a big electric hot water tank for bathrooms and kitchen: €500-€800.**

Looking for trouble

ble stone, in which case a full *chaux* rendering could look better. The best bet is to see what the local custom is. But here's a fashion tip: in many parts of France, *chaux* is making a comeback.

On some houses, cement render may have been used, which can be perfectly sound and trouble-free, but may cause problems. Quite apart from the austere grey colour of the older renders, they can be prone to microfissures, which allow water to seep into the wall and then get trapped there (cement renders are much more water-resistant than *chaux*). This means the wall can get damp on the inside with no prospect of drying out.

If there are signs of a cement-based render causing damp problems, the 'traditional' solution is to remove the render and replace it with a lime-based render, or remove the render and re-point the exposed stone using lime mortar. Another solution is to

JOINTING
With exposed stone walls, think about the proportion of lime mortar to exposed stone. Local style could see the stone almost, but not quite, hidden by mortar, an effect known as a 'buttered' wall. Elsewhere, the mortar sits deep within the joints, showing more stone.

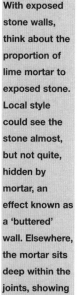

use air-permeable waterproofing agents (*hydrofuges*) which can be applied if necessary to exposed walls.

One other point is to check for climbing plants. Ivy is a serious problem, as its roots will penetrate the gaps between the stones and eventually move them out. Less worrying are clematis or virginia creeper, however, which use more building-friendly methods to grip on to stonework.

And finally, don't forget to check the roof as well as flashing, guttering, eaves and drainpipes, as they can also be sources of damp.

Internal walls
Inside the house, you might find some of the consequences of the faults you have already seen in the external wall structure. You are essen-

tially looking, and smelling, for damp.

If the internal walls have been lined with plasterboard or tongue-and-groove panelling, the damp problem may be simply hidden from view. However, humidity or mould growing at the skirting board level is a clue to what's hidden behind. Similarly, the usual signs of peeling wallpaper or discolouration are always a giveaway, as is the musty smell. If the house is still occupied when you visit with your estate agent, and it still smells damp, then the problem will get worse if it is not permanently occupied.

The work needed to solve problems associated with damp through the walls is straightforward for an experienced builder, and should not put you off buying a house (you may be able

to get the price down). In short, any interior wall that looks suspect may need to be stripped back to the stone inner wall surface, and a rough coat of a lime/cement/sand mortar mix (sometimes referred to as a *mortier bâtard*) applied to consolidate the walls in question, after undertaking any masonry repairs.

Consider insulating and lining with a new, additional inner wall constructed using various blockwork or panel methods. Lime-based paints are available, and can be the best and most attractive option for decoration.

Purists can apply limewash, in its most basic form, at a negligible cost, but test your mix and prowess first, as it could rub off on your clothing. A thick limewash will also take

The floors

weeks to dry out properly, holding up your building programme.

If the interior stone wall looks good, and is dry, then you could expose it, pointing it with a lime-based mortar.

As an added barrier against damp walls, you could also get a Field drain excavated on either side of your house, which will help take humidity away. Consult the experts to get this right, aiming not to damage your house's foundations.

Stone flags, terracotta tiles, beautiful parquet – these are just some of the reasons people fall in love with a particular house. But while a beautiful floor may have been in place undisturbed for the last 200 years, that does not mean you can cross it off your list of potential renovation jobs when you move in.

Underneath stone floors, you could find nothing more than damp clay, and below that, just earth and rock. For a house that was permanently occupied, with ill-fitting windows ensuring ventilation, and a fire burning

continually in the kitchen, you could just about get away with this kind of set-up. In hot summers, you would even benefit from the cool flagstones, acting as natural air-conditioning. However, if you envisage a house with energy-efficient draught-proof windows, a high level of interior finish and furnishings, and you don't want to spend a fortune on central heating, then the natural, 'breathing' floor is not for you. The house will be damp, cold, and prone to condensation. And if you want to leave your house unoccupied for periods of time, with

DAMP PROOF OF COURSE
How it's done: Compacted earth beneath the floor is dug out, and replaced by a layer of gravel and sand (and ducts for any cables or pipes). A PVC membrane goes on, then a steel mesh for strength. Concrete is poured and sets, then a smooth screed added, and finally, the floor covering.

books, bedding, clothes and so on stored there, damp coming up through the stone floors will be a real problem.

So it is essential to find out what's underneath. Unless your house is exceptionally well drained you will probably need to install a damp-proof course under the floors, if they do not have one already. (You will also need to do this for any kind of barn conversion where you are starting with an earth floor.) It is not as daunting as it may seem. (See page 76.)

If you have wooden floors on the ground floor, then there is probably a *vide sanitaire* below which keeps the air circulating and stops the floor joists rotting from below. If so keep it well ventilated as the original builders probably intended, paying attention to preventing shrubs or anything else outside from blocking any of the ducts installed for that purpose. If that area is accessible for crawling through for inspection, do your best to do so,

despite it being a dreadful task.

Upstairs floors in period properties will almost certainly be made of wood, and the challenge here is, like the roof timbers, simply a case of checking that the wood is in sufficiently good condition. Assessing this is another matter, though. Ceilings prevent inspection from below, while joists will be hidden by floorboards or even a layer of earth with fibre binders (straw, bracken etc.) providing a rustic 'antique concrete' over which tiled or stone floors were laid. This heavy earth composite helps explain why floor beams are often so massive – they had a lot of weight to support.

If the floor is rotten and the joists need replacing, it could be worth considering a number of alternatives to wood, such as an economic concrete 'pot and beam' system and other lightweight options.

These are discussed fully in Chapter 6.

Ceilings and exposed beams

If the exposed beams and joists are sound (again, check at the very least with a pocket knife) you may simply need to look at the material that sits in between to check it has not decayed. Renewing this is relatively simple. If the beams have been painted, don't automatically reach for the paint stripper or sand blaster. It is a time-consuming, unpleasant, and not always 100% effective job. If the beams are not too massive, painting them white against a white ceiling is extremely effective and lightens an interior. In any case you can always have another go when perhaps you have time and/or budget on your side.

WHITE BEAMS Stripping timber beams is extremely time-consuming. Painting them white, along with the ceiling panels in between, is much quicker and creates a light room.

Heating

If the house has no central heating at all, then how much you need to invest really depends on how you intend to use it.

The cheapest kind of heating in terms of investment is electric wall-mounted convectors. If you go for these, you will need decent levels of insulation throughout the house if you are to get value for money on running costs.

Oil-burning boilers are more expensive, but are the most powerful systems to drive water-filled radiators and/or underfloor heating. Installing from scratch also requires the oil tank, and possibly a new flue liner – which will obviously all add to your budget for the job.

Gas-fired heating is also an option, either mains (if you're lucky) or requiring a tank of liquid gas, which can be installed underground and which is rented from the gas supplier. With gas there is the advantage of being able to site a 'white-ware' style boiler (with option of balanced-flue outlet) in the

Electrical systems

SAFETY FIRST Rewiring a three-bedroom house, installing a new consumer board and all the regulation trip-switches, could cost around €5,000.

There are significant differences between the norms of electrical wiring in France and the systems we see in the UK. If your renovation project involves new floors or wall linings, then it will be the right time to rewire the house,

as you will be able to hide the ducting behind panelling or in new floors. A competent electrician will be able to make sure you have the right number of power sockets, lighting points and safety devices to meet the French norms. Even if you are just freshening up the house, you should still check the safety of the existing system. An ageing meter, or the absence of a typical consumer board with trip switches, is a sure sign that the infrastructure is ready for modernisation. (For more on electricity, see pp179-182.)

Circuit touristique

The UK-style electric ring-main is not legal for use in French homes, where separate circuits run from the main electrical source to each group of sockets and back again. The key reference is the French norm NF C 15-100, which specifies cable sizes, trip-switch ratings, and power outlets per circuit for all kinds of domestic installations.

Kitchens, bathrooms and plumbing

There is not too much mystique about renovating kitchens and bathrooms. It is possible to consider these as complete DIY projects, depending on your budget.

The recent trend away from fitted kitchens to more 'free-standing' ones helps preserve the look and feel of a room once converted, and blends in better.

The authors have examples of kitchens that are built by local joiners but which cost less and are in better materials than many 'cheap' fitted kitchens.

When looking at a house, check inside the kitchen cupboards for signs of damp. Sometimes, fitted kitchen units can stop a wall from breathing, and damp can accumulate in the kitchen units, causing chipboard-based fittings to degrade quickly.

French plumbing systems are always under mains pressure and use thicker-walled copper pipework with brazed rather than soldered connections. Hot and cold water both run at mains pressure, albeit with a pressure reduction valve generally fitted on the household side of the water meter. (This is therefore at your expense, and is not the responsibility of your water provider, who is responsible up to and including the meter.) Heavy duty compression fittings (the ones that bolt together) are also effective. They are relatively expensive to buy, but good for those keen to take on plumbing projects themselves, or who want just to extend an existing system. Polythene tubing systems are also widely used both by plumbers and DIYers.

The most tricky thing about these projects is finding a style that goes with an old house. Sometimes, ultra-modern actually works better than antique style fittings

LA CUISINE
You will need to decide whether to go for fitted or freestanding. The trick is to make sure it looks like part of the house.

or the slightly dodgy fake rural styles, which can clash badly with the genuinely old and rural character of your house.

Bathroom projects in France are generally fairly standard, though if you are considering a renovation project that involves

HEAT UNDER YOUR FEET
Underfloor heating is becoming popular for projects where a new floor has to be created. As well as the more common heated water systems, electrical systems (pictured) are also available, some of which will soon offer remote-control activation by internet!

kitchen or laundry area for example, without that whiff of fuel oil that oil-fired boilers would bring with them.

Of course, getting antique fireplaces into action is also tempting, but not always easy. If you renovate a house to reduce drafts circulating around it, a large fireplace will not draw so effectively. If it is only used occasionally, with the flue damp as well as cold when you light the fire, again this can cause it to fill your room with smoke. You need an efficient air intake, but even the best designs can cause a smoky result, or be a brilliant success. Don't rely on a big fireplace that apparently 'works' for heating, particularly in a small room.

A foolproof alternative is what the French call an *insert*, or a wood-burning stove that sits in the fireplace area. However, an unforseen installation cost could be the flue liner, which can be tricky to feed down narrow rectangular chimney flues in many old French houses. (More on this in Chapter 12.)

Looking for trouble...

re-locating a WC, this can be troublesome, and depends on the layout of your drainage system. A less good solution is to use a WC that pulverises and pumps the waste.

The question of where all that waste water goes brings us to the septic tank, which is the most common form of sanitation for rural properties which are not on the mains drainage system.

A septic tank is a system of chambers which treat waste from the WC and all other waste-water outlets — from the kitchen sink to the bath-tub. After treatment, the water is directed to a 'soakaway' which is a line of perforated pipes designed to release the water into the soil.

For everything you ever wanted to know about septic tanks, see pp188-189. However, when assessing a house to buy, remember that unless the septic tank was recently installed (within the last five years or so) with paperwork to prove it, it will be diffi-cult to assess what kind of condition it is in.

Older houses some-times had a septic tank for treating the WC waste only, and if this is the case in the house you buy, you will defi-nitely need to upgrade to a modern system, which will probably cost from around €3,000.

If you are buying a remote barn for conver-sion to a home, you should check that there is enough space to install the tank itself and the 'soakaway'. A soak-away typically needs 45m of pipework, as well as a suitable soil profile to allow the waste water to drain away properly.

Windows, doors & shutters

consuming. Stripping or scraping paint and sand-ing is a job that could quickly use up too many of your holidays in your new home in France.

Replacement made-to-measure windows and shutters that copy the original style are expen-sive, but worth consider-ing. New factory-made windows also exist that have a lot more charm than those available in the UK, and can some-times be ordered in bespoke sizes.

If the windows in the house you want to buy look as though they are at the end of their life, count them up and work out the replacement costs. Installation costs can vary, as other build-ing repairs can be revealed as necessary in and around door and window openings.

While original joinery, with its flaky paint and wonky geometry, may look charming, you have to offset this against its practicality.

Renovating old shut-ters, window frames, doors and any other joinery is extremely time

The right questions

This brief run-down should alert you to the kind of challenges you might face when buying a house in France. It won't turn you into an instant expert, but it should help you to ask the right questions and understand what you are look-ing for – and why. If you start to have a rough idea of the extent of renovation work required as you are house hunting, you will see a good deal more clearly which houses offer real value for money.

Tapping into the talent

The biggest hassle of all
We'll finish off this section on 'looking for trouble' with a quick thought about looking for builders. After all, for many people renovating in France, there is a deep-seated fear that 'Builders Equals Trouble'. But it doesn't have to be that way!

Finding the right builders can be the biggest hassle of all in a renovation project. You may have already come across the pros and cons of hiring British builders versus local French ones. Choose the locals, people say, if you want to integrate well into the community and make friends. Choose the Brits, though, if you want an easier time running your project.

In reality, this dilemma is no longer that simple, because there are so many second home renovation projects on the go at the moment in France. A good builder is not only competent and affordable: he is also unavailable, often with a waiting list. It is increasingly difficult to find British builders in France waiting for your project to arrive to relieve the boredom. They are all working like crazy.

And those local builders you want to cosy up to? If you move into an area popular with other restorers and renovators, then you could find yourself in a queue lasting weeks or months.

In fact, this thing about integrating with the locals by choosing the local builders is a bit overrated, and can lead to mixed results. A plumber may still not turn up, or get delayed on other jobs (bringing yours to a halt) – even if you have invited him and his entire family to dinner.

So if British builders are busy, and the local French ones are spoken for, what do you do?

First, decide how you plan to organise your project. In effect, you need to know if you are trying to hire a general builder providing project management too, or a series of tradesmen with different expertise. Then, ask around for recommendations, or failing that, use the yellow pages. And next, tackle the language problem.

The interpreter as middleman
If the project manager you find can speak English, this is a definite bonus. However, if not, there are other ways round this.

Good, bi-lingual builders are scarce. But there is no shortage of good French builders. And there are also plenty of bi-lingual people living in regions of France popular with the owners of second homes. The trick is to put these people together: to find someone who speaks both languages well, who has perhaps done a bit of work on their own house, and who can act as your interpreter.

There are benefits

THE RIGHT BUILDER?
If English-speaking builders are all booked up, try using a French builder and find an interpreter. But beware, there are risks.

and risks with this. On the plus side, it can be a rewarding role for Brits who have gone to live in rural France, and who have learned to speak French and perhaps picked up some experience of renovating along the way. It also allows you to tap into a big pool of non-English-speaking builders who have completed renovation work for French customers in your local area. And it means you can arrange to have someone on site, keeping an eye on how the project is progressing, and liaising between yourself and the builders. So work can progress without you actually being there.

The risk is that things can go wrong. If your interpreter misunderstands what you are trying to get the builders to do, then who is to blame? And if they are on site while you are away, who is responsible for decisions taken in your absence, or even a site accident? It is a role that puts a heavy, but generally unspoken, level of responsibility on the French speaker who agrees to help you, which is not always evident unless something goes wrong.

Finding the best builders
As we mentioned above, builders need to be available. People often say things like: 'My builders are rubbish. They never turn up when they are supposed to.' In reality, the builders may be brilliant, but their diaries are probably rubbish, and getting them to work to a schedule is hard for a first-timer.

You will find good builders through recommendation, or seek out recently renovated homes in your area and just go and visit the owners, or note the names on the vans parked on other people's sites. The next stage is to get around that diary problem. You will need either to find a professional to coordinate everything, or, and this can be difficult, take it on yourself to get a number of different tradesmen working as a team. We have more on this on pp190-193.

Chapter 3

THE APPROACH
PURISTS & IMPURISTS
TRADITIONAL VERSUS MODERN

Talking about 'the approach' to renovating a house may sound on the face of it like a bit of an unnecessary preamble to the real work. Surely you should just get on with it: find the builders, get it done, and enjoy. However, taking the time to work out how you want to approach the job will give you a better feel for what you will need to spend, and how long the whole thing will take.

Timeless harmony
This striking view of rooftops in Saint-May (Drôme) demonstrates the harmony that can be created when a whole village takes a bit of care over the building materials it uses. While the canal tiles themselves look beautifully weathered, the roof structures on the whole look pretty sound, with clean gutters and few signs of bending or warping, indicating good, straight timbers beneath. These houses have been well cared for, but still look as though they have changed little over the last century. The occasional metal chimney flue liner or satellite dish remind us we are in the 21st century.

Patched up
A charming thing about many old buildings is their weathered facade. These walls, showing a fascinating patchwork of repairs, exude character. A fresh new render is not always an improvement.

'Purists will pore over regional archive sketches of

There are probably two extremes when it comes to doing up property. At one end of the scale, you have 'purists' who will be determined to restore a house to its original condition, hunting down specialist craftsmen (and yes, you can find them in France), sourcing materials from local quarries, and poring over regional archives to see what local properties, outbuildings, and even gardens, really used to look like, both inside and out.

At the other end of the scale – and this is probably closer to the rest of us in real life – there are the people who will pore over the regional map to find the nearest DIY superstore, and then find the cheapest and quickest route to completing the renovation job in hand. Of course, we all want to do a good job. But sometimes just 'creating the look' at the lowest cost is good enough.

There's no ready term for this 'impurist' category, into which many of us identify ourselves at some point. The French word *bricoleur* relates to anyone who does DIY, though they may use the term *petit bricoleur* if the results are particularly laughable. A well-meaning neighbour with a reputation for being a *petit bricoleur* is probably not the best person to invite to help you with your project, even if you think this will help promote good relations in the community.

In reality, most of us are somewhere between the purist restorers and the *petits bricoleurs*. We all want value for money, and we all want to keep our building budget under control. But many people on arrival in France are bitten by the restorers' bug, expanding project budgets and time deadlines to suit as they seek out specialist skill and materials to create a first rate restoration project. The results of British projects in certain regions of France are frequently much admired by the local French community – even if they think there is a certain barmy eccentricity about it all among these Brits for whom, in French eyes, money is no object.

It is not true, though, that authentic restorations and modern materials cannot mix. They can. Beautiful restorations that incorporate modern materials and design are often seen in historic buildings open to the public, where a ticket office, information area, or auditorium is sometimes installed in an old barn or stable block, perfectly

Cafe culture
What would you do if you bought this cafe? Inventive decorators have painted on a ''half-timbered' effect, right down to the stone foundations, which are also made of, er, paint. It is clearly part of the character of the village street in which it sits, but if it was yours to renovate, what would you do? Strip off all vestiges of the 'auberge' and give it a sober render? Or recreate the brown and white paint job in all its glory? In an extreme way, this highlights the problem facing anyone trying to restore an older property. Houses evolve over centuries, with features added which, at the time, may have seemed out of keeping, but which years later seem to be just part of the character of the house. Modern additions that we make to old properties as we restore them can be part of a positive legacy that we leave to future owners. Though maybe dodgy paint jobs don't count.

imilar houses from 100 years ago. The rest of us will pore over the regional map to find the local DIY store.'

A tale of two roofs
If you put a new roof on an old barn, watch out for the effect it will have on the overall look of the building. The new roof pictured is perfectly straight: geometric, watertight, and well-made weather protection for the building beneath. It does, though, look as if it has been taken from a new building and put onto an old building. There is not much you can do about this if the existing roof was missing, or the timbers were unsalvageable. In time, the roof tiles will develop a patina, though machine-made tiles are highly compacted in manufacture and discolour less quickly than older, handmade tiles. Keeping the main timber structure of the old roof, and using reclaimed tiles, will give you a more timeless effect. The old barn in the other picture, with its weathered look and undulations at the eaves, is the kind of look many people would like from a new roof.

restored, with quite inspirational use of space. The new mixes seamlessly with the old: the addition of plate glass windows and frameless glass doors where old wooden barn doors used to be, for example. Or subtle lighting at floor level to highlight the relief of an exposed stone wall and bathe it in warm light – a modern touch that is completely in keeping with a sympathetic restoration. However these projects benefit from architects' and designers' creative and technical input: they are not as easy as they look.

Similarly, a very decent and economical renovation job, carried out with a sense of respect for the original building and carefully chosen materials, can also create a stunning result without having to bring in specially trained craftsmen to recreate 200-year-old skills. In any case, in all renovation projects, a willingness to adopt current French building standards and common techniques is vital.

A cheap and cheerful renovation will make your house habitable quickly, but may simply be stripped out by the next set of owners of the property – meaning in effect that you have added very little either to its appeal or its value in the long term. If you have been house hunting recently, think how many houses you may have visited and rejected because of their unappealing interiors, created a generation ago, or interiors more recently installed, and often botched, by well-meaning *petit bricoleurs*.

How far can the purists go?

People who are very serious about restoration can spend an infinite amount of time and money on a project. Here are some examples:
Roofing: A couple of hundred years ago, slates and tiles were less regular, so a roof would be built with subtle curves, so that it was slightly bowed (concave) both in the line of the rafters and along the ridge. In the days before slate clips or waterproof roofing felt was invented, this helped to ensure a watertight fit between the slates or tiles as it made the lower edge of the slate or tile touch the one below it for a better weather seal. To create a new roof like this today would mean briefing a specialist carpenter willing to build a frame with the

The new with the old
Once you install window glazing into large, arched openings (such as barn doorways) you are well on the way to create a quite spectacular interior space. Here, the room is bathed with light, while the shadows from the glazing bars play across the furniture. This is the perfect setting for a clever mix of the modern and traditional.

'Getting timbers specially made to create an 'authentic' undulating roof surface can be an expensive game

What's in a word? Many people use the words *restoration* and *renovation* interchangeably when it comes to doing up an old house. Some, however, would point out that the two words mean different things. Restoration means putting a building back to its original condition. Renovation by contrast is about making an old building new, with the option of using new materials that didn't exist at the time it was built. In reality, the two can work side by side. You may restore a *colombage* wall (pictured right) using original materials, but renovate the building as a whole, adding underfloor heating if you wanted.

right amount of bend in all the right places. Some carpenters will look at that willingly, particularly if they already work on historic buildings, but it takes time and is pricey.

Finding the appropriate tiles, whether they are new or reclaimed, is possible, or you could even get a batch made specially, to recreate the look. The result will be stunning, but subtle – with the contours of the roof brought out by a play of light and shade throughout the day.

But all this is an expensive game, as much for the benefit of a passing architecture buff as it is for the people inside the house. However, if the overall project is being undertaken meticulously inside and out, then such an approach could be justified. And if your property is a listed building (known as a *Monument Historique*), then a roof specifi-

'Any architecture buffs who stroll past will love it, but will the people who live inside the house even notice?'

cation like that may well be imposed on you. (For more on this, see pp202-204).

Masonry Replacing an interior or exterior lime render (*enduit à la chaux*) or pointing (*jointoyage à la chaux*), can lead people to undertake some local research over the 'authentic' colours, composition and textures required. Finding examples of existing renders and pointing nearby is usually possible. For this, you would need to look at the texture and proportion of the sand within the original chaux and do some small test areas yourselves, or ask your mason to do so. Masons may prefer a sieved, fine sand in their mortar mix, as it is always available and quicker to apply and finish. However, to recreate the look exactly, the avid restorer may source a coarser sand for more texture.

Local masons who restore with pride will handle this for you, but it is no foregone conclusion. They will have an obligation to provide a ten-year guarantee, which includes a guarantee against water infiltration, so you cannot force your mason to use a mix or a 'raked out' style of joint that they think is unsuitable.

Joinery Creating new windows is a severe test of nerve, and budget, for the purist restorer. If the existing windows are completely rotten and need replacing, the choice of materials on the market is wide, but the range that would satisfy the demands of getting that authentic look is much more restricted. If the defunct windows are original ones, then you could consider getting a joiner to make an exact copy of them, right down to using subtly irregular antique glass (which it is still possible to find) to create bespoke replacements. However, you may not be able to double glaze these as the original glazing bar dimensions are unlikely to be chunky enough to hold the weight of the glass. If eventually you come try to rent or sell your house to someone less sympathetic to your restoration cause, they may find it weird that you create brand new windows that are only single glazed. An estate agent or notaire may even knock something off the value of the property, despite its 'authenticity', as winter heating bills would be higher. (For more on windows, see Chapter 8)

Interior walls In some old houses, stripping back original wall coverings can have some of the excitement of an architectural excavation. Some people find sections of original hand-painted wall (if you do, you can leave a zone of this undecorated and frame it). Antique wallpaper, often hand-printed, maybe also be uncovered. Beneath these, you can find 'lining paper' made of old newspapers, which will effectively date-stamp the period when that work was done – and probably hold up your work by half a day as you browse through the local news from 1901.

Under this paper, there could eventually be a layer of clay, lime or plaster, mixed with fibres – probably some kind of animal hair, which has been applied to the inner stone wall.

Even the most purist builder is not going out to shave a horse to stock up on animal hairs, and more modern materials are really the only option. Ecological building materials exist, however, and there are new approaches to building using traditional materials that are

Pure and simple This bedroom shows the benefits of simple decor that brings out the fabric of the building to great effect. The walls are treated with an unpigmented lime render, which is applied to create a slightly textured effect. Note the absence of straight lines, particularly around the window opening – a feature that adds even more charm to the room, as does the small recess in the wall. The windows are new replacements, but in wood that blends well with the exposed beams and lintels. A mix of the old and the new, then, but which finishes with a timeless effect and above all else a cosy bedroom.

'Under this paper there could be a layer of clay mixed with horse hair, applied to the inner stone wall.'

very appropriate to the modern world.

For the really authentic look (pre-19th century), rendered walls should avoid straight lines. For the inept beginner, this approach is a real gift, given the challenge of creating an even surface with lime render or plaster, and getting it to stick properly. For best results though, ask a professional to do the job. Some will think you are nuts asking them to plaster a wall without straight lines. Others will be familiar with this 'back to basics' trend, and it is a good idea to ask them where you can see examples of similar work they have done elsewhere.

Using plasterboard or insulated panels to dry-line walls is a modern and effective solution, but one that some purists may also reject.

Floors The ultra-purists could argue that a traditional earth floor with stone flags or terracotta tiles will work perfectly well – allowing the house to 'breathe', and preventing humidity being locked into the lower part of the walls and floor (See opposite). However, a builder is likely to recommend replacing an earth floor with a concrete slab, under which is a damp-proof PVC sheet (and perhaps an underfloor network of drains). This is not because they are trying to create a big, expensive job: it is more to do with the ten-year guarantee of their work, and their obligation to upgrade to the current French standards. A damp-proof membrane will prevent damp rising from the floor into your room. If a builder does not install one, he could be sued for malpractice within the ten-year guarantee period if, for example, damp rising is proved to be detrimental (causing rot, for example). Would you really want to take that risk?

A mix of approaches

The most successful project is likely to combine a mix of restoration and renovation techniques, with a keen eye on practicality, the time you have available, and, of course, your budget. Eventually, you will sell your house and move on. It's always worth considering what you will leave on the house for future owners to enjoy.

Furnished to fit
This room has been sensitively restored, making the most of a fine bread oven set into the wall, hefty exposed beams, and a roughly cut stone floor, but keeping the rest of the place simple. This room works best thanks to the low-key furnishings: the antique cupboard with a wonky door, the plain kitchen table and chairs. In effect, getting a restored room to look right is in part down to what you put into it. Fill this room with modern furniture, and the stone floor would look ridiculously rustic.

Avoiding the big chill over a winter weekend

The cool summer home that never seems to get warm

Traditional methods of building and restoration have a logic to them when viewed as a system that uses the building materials in harmony with the climate, with the aim of keeping cool in the summer and warm in the winter. But a word of warning for second home owners: don't expect to be able to warm up an old stone farmhouse during the course of a winter weekend.

Consider two neighbouring and almost identical-looking holiday homes in the south of France, one owned by purist restorers, Mr and Mrs Stone, and the other by their more pragmatic neighbours, Mr and Mrs New.

The Stones have restored their house as traditionally as possible. They have left the old stone flagstones in place, under which is simply a layer of clay and earth. They have insulated the roof and installed central heating, but interior walls are mostly either exposed, or simply rendered with *chaux*.

The News, by contrast, have installed concrete floors and damp-proof membranes, with under-floor thermal insulation. They have dry-lined the walls throughout the house with insulated panels, and insulated the roof space.

CHRISTMAS HOLIDAYS

Both households arrive for a weekend. It has been a cold December. When the Stones arrive, the house feels, and smells, damp. The thermometer reads 8°C. They put on the heating, and wait for the house to warm up. They light a fire in the living room, but give up when overcome by smoke. The house remains cold, and by the time they leave, three days later, the temperature is only 16°C, and it is still humid. (Had it been permanently inhabited – and therefore heated – the walls would have kept warm through the winter.)

When the News arrive next door, their house is also cool, at 9°C. They too put on the central heating, and within 4 hours the house is at 20°C, and feels dry.

They invite their neighbours, the Stones, to dinner to help them to warm up.

SUMMER HOLIDAYS

The two families return in July, which has seen three consecutive hot weeks. The Stones arrive, and find their house a cool 15°C, though a little musty. They open the windows for a few hours to air the place, and then enjoy the cool respite the house gives them from the hot afternoon, walking on the cool stone floor in bare feet.

The News arrive to find their house also at 15°C, but once they open some windows, it is quickly 28°C as the warm air moves in, and it stays at that temperature for the rest of their holiday. The Stones invite the News for dinner, offering an escape from the searing heat outside.

THE MORAL TO THE STORY

You can't have it both ways. The Stones' house, with no insulation to hide its massive stone walls, benefits in the summer from the cooling effect of these walls (which bring water vapour from the ground into the room) as does the clay floor beneath the flagstones. However, such a house will never warm up quickly in the winter, because taking the chill out of the stone walls is a lengthy job – it takes longer than a weekend.

The News, however, can heat their house up quickly in the winter as they have banished water vapour from the floor with the DPC and have thermal insulation below it too. They have clad the walls with insulated panels, the air in the rooms is dry, and the central heating has simply to heat the air, not the whole structure of the house. In the summer, the News lose the cooling effect of the walls and floor.

This slow-moving cycle of walls heating up to store warmth, or cooling down to emanate chill, is sometimes referred to as the 'thermal flywheel' – capturing perfectly the notion that it's something that takes a while to get going, and cannot be stopped or started at will.

Traditional stone houses with stone or tiled floors laid over beaten earth were designed to stay cool in the summer and maintain warmth in the winter – if permanently occupied.

Chapter 4

USING RECLAIMED MATERIALS

If you're in luck, the house you buy in France may already feature roofing tiles with a beautiful antique patina, monumental stone fireplaces, richly grained parquet or wide-boarded floors, and ancient flagstones or terracotta 'tomettes.' If it doesn't, but you would like to bring a bit more 'authenticity' into your project, then don't despair. If it's architectural history you're after, you can quite simply go out and buy it.

'What keeps all these yards ticking over is a brisk trade in tiles, flooring and fireplaces.'

In the French yellow pages, architectural salvage yards are known as *matériaux de récuperation*, and on the internet, if you want to start your search there, you could enter keywords such as *matériaux anciens* (which covers 'reclaimed materials') or 'architectural salvage' if you want to hit the English versions.

Suppliers and dealers of of these materials are experiencing a boom at the moment, led by a very French interest in rural homes and architectural heritage. This suits British people too, and many of these websites have English translations aimed at UK and American buyers – which means keyword searches in English will take you there.

What keeps these salvage yards ticking over is a brisk trade in tiles, all kinds of flooring, and fireplaces. However, most will also be able to get hold of roofing timbers and beams, features such as statues, fountains and stone sinks, iron railings, pillars, staircases and even cobblestones. For many people working on a renovation project, the downside of using salvage is the time it takes to find what you are looking for, and the distance you may have to travel to bring it back. Not surprisingly some people prefer to visit yards, see what they have available, and then try to think of a use for it in the project at hand.

A quick guide to reclaimed materials

Roofing tiles

Reclaimed roofing tiles are much sought-after for their unmistakeable look – that patina of age and the colour variation that comes from the way in which the terracotta was mixed and fired. In fact, old terracotta is more open-pored, being hand-made and fired to lower temperatures than the modern, 'pressed' versions of terracotta tiles.

It is this relatively rough surface that allows bacteria to live on the tile's surface and create the patina of age, and to bring out colour variations in a way that is hard to beat with modern materials.

If you are going to use reclaimed tiles, you will need to forewarn your roofers, and include it in the specification when seeking estimates. If you are using local roofers, use reclaimed tiles from the local region if at all possible, so the builders know what they are dealing

Old with the new
Original canal tiles have been used here on a new roof project which incorporates modern insulated and waterproof under-tiles in undulating panels. The overall look is absolutely right. What's more, it uses only half the quantity of tiles, as the inverted tiles are no longer needed.

A tile in time
With a major renovation to the timber roofing structure, it is possible to re-use the existing stock of tiles, with reclaimed tiles added to replace those which are broken or missing. In such a project, your roofer may need some extra time to source the replacements. If you are planning to re-roof a building with reclaimed tiles sourced from elsewhere, get your roofer involved from the start, even to the point of helping select which stock of tiles you should buy. Of course, some property owners do not get too worked up about getting tiles to match (left) when doing a repair job. You could say it adds to the building's character!

Fired earth
Antique reclaimed terracotta, or *carreaux de terre cuite anciens*, or *tomettes*, come in a variety of formats. Typical ones are 16cm or 22cm squares, in peachy-orange blend, costing in the region of **€55-60 per sq m. Lighter tones and larger formats can approach €100 per sq m, as can very small medieval ones, 10cm square or even smaller. These are indeed rare, and best reserved for special restorations.**

with. Also, give the builders an idea of the quality of the tiles you have sourced. Having found a salvage yard that will supply the tiles, you could take away some samples with you to show the roofers who are bidding for the work. They will be able to assess the quality variation, and try to indicate how many may be unusable. Also they may well have some stocks of tiles of their own.

Cost wise, reclaimed tiles will probably turn out to be more expensive in comparison with factory made alternatives. In mid 2003, typical prices – before VAT – were around €1,200 per thousand for antique canal tiles, and €550 per thousand for antique flat tiles.

Watch out for reclaimed materials being unavailable just at the time when you need them: it is best to do the research in advance, and then pre-purchase if possible.

Not every roofing tile will be available from salvage yards. Slates often do not make it to a second life, but will be saved by roofers if they judge it worthwhile for their future projects. In some regions, frequently mountainous, where stone slabs (*lauzes*) are used for roofing, you may need a lot of persistence and luck to find such rarities.

Floor tiles

Antique reclaimed terracotta floor tiles are available in a wide range of shapes, sizes and colour tones, and are generally 20-30mm (averaging about an inch) thick. As with roofing tiles, modern terracotta is more compressed during manufacture, making it more resilient, but less prone to picking up a patina as it ages. Having said that, there are some companies which now specialise in terracotta made the old way.

Having bought a batch of tiles, you may want to pressure-wash them before laying. This is often the French way, whereas some British people tend to enjoy their tiles slightly grimy for added authenticity.

If the tiles have been painted in the past, they may need specialised cleaning which many reclamation yards are equipped to do, and may already have done before you buy them. Splashing about with tiles in an acid bath, wearing protective clothing akin to a chemical warfare suit, is quite an undertaking. However, you could do the paint-stripping yourself using DIY brands, if the surface area isn't too great.

'Wearing a kind of chemical warfare suit and scrubbing your tiles in an acid bath is quite an undertaking.'

New stone for old
You do not have to search out reclaimed stone to complete your renovation job, as there are plenty of sources of good, new stone flooring, which tends to be cheaper. These are either regional quarries (for example in Dordogne or Bourgogne), while good specialist distributors of floor tiles and stone flooring will be able to supply the complete ranges of stone if you ask them. Note that some of these firms call themselves 'marbriers de batiment' but despite the name, are not limited to supplying only marble. With limestone flooring, different finishes are available, including 'antiqued', otherwise known as *rustique* or *campagnarde*. New stone for flooring tends to be around 2cm thick.

No-one can pretend to enjoy this job, especially if it is carried out on a hot day. In all events it's a sensible precaution to wash the tiles repeatedly in water before and after laying them, to remove any impurities that can get absorbed.

If you are laying tiles in the traditional way on a mortar bed (which can compensate for varying tile thicknesses in a way modern adhesives cannot), they need to be completely wet when you install them, otherwise they will draw up all the moisture in the mortar bed, weakening it, with the risk that they become unstuck. If you intend to seal the tiles afterwards, you must let them dry off completely, or water in the tiles will cause the sealant to discolour or even blister and flake off. This could mean waiting months after you lay them. (Of course, if you lay them with adhesive, rather than mortar, there is only the grout which has to be left to dry out, so the drying process is much quicker, but you will still need to ensure that the concrete

Heavy duties
Antique limestone flagstones, left, can cost up to €300 per square metre depending on their age, thickness (up to a hefty 15cm thick) and where they come from. This kind of stone will be extremely heavy – weighing perhaps 350kg per square metre (the equivalent of five fully-grown adults). Transport costs will be high: you cannot put these in the back of an estate car, and you could easily pay more than €1,000 for the transport, and then need a crane for unloading. You could check whether the local mason, or even a local farmer, has the right equipment to unload.

the day, and then release that heat well into the evening, helping to create a warm terrace long after dark.'

sub-floor is completely dry before sealing the tiles.)

Stone floors

Before searching for reclaimed stone flooring, check with suppliers of stone to see how much newly-cut stone would cost in your area. The choice is wide in France, where a vast range of stone, particularly limestone, is quarried. In terms of prices for reclaimed materials, you could expect to pay up to around €300 per sq m for the most beautiful genuine antique limestone, 10-20cm in thickness, which is very rare. You may be able to have massive stone flags sawn down to a more manageable regular thickness (2-4cm) depending on their size and available stone sawing facilities.

At the lower end of the scale, reclaimed slate and new slate is easier to find (particularly in the Angers region from where it was originally extracted) and should cost below €100 per sq m.

Cobblestones

These are simply not available from shops, so if you want cobbles (or setts) you will need to use a salvage yard. They are simple to lay, but excrutiatingly heavy and back-breaking to transport and manipulate. Cobblestones should cost €30-€100 per sq m before transportation costs. Being made of stone, cobbles are not only very hard wearing, but also have terrific thermal qualities. If you put down cobbles on a terrace where you plan to eat outside, you will find that at breakfast time, with the sun shining, the cobbles remain refreshingly cold to walk on, as they will have chilled down during the night. They take a while to heat up, but once they do, they keep their heat for considerably longer than the air. So in the evening, as the air begins to cool, the cobbles remain warm, allowing you to linger over your dessert and coffee a little longer after dinner on the terrace. Thoughtfully positioned, cobbled terraces can act as a mix of underfloor heating in the evenings and air conditioning in the morning.

Timber flooring

Salvage yards usually have plenty of planks of wood in stock, which on closer inspection will turn out to be floorboards of various quality, or simply old planks – loftboards usually from barns. The quality is mixed and varied, and you can expect a high degree of wastage.

Decent hardwood floorboards with genuine antique patina are rare, and will cost well over €100 per sq m unless you find a real bargain. Many people may find it easier to go to a sawmill or traditional builders merchants to buy simple planks (oak, chestnut, or pine, for example) that can be laid edge to edge and then sanded, for cottagey or barn-style projects.

Planks, though, are not the same as floorboards, which are

'Old timber flooring quality varies: expect wastage.'

machined with a tongue on one side and a groove on the other, so that they fit together smoothly. If you buy reclaimed boards and the tongue and groove is tatty or damaged, it will be a difficult and maybe impossible job putting them together again. One option is to saw off the tongues, and fit the boards edge-to-edge. This does have a disadvantage in keeping the boards flat when they expand. The real reason floorboards are designed to interlock is that they can be held down with just one nail where each board crosses the wooden joist below. This not only keeps all the boards uniformly level, but allows them to expand or contract into the groove of the next board. If you use planks, rather than grooved boards, then the planks will buckle as they expand, creating an uneven floor (which looks particularly bad beneath a rug or carpet). Nailing the planks with extra nails will keep them flatter in the short term, but in the end the wood, which seems determined to shift somehow, will simply split.

Fireplaces

There are usually plenty of fireplaces on the market at salvage yards, but not always the kind that you think would fit best in your renovation project. The good ones are highly sought-after, and do not come cheap. If you are looking for a handsome antique stone surround, you will need to pay at least €1,000 for something fairly modest, or

In the groove If you are buying reclaimed flooring, watch out for the condition of the interlocking tongue-and-groove. If they look fairly tatty and damaged (unlike these pristine versions pictured above) you may end up having to saw them off, and if that is the case, you could have saved money by simply buying old planks (from a barn loft, for example) or new planks from a sawmill.

Old masters
A beautiful 18th century fireplace made from limestone could cost quite a few thousand euros, but, installed in the right kind of room, will add value to your house. The example pictured (top) is a regency-style piece that would cost upwards of €4,000. Below is another example from the 18th century, which will be closer to €6,000.
Don't despair, though, as you can find simpler, 19th century models from salvage yards from around €1,800 to €2,000.
And if you find someone locally selling an old kitchen fireplace, you could find one for even less.

Note that VAT (*TVA*) at some architectural salvage yards could be half its normal rate (ie, just 9.8%) if the salvage yard has not added any value to the item on sale – so has not repaired or rebuilt.
Remember that a stone fireplace lintel can be extremely heavy, but fragile too.

€5,000 €10,000 and over for a 250 year-old carved limestone surround with an over-mantel (*trumeau*).

On top of this, you will have to pay for transport and installation, the cost of which will depend on whether the fireplace surround is built into the masonry of the wall or not. However, installing a fireplace in an existing chimney breast could easily cost more than €1,500 and more if there are complications.

With the fireplace installed, you will not be able to guarantee that it will work effectively. Prevailing wind direction, air pressure, room size, and the flue design can all contribute to the creation of smoke rather than fire. Having said that, an antique fireplace does create a great impression and is generally considered an essential feature in a good many renovation projects. Just don't count on it to heat your house efficiently.

Other salvage items
For many people, the architectural salvage yard is a source of inspiration, with stone facings for windows, doors, or archways prompting people to knock additional holes in walls to add a new architectural feature to the property.

Salvage yards need not be your only source. Your local mason may also collect dressed stone from various projects, and may be an equally good source. In the same way, joiners sometimes keep a supply of old timbers that they can employ on new projects.

If you are looking for something specific, finding it in a salvage yard could take a long time, just as it could for any other antique. People can strike it lucky, but if time is short, the best advice is to do your research first, on the Internet and on the telephone. You will be surprised to find out how many of the French salvage yard operators speak English. Also, get your architect, designer, or builders involved as early as possible so you know that what you are buying will actually work and can be effectively brought into your project.

'You will not be able to guarantee that an antique fireplace, once installed, will actually work properly.'

Windows of opportunity
If you are in luck, your search through the salvage yards could result in finding a set of windows in good condition that are just the right size to replace the rotted windows in your old house. In fact, this may be easier than you think, as there is a degree of standardisation regarding the height and width of windows in many old houses from the 19th century. What is more likely, is that the window aperture in your wall may have to be adapted in size, which can be expensive. The alternative is to get bespoke windows made. Reclaimed windows, though, can be good value. The large green door and window arrangement (pictured) would probably cost several hundred euros in a salvage yard (unless it is completely rotten), and around €2,000 to have made by a joiner.

The white, 8-pane rectangular window frame to the right could cost perhaps €80 in a salvage yard, and a few hundred euros to have made. Installation costs, of course, are not included, and any new window will need a matching bespoke frame made to house it in your wall.

Chapter 5

ROOFS AND WALLS

A SOUND BASIC STRUCTURE

The heavy-duty work which helps keep your house weather-proof is the first priority in your building project. Until that is completed, most of the interior work can't get going. But you will have to bring in the professionals. This is serious, structural work that can be dangerous if it goes wrong. What's more, if you bring in the pros, you could be given a ten-year guarantee on the work. So you can sleep soundly in your bed, with no worries about a leaking roof.

A new roof
A major renovation of both the roof and walls of this house includes the installation of insulated sous-tuiles (under-tiles) with the original canal tiles refitted on top. The benefit of this system is a high performance roof, which will keep you cool in the summer and warm in the winter. From inside, the original timber structure of the roof will still be visible from the loft space, making it ideal for stylish loft conversion jobs.

Anatomy of timbers Depending on region, roof structures vary. But the basic construction pictured is very common, and comprises the roof truss (this is the A-shaped framework of timbers which runs along the building, resting on the side walls). This supports the purlins (or side-timbers) which run horizontally along the sloping sides of the roof, to support the rafters. The rafters run from the apex of the roof and down to the eaves.

We will not try to tell you, in this book, how to renovate your roof, as it's a job that relies on a careful examination and diagnosis, and depends entirely on the condition of the existing roof. You will really need to get your roof checked out by an expert, who will be looking both at the condition of the roof cover, as well as the interior structure and the walls that support it. Having said that, it's worth going into a bit more detail about how the various roofs are built.

THE ROOF

As we saw in Chapter 2, renewing a roof does not necessarily involve having to replace the original timbers and it can be preferable not to. A brand new frame for your roof will leave you with a very straight, very new looking structure that may be completely out of keeping with the look you are trying to achieve. An alternative, if part of the original structure is defective, is to try to find suitable reclaimed timber from a salvage yard.

It is almost impossible to generalise about roofing costs, but we will try to anyway. Typically, a new roof cover (which could include removal of the old roofing cover, plus the addition of underfelt if appropriate, as well as battens and the new roof covering) will be in the region of €100 per sq m on a typical house, including TVA and perhaps a skylight or two. If you aim to use reclaimed tiles, this could cost you more in time as well as money, but it will look the part.

Whatever the roof is made of, it will need regular and effective inspection. This is a good reason to do house hunting in France once the bad weather starts – you can find out a lot more about a house if it has been raining for a while. On the outside, check at the top of the walls for any degradation under the eaves. Gutters, incidentally,

'When house hunting, you can find out a lot more about a place if it has been raining for a couple of days.'

should be checked and cleared after the autumn leaves have fallen.

Repairing the roofing slates or tiles is bread and butter work for a professional roofer, and achievable for an experienced DIYer. The main challenges are access to the roof (and safety implications), spotting potential future problems, and avoiding causing damage as you attack what is a relatively fragile and sometimes brittle surface.

In the first part of this chapter, we take a look at the main kinds of roofing materials you'll come across in France and how to look after them.

Slates (*ardoises*)

Most common in northern and eastern France, and the Loire valley, slate tiles are relatively fragile, and need checking for cracks or the build-up of moss. Loose or missing slates need to be replaced promptly to prevent further damage and water ingress. If the nails or hooks are starting to deteriorate, they are all likely to be in a similar condition at the same time – meaning a re-roofing job lies ahead at some stage. Replacing a slate tile is best left to a professional roofer: creating a safe means of access to the roof itself, and avoiding breaking other slates, is the hard part. The detailing required at hips and valleys, often done with soldered zinc sheet 'flashing' is a skilled job and really not for a DIYer.

Natural slate tiles are generally 30-40cm long by 18-20 cm wide. Depending on their thickness, slates weigh between 27-70kg per sq m. Slate hooks used to be made in galvanised steel, although roofers now tend to use stainless steel, but the black tipped version is excellent for restoration, and does not twinkle in the sun as the stainless tips do.

Special effects The most fascinating use of slate tiles must surely be the creation of fish-scale designs, such as the roof in north west France (above). Known as *écailles* fish-scale slates are more expensive than the rectangular versions, and, being hand-prepared, would only be considered for fancy seaside architecture or authentic listed buildings. Top: reclaimed terracotta tiles, for an instant 'weathered' look.

Canal tiles
Antique reclaimed canal tiles (right) are a valuable commodity, if you can get enough of them. Look after them, and remember that when re-roofing you should keep as many as possible of the originals for reuse. They will stretch further if you use them as only the 'overs', with a more modern and cheaper substitute for the 'unders'.

Plain tiles, or nib tiles (*tuiles plates*)

Made of terracotta, plain tiles (pictured above) are moulded or extruded depending on age, and are either rectangular or scale-shaped. Standard sizes vary from 14x25cm to 18x28cm according to regional variations, with colours varying from beige, brown to red (and they can even be enamelled grey, blue or green). They are fixed either with wooden pegs, non-corrosive nails, or are simply laid straight onto the roofing laths or battens. The slope of the roof needs to be at least 45 degrees, and more in coastal and mountainous areas where the wind can whip rainwater into the gaps with some force. As shown above, the tiles are laid with staggered joints, with a generous overlap to ensure the roof is watertight.

Canal tiles (*tuiles canals*)

There is an amazing range of terms for this humble piece of curved terracotta: Roman tile, Spanish tile, mission tile (in America), barrel tile, hollow tile, canal tile – not to mention the graphic *tige de botte*, a boot-maker's term referring to the long tongue of leather, the shape of a shin-guard, that comes up behind the bootlaces. Whatever you prefer to call them, they all represent pretty much the same thing: the typical ochre or red Provençal tile, designed for the very shallow

he 'tige de botte' – a kind of prototype shin-guard.'

Understanding under-tiles

Under-tiles, or 'sous-tuiles' can provide insulation and water-proofing in one slick operation

1

The roof is prepared, having removed the old tiles (saved for replacement later). The original roofing battens are removed, and new battens installed to suit the dimensions of the under-tiles.

2

These under-tiles have a watertight outer skin, designed to interlock with the adjacent tile. Beneath this is an insulating foam core, mounted on a panel which will become the interior face of the new roof.

3

The panels slot together, overlapping at the sides and ends. You could choose uninsulated under-tiles (which are much thinner in profile) but they would need insulating from inside the roof space.

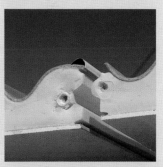

4

The finishing touch is to replace the original tiles, but with the under-tiles in place. The inverted tiles, which you don't see, are not required. The result is a cool summer roof-space, and a warm home in winter.

pitched roofs found in the Mediterranean, the south west, and central France. Their size varies from around 30-50cm long and 15-25cm wide, though this width will vary as the tile tapers from one end to another. They tend to be narrower in the west, wider in eastern France – so if you are looking for spares to fill gaps, check the dimensions. Canal tiles can be laid directly onto the roof battens, or between the rafters on sheets of mineral fibre or cellulose – which can also be insulated on the underside, ideal for loft conversions. (See the box: Understanding Under-tiles). Generally, canal tiles are pre-drilled for easy nailing or hooking, or wiring – but they can also be fixed in place with mortar, especially in areas of strong winds, which include areas towards the Atlantic coast, as well as the south of France. Elaborate overhang detailing, involving several layers, looks particularly attractive (see our picture on p69).

Standard 'mechanical' tiles (*tuiles mécaniques*)
Purists may deride these tiles as tacky modern lookalikes, but they have numerous advantages. Firstly they are reasonably cheap. Secondly, their construction in moulded, pressed terracotta, with ribs and channels, allows them to interlock firmly, ensuring a waterproof

'Elaborate overhang details look particularly good.'

The thatcher era
If you buy a house with a thatched roof that needs replacing, then beware: it could take longer than you think. Thatchers do still exist in France, of course, but their numbers are few, and with an increasing number of French (as well as other nationalities) renovating country homes, the demand for their services has been on the increase. The authors have records of one project where the owner had to wait nearly a year to get the thatcher to start work. However, the delays were just beginning, as the thatcher tried to work on several projects simultaneously, with the result that the job then took a further 12 months to complete. As no internal renovations could be completed until the roof was finished, the whole project was held up dramatically. Of course, this should not put you off buying a *chaumière* in France. A thatch can last up to 40 years.

Just get the roof checked and find out how old it is.

surface with less overlap (so you use fewer tiles). They are lighter too. Like canal tiles, they vary in colour from brown to red (even grey or bluish sometimes), though their highly compacted construction means they will not develop quite the same patina as terracotta tiles made the traditional way. Also known in French as *tuiles à emboîtement* or 'interlocking tiles', they come in a range of sizes (30-50cm by 15-25cm wide), and can be nailed or hooked directly onto roofing battens. Look out for the older versions, which did not seal adequately, as they will not be watertight enough for the ten-year guarantee.

Basic maintenance
Looking after any of these terracotta-based roofs described above is relatively simple. If the tiles are building up a layer of moss (this generally happens in more temperate regions or on the north-facing roof pitches) you can clean them off (from above) with a high-pressure water jet. Replacing a tile needs brute force employed with a degree of finesse – when the tile is nailed or wired in place the only way to remove it is to smash it with a hammer. So proceed with caution to avoid smashing neighbouring tiles. Professional roofers have clever gadgets and skillful techniques, and it is often wise to get them in on

'Ridges can be planted with irises, helping to bind the thatch.'

the job. Regular, careful observation of the state of your roof will pay off in the long run, as you can spot problems early.

Thatch (*chaume*)

Made of reeds or straw, a thatched roof, typically 20-30cm thick, provides good thermal and acoustic insulation. The ridge of a thatched roof is often covered with a thick layer of clay, and planted with irises and sedums – a move which is not purely decorative: the roots help to hold the fibres of the thatch together, as well as stopping it drying out and disintegrating. Obviously, a thatched roof does not have gutters at the eaves. Instead, people generally put in a thick layer of gravel around the house to drain away rainwater.

Thatched roofs used to be the cheapest option of all roofing materials because people had the right to gather up reeds for roofing free of charge, right up to the 19th century. Today, the raw material itself is not that expensive, but finding the skilled artisans is, and can give the roofing job a long lead time, and result in a hefty bill. Having said that, a thatched roof could last for 40-50 years, depending on a number of factors such as the slope of the roof, the level of ventilation in the roof space, and, of course, how well it is looked after. Look on it as an architectural legacy for the next generation.

Roofing stone (*lauze*)

This is flat, sedimentary rock (such as schiste, a rougher, more rustic version of slate) in various sizes that gives the effect of the roof being covered in flat stones, and is most commonly seen in mountain regions, the Massif Central and Corsica. Extremely heavy, these weigh around 90kg per sq m, so the roofing timbers need to be robust. The weight of *lauze* means it helps insulate against cold in the winter and heat in the summer. As with regular slates, lauze is fixed with nails, or on shallow pitches, by its own weight.

No time to lauze
If you buy a cottage in the mountains, you could end up with a rather rare roof covering to deal with: *la lauze,* which is basically made of chunks of stone that are carefully fitted together. The overall effect is a house that has somehow 'morphed' its way out of the bedrock. Beyond the fairy-tale looks, these roofs are a tough challenge to renovate, as the raw materials are hard to find and, if you do find them, heavy to transport. If your roof is beyond repair, you could always sell your old lauze to use on other local projects, and then build a new roof using natural slate.

'Inverted canal tiles rest in the space between each of the battens and are nailed or wired in place. The

What lies beneath
This roof is being taken apart for complete replacement, and this shot shows the extremely simple and efficient way in which a typical canal tile roof is constructed. The round timber of a rafter is visible running beneath the rest of the roof construction, heading down to the eaves. Running at right angles to this, we can see one of the support timbers, or purlins. The roofing battens run in the same direction as the rafters (compare that with a slate roof, where the battens run horizontally), and are spaced to allow a line of inverted canal tiles to rest in the space between each of the battens, before being nailed or wired in place. Then, the final canal tiles are put in place, running up the line of the roofing batten and covering it completely, and in this case, are held on to the lower tiles with mortar. This technique remains simple and efficient, and even if the void underneath the roof is too small to be converted into a room (as is often the case because the pitch of the roof is so shallow), insulating the loft space from within is a perfectly good solution.

final canal tiles are put in place running up the line of the roofing batten and covering it completely.'

'Push the mortar too far into the joints between the stones, and you could end up with a finish where it look

Because *lauze* is so heavy, needing extra-strong roofing timbers, means it has gradually fallen out of favour over the last few decades and it is extremely rare to find a new roof in this material. However, if you are lucky enough to buy a house with such a roof, bear in mind that repairing the roof will be a challenge, as you will have no choice but to find replacement lauze locally or from salvage yards. This could make the job time-consuming and expensive, especially in transport costs. A 4m by 4m section of roof, for example, would require a hefty 1.5 tonnes of lauze.

Cement and concrete-based tiles

As a cheaper alternative to slate tiles, fibro-cement tiles (made of cement with mineral fibres and/or resin) are a good deal less elegant than natural state tiles, but they can be a sensible choice if budgets are tight. They come in various colours such as grey, dark blue, and terracotta.

Similarly, you can find concrete-based versions of flat tiles and canal tiles, and there is strong evidence that manufacturers have made great inroads in the look and feel of these tiles over the last few years. They also have good resistance to frost.

Guttering and valleys

Known in the building trade as 'rainwater goods', these are essential to the well-being of your house. If they are defective, they will leak water down your walls, creating damp patches inside the house. By the same token, if the valleys (between different slopes of roof) are not secure, the roof itself will leak.

In France, zinc guttering has been used for generations. It is attractive, and gives a 'French' traditional appearance. However, it is not a DIY job to learn how to do the complicated work to the kind of quality a French trained roofer would achieve.

Generally, PVC has always been the poor relation in the range of materials, thanks to its poor resistance to frost and sunlight, and its generally clunky appearance. However, recent models are better, and even come in more subtle colours to blend in with your house.

Sun-kissed stone A Lubéron village basks in the evening sun, with the stone walls thrown into relief. Some of the houses visible under the castle ramparts have retained a render on the facade, while others have stripped it back to the stone. All these properties are in a protected zone around an ancient monument, and their owners will have had to take advice on the exact chaux render mix to use. The result harmonises perfectly with the local stone. Those who have exposed the stone have also followed guidelines on the kind of jointing required in terms of depth and colour.

...s if fake stone facings have simply been stuck onto the front of your house as a decorative afterthought.'

Obviously, they are no match for a fine, copper gutter, but are a fraction of the price.

A word on safety: If you are inspecting gutters, don't assume they will be strong enough to support a ladder without cracking – lean the ladder against a wall. Whether you choose to clean out the gutters yourself, or if you hire people to do it for you, make sure the working environment is safe – which generally means a scaffold platform with a safety barrier at the top.

THE WALLS

France has a multitude of different methods and materials of construction, and they are usually linked to whatever building materials are found, or used to be found, in the local area. When working on the exterior walls and façade of your house, it is well worth getting some advice to make sure what you are planning fits in with the local style. A good source is the regional CAUE, (the *Conseil d'Architecture, d'Urbanisme et d'Environnement*) which may have leaflets on the local traditions, colours and materials.

Stone walls

Stone walls are what French rural architecture is all about, even though it is impossible to talk about stone as a single kind of materi-

Dressed stone
If you need to repair dressed stone (such as these fine blocks used to build this tower) there are two options. Small cracks can be filled with a lime mortar to match the existing one. Larger missing chunks are best repaired using a fragment of stone, a fiddly job that takes time. Otherwise, you will need to call in a stone mason.

Lime renders:

'Humidity can usually rise through the stone wall from ground level.'

al. If you drive north-to-south, or east-to-west through the French countryside, the colour and texture of stone walls evolve, along with the landscape, crops, and the intensity of the blue sky.

There are two main types of stone wall. Dressed stone (*pierre de taille*), which is the quintessential stone wall – large, regularly-shaped blocks with very fine joints. The other kind is the irregular stone wall (*pierre apparente*) which is the most commonly found all over France. Sometimes this will be hidden behind a layer of lime render.

In most older houses, such walls are likely to be better built on the external faces than in the middle. where a mass of clay and stones fill the void. These walls will typically be implanted directly into the ground, without any foundations or any damp-proof protection to the walls. This means that humidity can usually rise up through the stone from ground level. Ensuring a suitably impermeable external surface is the job of the mortar joints between the stones, while stopping rising damp problems is more complex. One part of the solution is to make sure the ground beneath the walls is well-drained, and that there is room for the walls to breathe (so they are not blocked by large shrubs or climbing plants). It is also possible to apply a waterproof render to the lower section of the wall (if it is below ground level), a technique known as tanking, and also to block out damp with a secondary wall inside the house.

The external face of the wall may be rendered with lime-based mortar, (see box). Alternatively, the joints between the stones on the

La chaux must go on

Back in the days before cement was invented (which happened around the start of the 20th century), there were three main substances suitable for binding building materials together: plaster, clay, and lime – what the French call *chaux*. Used with wood (filling the gaps between the timbers in 'half-timbered' houses), with bricks (as the mortar) or with stone (as mortar for the joints and as a rendering across the surface), chaux was one of the most important building materials of all, and used everywhere in France.

When cement took off commercially, it looked as if the chaux, as it were, was over. Cement was cheaper to make and easier to apply. Lime kilns across France shut down, or were transformed into museums, or even converted into stunning second homes built around cavernous, soaring stone furnaces, instantly knocking into a cocked hat any neighbours daring to brag about their restored bread ovens.

Today, though, chaux is making a comeback. Part of this is down to French home owners putting much more value on traditional materials. But there are other reasons. Cement-based products are not always best adapted to restoring old properties, either in terms of looks, or their technical properties. Chaux, after all, is a breathable material, well-adapted to stone-built houses. It is a bit like a natural version of high-tech hiking gear: it keeps the rain out, but allows humidity in the walls to escape. Damp is never trapped permanently inside the wall – it evaporates in dry weather. What's more, chaux provides good thermal and acoustic insulation. It can absorb slight movement, and is even fire resistant. So the chaux, you could say, must go on.

What you always wanted to know about chaux...

What is chaux made of?

So here comes the science bit. Chaux is a kind of binding material for mortars and renders, created by the high-temperature firing of limestone. If the silica content of this stone is very low, then the chaux is said to be *calcique*, and is classified as 'CL' under European standards. It hardens by absorbing carbon dioxide in the air, which is why it is known in French as *chaux aérienne* (and in English as non-hydraulic lime). There is another type of lime, which is rich in silica and aluminium impurities, and which hardens in the presence of water. This is known as *chaux hydraulique* or natural hydraulic lime, with the 'NHL' classification. Hydraulic lime is harder, and sets more quickly, than non-hydraulic, but is less flexible and less good at allowing water vapour to escape.

Aérienne or *hydraulique*?

Chaux aérienne actually hardens rather slowly. It is applied in thin coats, each of which must be allowed to harden properly. Sold either as a powder or as a kind of putty, it has excellent adherence and a fine grain. It is very, very white in its natural state, and is coloured either with natural pigments, or is mixed with naturally coloured sand.
It can be ideal for indoor plasterwork.

Physically, chaux hyraulique behaves much more like cement, hardening on contact with water. It is often used as the main body of a render, (before the final coat) and dries more quickly than chaux aérienne. In building stores, you will see a range of different kinds of NHL, which are designed to do different jobs, with 'NHL 3.5' the most common and general purpose variety. It is available in powder form.

Some tips on how to use it

Whether you are renovating or building something new, chaux is a great material to work with, though can require patience and a degree of skill. It has very good adherence, and is one of those rare materials that allows you to correct your errors as you go along – particularly with the versions which take longer to dry.

The best time to work on chaux is spring or autumn. Avoid extremely hot days, or winter frosts, which could provoke surface cracks.

When rendering a stone wall, you start by brushing out all the dry material. Dampen the wall down the night before, and again a couple of hours before you start work.

Most builders apply two coats: a main render coat, which is often created using chaux hydraulique, followed by the thinner, top coat in chaux aérienne. If using the latter, mix in the water the night before, so that it is nice and oily and easier to apply.

Keep the proportion of powdery material (such as pigments) to less than 20% of the dry volume. If you don't, you could end up with a powdery surface that comes off on your clothes.

Generally, even after being applied, chaux aérienne remains fairly malleable for a few hours, so you can go back and tidy up mistakes after the first pass.

Chaux also needs to be tamped down the day after application, to eliminate any air bubbles and cracks, and to make it as compact as possible. After this, the surface finish is created by smoothing it all over with a wet sponge, or the back of a trowel. To be avoided, though, is the practice of scraping or combing the surface, which can make the surface less resistant to water infiltration.

NATURE'S COLOUR PALETTE: THE WARM EARTHY TONES OF YELLOW OCHRE AND 'TERRE DE SIENNE'
The characteristic colours of houses in the south of France, and across into Italy, come from the local minerals such as ochre or *terre de Sienne*. The colour of your chaux will depend on whether you go for a naturally coloured sand, or add a natural pigment to the chaux and sand mix. Chaux gets paler as it dries, so test the colours first, to make sure that the deep red hue you want does not become a disappointing peach colour after a few days. In Roman times, other ingredients were added to improve the mix – and colour – including eggs, milk, and even blood and urine!

outer wall are pointed to leave exposed only the face of the stonework.

There is more skill and finesse involved in filling the joints between stones than you might think. It's worth looking at neighbouring houses that appear particularly authentic (if in doubt consult the CAUE or local experts) and take this as a benchmark. The typical style varies across regions. In some parts of France, the mortar is more or less flush with the face of the stone, an effect known as *beurré* or 'buttered'. In others, it is pushed right into the gaps between the stones, leaving more of a relief effect. It is worth doing some research to make sure you get this right. If you try too hard, you can end up with an extremely clean definition of each stone, rather like the walls of the Tower of London: if you go too far, you could end up with a finish where the stones can look as though they have simply been stuck onto the walls of the house as decoration. Also, renovating a façade needs be done with the appropriate regional stone. Otherwise, you could end up with trouble in terms of resistance to rain or frost.

Bricks

Like stone walls, brick walls need careful maintenance of the pointing to work as an effective barrier against rain. For repairs, your local mason may know where to find a stock of bricks that resemble those in your own property, and there are strong regional variations in terms of brick dimensions and colours. The patina that bricks develop depends largely on the kind of minerals and metallic compounds to be found in the earth from which they are formed.

Generally, new bricks are sold in palettes of 450, though you can

Timber frame
Half-timbered houses are built on a stone or brick plinth, though it is the timber frame itself that provides the rigid structure. Between the timbers, the infill panels were often built up from a mix of clay and straw. Today, bricks or chaux provide the standard basis for such panels. Cement should be avoided, as it is too rigid and can be prone to cracking.

understand the materials. But after surviving so many centuries, it is what these fine old buildings deserve.'

always buy smaller quantities (at a higher unit cost) for smaller jobs. Salvage yards will also sell reclaimed bricks, which look great for their patina and character, but check the selection to avoid getting a load of broken bricks, or those encrusted with old mortar.

Timber-framed houses

The majority of timber framed houses in France are what are known as *maisons à colombages* (the equivalent of 'half-timbered' houses that we see in the UK) with some dating from the middle ages.

This kind of architecture uses a timber frame and infill panels of clay and straw, sometimes known as *torchis*, or brick, stone or even tile infills. This method of construction, found almost everywhere between the middle-ages and the end of 16th century, was eventually banned at the beginning of the 17th century. The reason? Fire risk. From that point on, facades had to be covered in a rendering as protection against the whole lot going up in flames.

In effect, these wood framed houses are all built on the same principal: the footings are made of stone or brick, but the rigidity of the house is entirely due to the timber structure. Buying such a house to renovate is a specialist business, and help from voluntary organisations such as *Maisons Paysannes de France* can be useful, as will certain specialist architects and artisans. On some houses, the infill panels have been rendered with cement which lacks the suppleness of traditional materials and can even make the timber frame rot. However, it is still possible to find craftsmen who understand how to repair and replace these walls, which is what these fine old buildings deserve after surviving for so many centuries.

Chapter 6

SORTING OUT
THE INSIDE

Right then. Time to get into some old clothes, wellies and a hard hat. In this chapter we're going on site. Up to now there have been plenty of pretty pictures in this book, designed to inspire you to create wonderful things. There will be more. But first, it is time to take a look at some proper building work. We are talking about new floors where there were none before. And ways of getting your interior walls sorted out. So be warned: there will be a fair amount of wet, grey concrete over the next few pages. You could learn to love it!

Getting the interior of your house sorted out will probably involve two fairly challenging types of building jobs. One will be dealing with the interior faces of the main walls that support the house. The other involves making good the floors, both on the ground level, and upstairs.

The ground floor

Let's start by talking about the floors. We have already mentioned that in some older French houses, the ground floor is almost exactly that: a floor which is basically laid directly on the ground or earth beneath. In old barns, outbuildings and so on, the ground floor will simply be 'terre battue' or compact, and completely bare, beaten earth. We have already talked about why having a floor of flagstones laid directly onto the earth is a sure recipe for absorbing, and then transmitting, damp into your home. And the solution to this is a proper damp-proof course, or DPC, laid beneath a concrete floor.

Getting a damp-proof course installed will be a simple task, as any respectable builder will be able to do this for you. However, you could save money by digging out the existing floor yourself, though discuss the correct depth required with your builder, who is of course better equipped for excavating and removing the spoil.

Plans and a cross-section should be drawn showing both the ground floor and upper floor to check the room height after the new floor is in place. Agree on the levels with everyone involved, and make any revisions before starting work. Underfloor heating will need a slightly different approach.

One important thing before you start is to work out if underfloor drainage may be required. One project the authors have seen involved a barn conversion where the floor of the barn used to get a small trickle of water running across it during the wet winters. This did not stop a DPC being put in, but it did mean that a drainage system of pipes and gravel was installed below floor level to take the flow of water through the barn and away.

The technique to create a DPC is fairly straightforward. The

'Drainage matters: on one barn conversion project...'

1 The original floor covering is removed, and the compacted earth below is dug out to a depth of around 25cm. The bottom is lined with hardcore, and on top of this is laid sand, which is smoothed to create a level surface. Any service ducts are installed now.

2 This will be an insulated floor, so the next stage is to place a layer of plastic over the sand, followed by the insulation panels. If the floor is not insulated (and most are not) then you just lay the plastic sheet – which is the damp-proof course – and then jump ahead to picture 4.

3 A layer of plastic is then laid over the insulation panels, allowing plenty to rise up around the edges of the floor. The builder will trim these off after the concrete has set.

4 Next, the reinforcing mesh is laid over the panels, which will add strength to the floor. As this is a large space, timber uprights are being installed (held in place with cement, and checked with a spirit level) to help keep the floor surface level after the concrete is poured.

5 When the cement holding the timber uprights has set, the concrete is poured, and smoothed to a roughly level surface.

6 It is then carefully evened out, which is a two-man job using a levelling bar. When the concrete has set, the final coat is a smooth levelling screed, followed by whatever kind of flooring finish is required.

ground is first excavated to a depth of around 30cm. This will create for you a little mountain of earth, so it could be worth incorporating this part of the job with a bit of garden landscaping, to cut down on the number of wheelbarrow loads of earth you end up carting around.

At the bottom of the excavated floor, you lay broken stone, (which must be designed not to settle) and an underfloor drain if required, made of perforated tubes sloping towards the external drain. Above this, you unroll a layer of geotextile, to stabilise the surface, and then pour on sand, which must be smoothed out to create a layer about 4cm thick. Onto this goes the damp-proof membrane: basically a giant sheet of PVC, which is cut to the size of the floor with some excess, so it folds up against the wall on each side of the room by 30cm or so.

The next part of the floor is the insulating panels, laid on the plastic film, and cut to fit the whole floor. On these will go the reinforcement mesh (known as an *armature* or *treillis* in French), and once this is in place, the concrete is poured on. Note that over a large surface, wooden battens are mortared in place first, which provides a way of ensuring that the surface is level, as the concrete can be smoothed to the height of the battens.

The concrete will take nearly a month to set, or cure, completely, and releases a great deal of moisture way beyond this period. Once set, the next stage is relatively simple. The surface is screeded level, ready to receive your choice of floor covering (regular tiles, fixed with adhesive, or floating parquet floor etc.). Traditional terracotta tiles or stone flags would be laid using the old-fashioned mortar bed technique.

The upper floors

The biggest job you could face is renovating a property where the upper floors are in such a bad state that they need to be completely replaced. Alternatively, you may be renovating a barn or outbuilding where upper floors are being created for the first time.

'... a mini-stream ran across the floor every winter.'

1 The starting point: the empty shell of a stone house. The roof has been replaced, and the walls made structurally secure. The plan is to make a new first floor level, creating a genuine wood beamed ceiling on the ground floor. You need experienced pros to do this, who are used to manipulating these extremely heavy weights.

2 The walls have been prepared to accept the massive cross beams. These will be supported mid-way up the wall, which has been strengthened with reinforced concrete where necessary. The first of the oak beams is brought in. Measuring around 6m in length, and with each side around 30cm, each beam weighs 400kg. Seven are required.

3 The beams are hoisted into place, then jacked up to the correct height, before being fitted into the wall. The masonry must be up to the job, and the ends of the beams protected from damp. For a project like this, reclaimed, seasoned timber is less prone to expansion or contraction. You could even use concrete beams, clad in antique wood.

4 The next stage is to fit the load-bearing joists (which have a profile of around 15cm square) into the slots, or mortices, cut into the beams. Other methods exist, such as the joists going over the top of the beams. All the wood should be pre-treated whilst it is still all accessible.

'This is a mix of old and new technology. The supporting framework is made of fine timbers, to give you a

There are several techniques available. First and foremost, you will need to get qualified professionals on the case, as a botched job where a ceiling collapses could be fatal. But what are the options, and the costs? If you want to achieve a ground-floor ceiling that has genuine supporting wooden beams, then you will have to invest in some high quality and well-seasoned timber. The technique is shown in detail above, and is a mix of old and new technology. The supporting framework is made of beautiful timbers, but the floor above is created with insulating boarding, onto which is poured a lightweight concrete floor. It is the best of both worlds. The obvious benefit is the impact it creates on the ground floor, with a genuine beamed ceiling. You could typically expect to pay around €500 for each of the major cross-beams in a structure like this, so it does not come cheap.

There are of course cheaper alternatives using modern technology for those who are willing to do without a beamed ceiling. The so-called pot and beam technology uses reinforced concrete beams which are spaced around 40-60cm apart, with specially designed blocks, some of which can be insulated, slotting neatly into the space

5 The framework is almost complete, with an access space left for the staircase. Obviously, the entire upstairs room layout has already been planned out in advance.

6 Ceiling panels are then laid on the timber structure. Sometimes an electrician will have run cables in grooves in the joists, and the vertical posts too. A lightweight concrete floor will next be cast over the ceiling panels, with plastic sheet and reinforcement mesh.

7 The floor above is cast, and the timbers are supported with props to prevent them sagging before the concrete slab develops its own rigid strength. The traditional appearance of the ceiling is now evident.

8 The contrast with this is when you look at the upper floor: a tough, rigid, concrete slab with good acoustic and thermal insulation, designed with appropriate reinforcement and expansion joints. and rigid enough to support any kind of floor covering.

eamed ceiling. The floor above is a lightweight concrete slab on ceiling panels. The best of both worlds.'

in between (shown on p80). This is completed by casting over with a suitable concrete floor, onto which the final parquet or tiling is added, with underfloor heating if this is required.

Finishing the floor

In Chapter 4, we discussed the possibilities offered by reclaimed materials, including wood, stone and terracotta flooring. However, if the prospect of scouring salvage yards is too daunting, it is still possible to create the look with factory made reproductions of antique materials. The market is expanding, and with their convincing patina of ageing, these can often look as good as the real thing. And because they are new, and regular in format and thickness, they are usually much easier to install with resulting cost-savings in labour.

It would be fun to be able to tell your friends that the parquet in your home in France once belonged to a 17th century coaching inn – that it is 350 years old, and still contains authentic bloodstains from the many animated disputes that took place between travellers at the time. And especially fun if the story were pure fantasy.

Pot and beam
This is a structural floor system using concrete beams and some kind of insert, often concrete, (or, in the case below, insulating material) over which is cast a structural reinforced concrete slab. Builders' merchants often have an arrangement with pot-and-beam manufacturers, who will do a costing and work out what is required, given a set of plans. Small masonry firms rely on the manufacturer to supply the structural elements as a kit. The beams are sometimes supplied cut to length and prestressed, and are either housed in a groove cut into the wall, or placed in sockets.

Some people treat this as a DIY job, though there are obvious risks. The role of the planning authorities in France does not include structural inspections, so an inexperienced team could get it wrong and create a highly dangerous structure.

Our advice: get a professional in on all structural work.

These days, you could almost get away with it using reproduction antique parquet. Technology now exists to 'age' wood very convincingly – using oxidation, running the wood between rollers, and then leaving it in a humid storage area before waxing it. In effect the wood appears to take on 150 years of wear in just a few days, showing all the effects of wear and tear over the 'decades' as well as a dark patina of age. The only downside is that this ageing beauty is quite literally skin deep, and can get worn away with time. And if you sand the wood, you end up, of course, with bright, brand new boards once again. In addition, any new timber will be more prone to movement than a genuine antique.

How to repair a terracotta floor

Many people fall in love with an old house in France because of the stone or terracotta floors – worn and uneven with the passage of time and the passing generations of householders. But if the floor is dirty, broken and needs serious work, how much of it can be salvaged? The answer depends largely on how the tiles have been laid. Traditionally, they are simply placed over a layer of sand, clay or a weak mortar, which in turn sits on the earth beneath – allowing the floor to 'breathe' (but becoming also a source of damp). These are relatively easy to remove with the aid of simple hand tools. You can then repair the floor (installing a DPC and concrete slab, and renewing underfloor services if necessary).

In houses that have at some time been modernised, the tiles are more likely to be fixed with cement-based mortar or a modern adhesive to a concrete base, and are much more difficult, or impossible to lift without breaking them.

They could also have stubborn bits of mortar stuck to the bottom, making them harder to re-lay and more prone to breakage.

If there are tiles missing, then you will probably have a hard job finding lookalike replacements at a salvage yard, unless the owners kept the spare tiles from the original tiling job somewhere else in the house. An alternative would be to re-integrate the flooring into sections – some areas being covered in the remaining original tiles, the other in some kind of contrasting material.

Once the tiles are lifted, you can then set to work cleaning them up (described on p50). It is important to rinse them thoroughly in water after treatment with chemical agents, and then seal the tiles with a wax or oil once they have been laid and fully dried out. Other non-waxy finishes are also available, perhaps less sticky than wax or oil. Keeping the tiles clean in the future is simple, and you can use soapy water, or further coats of sealant.

Cement or 'encaustic' tiles

Made of a mix of cement, sand, and fragments of marble ground to a powder, cement tiles first appeared in the mid-19th century in south east France. They gradually caught on everywhere, thanks to their potential for making incredible, geometric and colourful surfaces which are also incredibly hardwearing, as the vibrancy of the colour runs throughout a significant part of the tile. From the 1950s onwards, these *carreaux de ciment* were gradually surpassed by cheaper, quicker-to-lay flooring such as lino, though over the last few years they have been making a comeback. A number of suppliers are now stocking versions of these tiles with traditional motifs or in plain colours, which allow you to create your own chequerboard patterns. The standard way to lay these tiles is on a cement screed over a concrete base, fixing them with mortar or adhesive.

Random walk With a natural stone floor, or a good reproduction composite version, you may opt for a random laying pattern, or *opus romain*. It is not quite as random as it looks, as the eye can pick out the repeat in the format, especially in bigger rooms. Whether you choose new 'antiqued' or reconstituted stone, the slabs will be easy to adhere to a screeded surface.

If you have *carreaux de ciment* in need of renovation, this can be straightforward. Freshen up the surfaces by hand with extremely fine-guage glass paper, or use an electric sander with great care. Then apply a sealant (otherwise the surface is porous) and finally apply a clear wax – something you will need to renew periodically. In everyday cleaning, avoid detergents as these will strip off the wax and the sealant. Ordinary soap-based floor cleaners will be good enough.

DEALING WITH WALLS

However good your house is on the outside of your house – in terms of pointing the stonework, or the integrity of the rendering, or the drainage of the land next to your walls, or the good maintenance of guttering and roofing – you can still end up with an interior that tends to be cold, and prevents your home from from being readily warmed up (see 'Cold in Winter', p45). If this is the case, you may choose to line walls with insulated panels, or build up a more substantial 'inner wall' from blocks to do the same job. In both cases make sure the surface of the existing stone wall is made good, and leave a gap between the stone wall and the lining wall, to allow air to circulate and stop damp from hanging around in this space.

Beyond these measures, you may also choose to create new partition walls to re-design the room layout – with the option of using insulated materials (thermal or acoustic insulation) for added privacy, warmth, or simply to hide the noise from a heating boiler, for example.

There is a wide choice of materials, from bricks designed for building a new, lining wall, to the familiar plasterboard or similar panels which will do a similar job. Here is a brief run-down.

Plaster bricks (*carreaux de plâtre*) are aimed at the bigger renovation jobs, and need decent brick-laying skills to use properly. For lining a damp wall exposed to the north (you leave a gap for the air to circu-

'However good your house may be on the outside...'

1 There is an extremely wide range of materials available to insulate a wall, from the mineral fibre padding shown here, to rigid panels that fit onto a metal framework behind dry-lining (such as plasterboard panels). If the walls are dry, the technique illustrated is fine. If you are worried about damp, it is better to use rigid insulated panels and keep an air gap between the panels and the wall itself, and ventilate the space too.

2 This type of insulation is easy to fix, using a system of plastic plugs that are hammered into holes drilled straight through the insulation. Don't skimp on supporting soft insulating material: if it is not properly supported on the wall, it can start to sag or even come off, leading to a messy pile of compacted insulation behind the neat plasterboard or blockwork walls that you create.

3 The thickness of an insulated wall will inevitably compromise some element of the room. It will. of course, reduce the dimensions slightly, but more importantly, you could lose some of the attractive details around doorways or windows. The thinner the insulation, the less this is a problem, but high performance thin insulators can be more pricey.

wall with insulation

4 The final wall here will be built of blockwork: in this case, *carreaux de plâtre*, or plaster blocks. To start the wall, a metal profile is fixed to the floor. This not only provides a level start for the wall, but it also prevents damp getting into the plaster blocks, helps to spread the weight of the wall across the floor, and keeps the wall straight.

5 Blockwork builds up quickly, with frequent checks that it is vertical. Alternatives would be any kind of dry-lining system such as plasterboard or fibro-cement board. The tricky bit, as always, is finishing off the edges between the new wall and existing walls. Use a saw designed for cutting up these blocks to get the best results.

6 The gap between blockwork wall and insulation is fairly wide here, because part of the aim of this job was to square up the room. You don't need to leave an air gap this wide, though. The blocks are fixed together with a plaster-based adhesive. When completed, a decorator will add a skim coat and sand down the joints, before finishing the job, typically with a primer and water-based emulsion paint.

late) be aware that the bricks too can suffer from damp and in turn prove a difficult support for paint or papering to remain in good order. They are thick, dense, quite heavy, and thus excellent as acoustic barriers too, but need a strong floor to support them. **Hollow clay blocks** (*briques plâtrières*) are also laid like a brick wall. Again they are ideal for lining a wall exposed to cold weather or driving rain (such as on the Atlantic coast in the winter) or where there is damp coming up from the ground. They are not so good for sound-proofing, though. **Plasterboard** (*Placoplâtre, or 'placo'*) will be a familiar material to most experienced DIYers, and is quick and relatively simple to use. You need to take care with fixing objects to the walls once they are up: there is an enormous choice of fixings available in DIY shops, but you need to find the right size and design for your wall. Plasterboard can sometimes deteriorate in damp conditions, so a more sophisticated, robust and expensive alternative is **gypsum fibre-board** (*plaques de plâtre renforcées en fibres de cellulose*), which also has good damp resistance when used to line walls.

Lightweight partitions

We are all using the space in our houses rather differently these days compared even with just a couple of generations ago. The dining room is an endangered species. The kitchen instead is becoming the main focal point in many houses, enlarged whenever possible. People providing guest rooms today often think of installing an adjoining shower room and WC. So part of the renovation job can involve redefining how the rooms fit together. Putting up new non-loadbearing partition walls downstairs gives you plenty of choice in materials, providing there are few constraints on how much weight can go on the floor. Upstairs, however, you may be limited to more lightweight options. Timber frame studwork (*ossature bois*) is being largely overtaken by plasterboard on a metal frame (unless for some traditional designs where the frame itself is a feature, or where you

'...you can still end up with a cold wall on the inside.'

Rendering a wall If a stone wall needs rendering, one option is to fix a mesh to the wall to help the render key into the raked-out jointwork, and to stabilise the whole surface, reducing the risk of cracking dur-ing drying and afterwards. In this example, the first, rough coat is applied with a pump, which means a large quantity can go on in a short time. The manual alternative is the traditional method, flicking it with dexterity off a trowel. Interior walls could then be painted, or clad with dry-lining panels. Or a second, lev-elling coat, or a traditional plas-ter, will complete the finished surface.

use some kind of wooden panels. The metal frame, though, will give you extremely flat and rigid partition walls (if you do it properly), with the opportunity to add insulation between the two panels. If you choose waterproof panels (*plaques hydrofugées*), you can use this system for bathrooms and kitchens.

An alternative for upstairs partitions where you want good sound-proofing is lightweight **concrete blocks** (*béton cellulaire*) which are built up using a mortar-like adhesive.

Exposing stone walls

When your house is built of stone, it is hard to resist the temptation to strip off some of the wall coverings to show off the stone in all its natural beauty.

If the stonework is really good, there are hardly any downsides to this – except that stone walls can be prone to creating dust, so you either need to vacuum a bit more often, or else treat the stone with a clear sealant, or repoint the jointwork to keep it together.

However, the stone in a wall will not necessarily look good. Stripping it back could leave you with a dull, messy-looking wall of rubble. Even if the stone does look OK, you will need to work on the joints between the stones, taking out the loose material (and there can be a lot of it) using a pick-like hammer and a wire brush, and then jointing the whole lot with a lime mortar in a natural colour that com-plements the stone. In any case, it's best not to overdo the exposed stone. Pick the best, warmest walls to expose, perhaps those panels to either side of a well-built stone fireplace where the original masons needed to build carefully. You could dry-line or render the others. Walls newly hacked-off frequently reveal treasures like wall cup-boards, carved stone niches or doorways from the same era as the fire-an exposed stone wall makes the stone look even more stunning. Subtle lighting will complete the effect.'

place, often in the same stone. It's exciting stuff. Also, a clean, freshly plastered wall next to an exposed stone wall makes the stone look even more stunning. Warm lighting that shows off the relief of the stone is also highly effective.

Rendering walls with chaux

France is going through something of a revival of traditional materials, led by the famous *chaux* or lime render. Breathable, natural, and clean, chaux is becoming popular for interior decor too, not least for its ability to take great colour pigments (derived from sand or natural minerals), as well as its matt feel and resilience. You can repair it easily, so it is ideal for old buildings prone to slight movement.

Depending on the look you want to get, (from a thin paint, right through to a thick render) you simply dilute to taste. The thickest, known as *chaulage* is generally unpigmented, while the chaux *enduit* or

Options for walls A deep and richly pigmented chaux interior (left) adds warmth. The unpigmented rough render in natural white (top) keeps the vague contours of the stone beneath visible, but at the same time adds light to the room. Meanwhile, the dining room (above) has opted for exposed stone, which is carefully jointed and very much in relief.

Better buttered

A successful stone wall should be seen as an overall beautiful surface, rather than a surface made up of countless individual stones, however attractive they all may appear to be. Despite the rather 'buttered' appearance of this wall, which may not be everyone's ideal of an exposed stone wall, this kind of surface looks good and is more practical than one with sharply recessed joints, which is much more time-consuming to achieve. Also, hundreds of small ledges on an interior wall will gather dust, while on an exterior wall, they could easily harbour damp and provoke rain infiltration.

rendering is a more traditional plaster-like render, and *badigeon* is a limewash, that goes onto a primed surface (some modern versions may indicate a couple of coats of acrylic paint, or a limewash primer).

When you buy chaux, you will find it either in a ready-mixed form, which is like a kind of putty you can then dilute, or in powder form, which takes a little longer to prepare but is easier to adjust for colour and thickness. When adding natural pigments, it is best not to let them exceed 10-15% of the quantity of chaux. At this level the colour is already saturated, so it won't get any better, and beyond this level, the chaux can become too powdery and flake off the wall, and onto your clothes – a factor that puts many people off using chaux for interior walls.

Applying chaux in render form to a wall, like plastering, is a skill, and it is usually worth hiring someone to do this and any preliminary making good of the wall beforehand.

A DIY alternative is the increasing number of faster-drying chaux lookalikes, in the form of factory-made renders which will seal up a wall and provide the finished surface at one pass, though they will be less 'breathable' than lime render. The colour is created in one of two ways. Either the render is pre-coloured with pigment, or you can paint a layer of coloured wax over the finished render. This is an interesting option, as with pre-coloured render the pigment is more or less uniform, whereas if you use wax, the colour density will vary according to the look you want to achieve.

Waiting weeks for a thick chaux layer to dry off inside your house will hold up a lot of other jobs as the humidity level will remain too high. Nevertheless, taking time to allow the job to be done properly is a good maxim for long-lasting renovations or restorations. And who wants to re-do rushed jobs a few years later?

Exposing beams This can be tricky, exposing also a spider's web of electrical wiring, flaky plaster and insulation. Also, stripping paint from beams is usually a drag: you hire a sand-blaster, or use paint stripper and a wire brush. There is, though, a new method involving a gauze sheet impregnated with stripper that is applied to the beams, then peeled off. Alternatively, paint the beams white, to create a fresh, bright ceiling (top picture).

'Dusty chaux render marking your clothes can be avoided. Check the mix of the 'potion' and test it first.'

Chapter 7

MAKING WOOD GOOD

DOORS, WINDOWS, SHUTTERS

Anyone who has visited a few old country houses in France will be well aware of how much wood takes on character as it ages, adding to the overall allure of your home. Up to a point. But if wood is too far gone and your joinery is falling apart, you get into this dilemma: renovate or replace? It's a dilemma because renovating doors and windows can take forever and hold up your project. But many people worry that replacement versions will spoil the look. The good news: they don't.

More off than on
The cycle of intense heat in the summer and winter rain and frosts will ravage even recent paint-work, and if you buy a place that has been neglected, woodwork like this will be waiting for you. It is not necessarily beyond repair: if the wood is still sound and the framework straight, then you could consider a restoration job, involving scraping, sanding, priming, filling, and painting. The downside: very time consuming. It can be therapeutic and enjoyable at first, but a painful task by the end.

French windows (and we are not talking about patio doors here, but the basic *fenêtre*) are brilliant inventions. Large frames, opening inwards, easy to clean, bringing plenty of light and air. And then there are the shutters. Even the old ones, on antiquated rusting hinges, will close up at night to keep your bedroom dark well into the morning, allowing you to oversleep to an extent unknown since you were a teenager. Doors, too, show a kind of simple practicality. If you want to remove a door in Britain, you usually need to take out a dozen long screws, and it never seems to go back in quite the same way again. In France, you just lift the door off its hinges. If there was a word for that, it would have to be 'hingenuity'.

These kind of joinery fittings generally have a long lifetime, and what's more, the older some of these doors, windows, or shutters get, the more characterful they are. This brings us back to a recurring theme in this book – how *not* to over-renovate your house in France.

Shutters that shut, even though they are not quite straight, or windows that are tough to close but still close, or a front door with a draft underneath that can be blocked by a large rug and perhaps a large dog too: we can all live with these little inconveniences, and it is part of what having a rural holiday home is all about.

However, if you buy a place that needs total renovation – where the windows are missing, or completely rotten, or impossibly drafty, and the shutters are in pieces and the metalwork looks like something dredged up from the bottom of the ocean – then it is time to consider investing in something new.

Before we move on, a word about materials. Wood is the traditional choice, but good joinery can be expensive. Tropical hardwoods are not necessarily as rot-resistant as they are made out to be, and are also decimating the world's natural resources. Oak is a fantastic material and wins hands down against modern plantation-grown pine which has little rot-resistance. And, while not a wood, PVC is becoming

'Wonky shutters, drafty windows... they are just part of what having a rural holiday home is all about.'

Early doors

What is the best wood for a front door? Oak is hard to beat. However, all timbers can be sensitive to changes in temperature and humidity, which can cause warping and cracking. This can be avoided if the door is made in a well-proven traditional way. In some regions, two layers of tongue and groove panels – vertical on the outside, and laid horizontally on the interior, seem to last for ever. Maintaining a door like this requires a wood-protection coating, which needs to be sanded down and re-applied every three to four years. Avoid varnish, as this suffers when exposed to sunlight. If your door will be exposed to heavy rain during the winter, your joiner may recommend hardwood, which is naturally resistant to damage from humidity or sunlight, and is not prone to cracking. The best finish for this is paint. For example, a typical Basque red, a Provençal green, or the characteristic light blue of the Atlantic coast and its islands. Old whites are also good for unassuming simplicity.

91

'Decent joinery is a worthwhile investment. It is what people notice when they are buying a house.'

more and more popular in France for budget-priced renovations. However, despite attempts to copy traditional styles, the PVC solution never really looks the part when viewed up close.

While the floors and well-insulated walls that we talked about in the last chapter are part of the invisible fabric of a house, joinery, in terms of doors, windows, shutters and so on, is very much the opposite. When you come eventually to sell your house, it is part of what will make an impact on the buyers, almost a kind of jewellery, designed to attract compliments. With this in mind, joinery is worth investing in. It does not take an expert to spot good quality. Great doors and windows, like a great fireplace or a great floor, will be a major selling point.

Doors

The exterior door, your front door, must at the same time offer durability against the weather and security for your home. A new front door could be made of oak or hardwood, though the choice could be influenced by the kind of weather you expect and its exposure to prevailing winds. A solidly built made-to-measure door could cost you upwards of €700. An authentic old door from a salvage yard is an option, but can be a labour of love to integrate, perhaps with a new frame to make. You could find that the time and money required to get a good joiner to adapt a reclaimed door could have been better spent on a completely new model. Wooden doors at a salvage yard could cost from very little to between €500 and €1,000.

Generally taken for granted, doors actually play a major part in creating the general ambiance of a room. And a French country house is typically the kind of place where we go out of our way to create a warm, comfortable atmosphere that has a bit of history about it somewhere. If you're keen on antique sales, you could be lucky enough to get hold of an imposing oak or cherrywood cupboard, or an oversized kitchen table with a hundred years' worth of stains and scratches running through it. But put this kind of furniture next to a cheap, modern door, and the effect is lost immediately.

If you are rearranging rooms and putting up new partitions, you

Unlocking language Finding the right fittings and metalwork for doors and windows is a linguistic challenge. Any kind of catch for a window or door is un loqueteau, while the vertical locking mechanism for a casement window is known as an espagnolette bolt, or une crémone or une espagnolette. A typical French door hinge is une charnière or une paumelle, while a UK-style hinge is une penture anglaise. A door handle is une poignée de porte. The hook and hinge of a shutter is un gond et une penture. General locking hardware is la quincaillierie de condamnation, which includes the lock, la fermeture or la serrure, which if for a window is la serrure de crémone. A deadlock is une serrure a pêne dormant, while a high security door latch is un verrou haute sécurité. A mortise lock is une serrure à encastrer, or à mortaise.

'High quality new joinery looks particularly appealing in an old house.'

will need to think about interior doors. Sometimes, there might be a serviceable door hidden away in an outbuilding. More likely, however, you will need to buy some new ones, or get some made. And if this is the case, it is worth remembering that interior doors play their part in keeping rooms warm, or quiet. The cooler and draftier your house is, the more robust the interior doors should be.

Replacing an interior door

When we talk about a door, we really mean two elements: the door itself, and the door jamb, or architrave, which fits into the masonry of the wall with cement bonding. In a renovation job, you could find yourself replacing the whole thing (the *bloc-porte*) or just the opening part of the door itself. In the latter case, you will face the problem of a brand new door sitting in an old, and perhaps a bit battered, architrave. You will probably therefore need to work on the architrave to strip back paint and sand it down, so that it does not look 100 years older than the new door, though this is a time-consuming job. The quicker alternative is to invest in good quality new joinery for the architrave as well as the door – in other words go for the *bloc-porte* option. New, high quality joinery can harmonise extremely well with an old house.

If you are trying to keep the look authentic, re-use the hardware (the door knob, keyhole and so on) or if this is impossible, either find something in an antique market or in a hard-

A breath of air
Typical inward opening casement windows: great for bringing in the gentlest breeze on the most suffocatingly hot day. They are easy to clean too. French people are astonished at the outward-opening UK versions.

Prepare to be pleasantly surprised by the quality and finish of double glazed window units in France, available in traditional styles.

Old, uneven casement windows, with peeling paint and flaking wooden shutters are another element of the rural charm of so many French cottages. However, in terms of doing what windows are supposed to do (such as keeping out drafts, or heat, or robbers) the more charming the windows, the less effective they tend to be. Many people are prepared to live with this. But it is also possible to have decent windows – either by renovation or replacement – that do not spoil the charm of your house.

Obviously, there is no point renovating window frames if they are too warped to ever shut properly. Generally, the outer wooden sill, known as the *jet d'eau* is the most easily damaged by weathering, and usually rots underneath, where it meets the stone ledge. Making good in a long-term manner involves removing the frame, and even grafts to the side verticals. Making a new frame is often the best option but may be expensive.

Draft dodging

If the window does not shut properly, then it is obvious where the drafts are coming from. If it shuts but there are still drafts, then there could be gaps between the edge of the window frame and the masonry of the wall. Running your hand around the edge of the window can help find drafts – which can then be dealt with either by filling cracks with a silicone mastic, or, for bigger cavities in the masonry, with a polyurethane foam which doubles in volume as it hardens. This is available in a number of different forms, including aerosol versions, and can be cut, sanded and painted once

dry. If air is whistling in between the opening part of the window and its frame, then you can use a band of foam insulating strip, or alternatively use rubber strips, cut to fit, and fixed on with silicone adhesive.

Double glazing

While it is possible to buy new wooden or aluminium windows faced with wood, in the traditional style, and which incorporate double glazing, it is much more difficult to upgrade an existing window to double glazing. If the window is in excellent condition, and the framework is strong enough, it is possible in theory to replace a single piece of glass with double glazing. However, where the frame is too weak or too thin to support this (and that is more often the case, because these double glazed panes are heavy) your builder might suggest inserting double glazed panes, in their

In this Luberon renovation, new cast concrete window housings have been installed, together with new windows, and shutters that close flush to the outer surface. Painted white, it all fits in surprisingly well with the traditional stone wall.

own frames, inside the existing frame. Aesthetically, this is not a great idea, as the window frames will then appear much thicker than they were before, and you will get improved insulation at the cost of losing a good deal of their elegance and charm.

Secondary double glazing is an option, depending on the configuration of the interior walls, and again, it does not always look great.

Other options

Keeping the original window frame intact If the frame or chassis of the window is in good condition, you can replace a window with what is known as a *bloc rénovation* which consists of the opening part of the window, within a slimmed down version of the outer frame. This is made to measure, and fits inside the existing frame, making it quick to install as it does not involve ripping out all of the old window and tidying up the masonry.

The problem with this technique is that the window ends up with a bigger total outer-frame size, and a smaller glazed area – with the risk that it won't match your other windows, and will reduce the amount of light that gets into your rooms.

If the main frame of the window is too damaged, you could replace the whole window. This will cost more, but you get a window that is perfectly sound, double-glazed, will eliminate drafts and conserve heat in the winter.

ware store (*quincaillerie*) where you can find some convincing-looking reproduction models on the market today.

Staircases

A rickety farmhouse staircase has a lot of character, and is usually worth preserving, but if you are creating space in the roof, or starting with a 'shell' of a house with the upper floor missing, you will need to create a staircase from scratch.

Even something humble and utilitarian like a staircase has its charm, but will need to meet a certain number of hard criteria: safety, the amount of floorspace it takes up, the steepness, width, and depth of each step. If you are briefing a joiner to design a staircase, there are a few things to think about: How often will it be used? Where does it go – to a bedroom, or down to a cave? Who is going to use it – children, great-grandparents, party-goers? And how do you want it – spiral, with a turn, straight up? And will it have to be big enough to take bulky furniture?

The height the staircase has to climb will have a direct effect on how long it is in a horizontal direction, as there is a clear maximum comfortable height to a riser, and a minimum practical width of each stair. So the number of stairs will, of course, be proportional to the height you need to reach. Equally, a staircase should not go up more than about 2m without a break or a landing of some sort. That takes even more space. For more on staircases, see p209.

Renovating shutters

Wooden shutters have a hard time, enduring the intense heat of the sun during the summer, and rain, wind, damp and freezing temperatures during the winter. Not surprisingly, it is rare to find an old

'Shutters have a hard time: intense heat in summer...'

house that does not have shutters with some kind of problem: they won't open, or they won't shut, or they are too tight, too loose, warped or wonky.

Sagging: The most common problem with wooden shutters is that they tend to sag under their own weight, to the point where they are too low relative to the window and window ledge, and will not close. Often, by this time, they are a lost cause, though it is possible, if you catch the problem early enough, to repair the shutters. It is time-consuming, and involves taking the shutters apart plank by plank, cleaning up the tongue and grooves, replacing any which are damaged beyond repair, putting the whole thing back together and painting it. If the shutters are not too far gone, a simpler solution is to add an extra reinforcing strut across the width of the shutter door (such a strut could be made of metal).

Flaking paint: This is an inevitable problem considering what a wooden shutter has to live with, and repair is a standard process of stripping the loose paint (or all the paint or varnish if you have time) and reapplying a suitable replacement. This could be wood treatment; or marine varnish for wood exposed to sea air; or micro-porous paint (which allows the wood to breath) for exterior joinery.

Rust: A major problem for home owners who live near the sea, rusty metal fittings on shutters will quickly drip a red stain down across the paintwork, or even burst open the stonework (as on the lintel above the doorway pictured left). The only solution is to be quick in spotting any faults in the paintwork, brush away any existing rust with a

Open and shuttered New, brightly painted shutters are a hallmark of the renovated house in France, and are one of the simpler and relatively inexpensive jobs. Bespoke pairs of shutters like the orange ones (left) could cost around €350 per set if you opt for pine, which will not last forever, but certainly creates the look.

'...wind, rain, damp and frost throughout the winter.'

'PVC shutters: technically efficient, yes, but charming they are not.'

steel abrasive or brush, then treat the metal with a rust-retardant, followed by a fresh coat of paint to finish.

Replacing shutters

Traditionally, wooden shutters were made of oak, or other durable timbers, though this is now less and less common, both because of cost, and the need to make them in a traditional manner. Oak is heavy, and when it is wet, it is heavier still, which means the wide hinged arms that hold the vertical planks together must be very strong. Many people today turn to cheaper, lightweight pine for shutters – not robust or hardwearing, but it does the job. Unfortunately, all today's fast-grown timber lacks durability.

If you are seeking replacement **wooden shutters**, it is likely you will have to get them made-to-measure, though this does not necessarily mean going to a specialist joiner. Certain big DIY retailers will create bespoke wooden shutters for you. And some manufacturers of wooden shutters will also make bespoke sizes, with the option of supplying them in an unfinished state ready for painting, or offering the usual range of factory finished paint or varnish. The price of this bespoke service is surprisingly low – a premium over the cost of the standard shutter itself of as little as €40 per unit.

Even **PVC shutters** are also becoming available in bespoke sizes from certain manufacturers. Technically efficient they may be, but charming to look at they are not.

The alternative to the standard shutter are folding shutters (*persiennes*), made of a series of panels of wood, PVC or metal, each around 15cm wide which are hinged vertically, and which fold back on each side of the window. These are light and easy to install, fixing onto the window's side jambs, and when they are folded back they are virtually invisible.

In many older houses, there is a tendency towards rather gloomy interiors. This is fine on a really hot day, but at other times, the low ceilings, not to mention the small windows can create a desire to break open a wall and let in some light, and often a great view too. It sounds relatively straightforward, but it can be difficult to get the balance right when creating new windows without spoiling the look of the house.

A sense of proportion

There are no hard and fast rules about window dimensions and proportions, due to regional variations, though a good many houses seem to have remarkably similar-sized windows.

Generally, a typical 'French' window in older country properties is around a metre wide by around 1.6m high. These tend to create a harmonious façade, and let in plenty of light. Bear in mind too that the higher the windows are from the ground, the more light they will bring into the room. Purely going on looks alone, a vertical window (or 'portrait' as laser printers would have it) gives a feeling of balance and finesse, whereas a horizontal 'landscape' window tends to give a feeling of being squashed down in a room where the ceiling is too low. It is partly for this reason that widening an existing window can change – for the worse – the look and feel of a façade, and the living space behind it. A better idea is to create a 'twin' window of the same proportions as the original, making sure there is enough space to open the shutters completely on both windows.

With old cottages which have a low ceiling, a narrow vertical window will look better than a new window which is wider than it is tall.

The difficult north face

A typical feature of French houses built between the 17th and 19th centuries is that they tend to turn their

backs towards the north – or towards the prevailing winds – with the rear façade having few, if any windows. The practical benefits, of course, were to keep out the cold and wind, even if this meant depriving that side of the house of light. For households at the time, just one side of the house letting in the light was seen as being perfectly good enough.

These days, opening up the north face of a house will not let much sunlight in, though it will add to the ambient light in the rooms. It will also tend to make the house feel colder in winter.

The most practical solution is not to go over the top in creating too many windows, get them double-glazed, and put up thick curtains during the winter to help insulate rooms.

Symmetry

Many older rural houses have already been chopped around over the previous century, with windows and doors added or bricked up – adding to their quirky charm. This means that a strictly symmetrical façade is not a necessity – and in fact asymmetry can look good too. It's a question of thinking about the context. Symmetrical facades can look out of place in a very rural setting, though are completely appropriate to a manor house or chateau from recent centuries.

At the same time, the simpler the design of a house, the more impact the windows will have. It is worth noting that upstairs windows are often narrower than those on the ground floor, where the demand for light is the greatest.

And if you wish to add more light to the upstairs rooms, it is worth considering additional windows in the roof, in whatever style is appropriate to the region (such as *lucarnes, chien-assis, oeil-de-boeuf* etc.). You could even consider a 'light-pipe' which provides a conduit for light from the roof down to the ceiling of one of your rooms.

If in doubt, consult a local architect, or an organisation such as *Maisons Paysannes de France*, which has a network across France ready to give advice on how to respect local architectural styles.

Not every house will have a 'face' quite as striking as this mill, but the overall look of where the windows are on a façade generate a good deal of character in some older houses. Adding a new window opening is a bit like hanging a new picture on your wall, except that if you get it wrong, you cannot just take out the nail and try elsewhere.

WHAT'S INVOLVED: OPENING UP A NEW WINDOW

Opening up a modest-sized window often involves opening up a vast hole in the wall. Masons start at the top, with a small hole that is supported as soon as possible by heavy timber sections on Acrow props, screwed to the timber. As the hole is enlarged, more supports are added. Opening up a large space allows masons enough room to build up the stonework and then cast a reinforced concrete lintel above the window opening (in this case, behind a timber beam), and which supports the structure above. Here, the window openings and their interior reveals are in limestone. A cheaper option is to build up in concrete blockwork, if you know that the interior finish is to be rendered, plastered or dry-lined. We don't want to nag, but these masons should be wearing hard hats.

Chapter 8

LOFTY AMBITION

A ROOM IN THE ROOF

Converting loft space (in French, this is *aménagement des combles*) has become a major trend in France, and most estate agents selling a house will make a point of drawing attention to whether or not the loft space, or *combles*, is suitable for conversion. In many older properties, the results can be stunning, not least because of the presence of the roof timbers, creating what some people like to call a 'cathedral' roof. Whatever you call it, a room in the roof can be a major feature of a renovation, and – as it adds space – it is also likely to increase the value of your house.

Loft story

If you have great-looking timbers in the roof space, a loft-conversion will look stunning. The biggest potential snag is a roof structure that limits headroom or which simply gets in the way of the living space you plan to create. No such problems with this bathroom project, beneath a roof which at its highest point rises to nearly 4m. In projects where headroom is more limited, the best option is to use the eaves space at the side for storage, and for the bath, and mount a shower unit on the far wall where the headroom is highest. The limited-height side walls are often an ideal place to install low-level radiators.

'The vendor says the loft space can be converted. But is it just a case of putting in partitions, floors, insulation

Mind your head
The arrangement of the structural timbers for the roof will in large part dictate the viability of your loft conversion project. If major structural reworking is needed, costs can get out of control. But don't write off a loft space just because there are hefty timbers that limit headroom. As this room shows, you can work around a massive cross beam and still create a comfortable bedroom. You just need to warn your guests to take a bit of care if they are stumbling around at night trying to find the bathroom.

The question of what makes it possible to convert the loft space depends, of course, on the nature of the roof. Broadly speaking, in the south of France the slope of the roof is relatively flat, so there is often not enough head-room to do the job properly. Where roofs are steeper, you will have greater potential headroom.

Inside the roof, you are looking for the standard timber purlins and roof truss construction, while hoping that the existing structure lends itself readily to the kind of adaptations implied by adding roof windows, flooring, furniture and so on. Lightweight pre-fabricated roof structures are generally unsuitable for loft conversions unless radically transformed, but are unlikely to be seen on French houses built before the 1950s.

The structure of the roofing timbers may not immediately suit a loft conversion – it could get in the way, or be such that the height to the ridge only allows a narrow corridor where you can walk up and down, with the pitch sloping away on either side. It is possible to sort this kind of problem out, but it will need expert advice. Obviously any changes or repositioning of timbers must not endanger the stability of the structure.

The other solution involves changing the slope of the roof on either one or both sides of the ridge. This is dangerous territory in terms of how your house will work afterwards, and the extra space gained is often not worth the costs involved. Going back to the basics of what is the right kind of house for you, the answer is partly going to be: one which is big enough for your requirements, but without having to shoe-horn additional cramped rooms into unsuitable spaces, very often at a ridiculously high cost.

If structural timbers are in the way, it is possible to take them out, usually replacing them with other structural elements (such as a raised or lowered tie-beam, or special additional struts).

Alternatively, in changing the pitch of the roof (to make it less steep), the structure is effectively rebuilt, keeping certain parts of the structure and replacing others. This can also necessitate raising the height of the walls, or building a 'mansard' roof. Evidently, this is major structural work, which will make the creation of a loft room extremely expensive for the actual space provided. So when considering buying a house where a loft conversion is claimed to be possible, check whether this means simply putting in a floor, partitions, ceilings and insulation, or if they mean you would need to more or less completely rebuild the house. It makes a huge difference.

Avoiding noise

On the next page we look in more detail about partitions and insulation. It is vital not to neglect acoustic insulation throughout a loft conversion project, so that every new partition wall is, in effect, a sandwich with insulation in the middle. However, if you have a loft already converted, where this has not been done, you could add a layer of insulation and a second plasterboard or wood panel against the existing partition wall.

To reduce noise coming through via the floor, floor panels on a bed of dry screed (a layer of granules) have good acoustic qualities, as does a lightweight concrete slab. Seek professional advice before you start.

If you are planning either a floating parquet floor, or one which is glued down, use a layer of insulation below it. Leave a gap between the edge of the floor and the partition walls, not just for expansion of a floating parquet, but to reduce the transmission of noise from the floor into the walls of the adjacent rooms. If you need to, for a complete belt-and-braces approach, consider adding a false, insulated ceiling to the rooms below.

Loft insulation and partition walls

Insulation

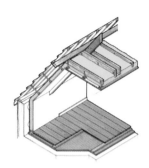

INSULATION

A typical set-up where the roof timbers will not be too evident. Insulation (18mm) is behind plasterboard, screwed onto metal profiles. The vertical wall section is a one-piece insulated plasterboard.

The roof will need to be insulated, or the loft space will become like an oven in the summer, and very cold in the winter. The most radical option, if you want to really appreciate the quality of the roofing timbers, is to insulate the roof from the outside. This means removing the slates or tiles entirely, adding insulation (see p63) and then re-laying the roof. If the roof has to be rebuilt anyway, this is worth considering. But note that the thickness of the insulating layer can subtly alter the way the roof meets the wall tops at the gutter height..

Of course, you don't need to have so much roof timber visible and most French builders will suggest the more usual option of insulating from the inside. It is a compromise, because it invariably means hiding a certain amount of the wooden structure that you were keen to expose in the first place. You will also lose several centimetres from the dimensions of the room, including, of course, headroom.

Before adding insulation, check and treat the wood, as once insulating panels are in place, you will no longer have access to the timbers. Keep the receipts or guarantees as this will serve as proof that the checks have indeed been made before cladding everything in panels.

It is possible to insulate from the inside and leave part or all of each principal rafter visible – more if using a specially designed *isolant mince* or fine-gauge insulation. This is only around 25mm in thickness (instead of the standard 20cm), but has similar thermal insulating qualities. It is particularly suitable for installation behind plasterboard or tongue-and-groove finishes, or awkward spaces such as alongside dormer windows.

There are other very effective insulators too, some of which are integrated with the finished surface ready for painting. Rockwool or 'glass wool' (*laine de roche or laine de verre*) are generally available as semi-rigid glass-reinforced panels that can be suspended below the roof slopes, or as a soft roll

Partition walls: Using plasterboard and insulation on a metal frame

1

The aim here is to divide up the space into two rooms, separated by a doorway. Here, the roof timber has provided a suitable point where this will happen. The first step is to drop a plumb-line to the floor, to mark the baseline of the partition. Note that plasterboard on metal frame is ideal for wooden floors.

2

A complete door and frame unit (a *bloc-porte*) has been bought, and the frame is the first thing to be installed. Then, the metal profiles that will take the plasterboard are cut to size and screwed to the floor and the timbers, as well as to the door frame.

3

Two sheets of plasterboard will be fitted, with a layer of insulation between. After the first layer is fixed, the electrical wiring is installed, then the insulation is fitted into place, before the second layer of plasterboard is screwed on.

4

The fiddly bit: filling the uneven gaps between the various timbers. This takes patience and careful measuring, and these sections are also insulated. Finally, the joints between boards are taped up, and the gaps between the edges of the boards and the visible timbers sealed with a flexible filler.

THINSULATION

An example of a thinner type of insulation (the green layer) behind tongue-and-groove panelling, keeping the side-timbers exposed. The floor is a pine parquet placed over panels of particle-board (the orange layer) resting on insulating strips on the joists.

Partition walls

which is stapled directly below the rafters – the latter being the most common DIY solution.

Also available are panels of plasterboard backed with insulated material, fitted directly to the rafters and beams, or polystyrene panels that simply clip into place.

The underside of the slates or tiles must be ventilated, so leave an airspace and install some roof vents.

If you have enough space to create a number of rooms in the loft space, then lightweight partition walls will be the best solution to avoid adding too much weight. What most people are seeking are lightweight panels that are good sound insulators: a technical challenge to the laws of physics, in fact, but this is what's available.

Wood frame & panels:
A simple wooden frame, clad in wooden panelling, sandwiching a layer of mineral wool. Consider using oak or chestnut, which looks good. This is a lightweight and economical solution within the scope of a competent DIYer. Movement in the timber, though, can cause splits in the wood and panels.

Metal frame and plasterboard:
Metal rails that form the frame create a space for plasterboard on each of the two faces of the wall, plus insulation in between. The result is an even, rigid wall, great for bathrooms if you use waterproof panels.

Cellular concrete blocks:
They are built up in the style of a brick wall. However, this is best carried out by someone who has practiced their technique, rather than a first timer. The blocks provide you with both a partition and acoustic insulation at one and the same time.

The floor

You can generally expect the floor of the loft to be already insulated, with rolls of mineral wool, or granular polystyrene, or even cork between the joists. Above this, you would need to create a light-weight floor using, for example, a double layer of plasterboard, or sheets of particle-board as the base. Parquet or natural flooring add the finishing touch, while tiling is possible only if the floor is very stable.

Partition walls: Using cellular concrete blocks, bonded with adhesive

1

A similar kind of job, with the blocks being used to create a room partition underneath cross-members of the roof structure. This is less suitable for building on a wooden floor, as the blocks represent a dead weight, whereas the plasterboard panels are semi-suspended thanks to the metal framework.

2

The first course of blocks is built on a section of timber screwed to the floor, after which the blocks are sawn to shape as required and bonded with adhesive. These blocks have good acoustic and thermal insulating qualities, so may not need to be used with further insulating material.

3

Check the width of the blocks you intend to use. As the principal rafter may only be 8cm wide, you may decide to expose just one side of the truss. This may mean you offset the line of the partition, allowing you to add acoustic insulation and further panels (eg waterproof plasterboard for a bathroom project).

4

The fiddly bit: the small gaps between the blocks and the timber should be filled with a flexible mastic, while the larger gaps (for example between the principal rafters and the roof slope) are filled with bits of block sawn to shape. It is these small finishing jobs that are the most time consuming.

The new staircase

The main challenge here is to choose the location of the staircase opening (*trémie*) to ensure there is enough headroom for those entering the loftspace, and that it suits the room layout of the rest of the house. It sounds like common sense, but it can go wrong when all the other considerations of space planning are in the mix. At the same time, consider how the room will be used and what kind of investment is necessary in the staircase. Most people go for a standard budget pine option, in keeping with the informal feel of a loft space. However, all the usual security measures must be in place, especially if you plan to get guests with kids staying up there. Spiral staircases obviously save space and look cool, but will create problems when you want to shift furniture.

Skylights

These are the most economical way to get plenty of light into your loftspace, and have improved greatly in terms of their looks over recent years. Their only real disadvantage is that as they are directly exposed to the weather, they can be noisy during heavy rain, especially at night, while during hot summer days they will create a bit of a greenhouse effect in the loft. However, higher specifications to the glazing in skylights have become the norm in France, increasing prices but adding great improvements to overall performance. Some also have optional shutters integrated into the outer face of the skylight.

With steeper roofs, skylights tend to open by rotating on a central, horizontal axis, with the handle at the top. Where the roof is flatter, in the south of France for example, the more usual practice is to have the handle at the bottom and the skylight hinged at the top, known as the *panoramique* version. Incidentally, the flatter the roof, the longer the skylight needs to be, if you want to be able to see out of it. Both versions can find their place in the same home, as their characteristics provide useful alternatives when space planning.

Generally, skylights are positioned so that the lower part is around 90cm from the ground, and the upper part no higher than 2m, but

Blending in
Some 'purists' get a bit twitchy about skylights, seeing them as a modern feature out of keeping with a traditional house. Generally, they are fairly unobtrusive, and from street level, unless you are really looking out for them, they pass unnoticed. As this pair of renovated cottages shows, though, a black finish blends in better. If you want your skylight to fit in even more discretely, you can get a kit that fits the unit flush with the tiled surface of the roof.

'The flatter the roof, the longer the skylight needed to create a view.'

'If you have a village house with no garden of its own, and are willing to sacrifice an upstairs room, the

this can be dictated by the position of side-timbers in the roof structure. If you need it to go higher than this, it becomes difficult to access. An option is to go for a motorised version, but this will double the cost of a standard skylight.

A skylight can be installed in a single day, if the opening has already been created. You will find that in different regions, your supplier or roofer will supply a *kit de raccordement* or installation kit which suits whichever kind of roofing material (slate, flat tiles, canal tiles etc.) you have on your house.

Dormer windows (*les lucarnes*)

Architecturally, there are dozens of variants of the *lucarne* across France, and they vary from one region to another, each with their own particular charm and terminology. How good they are at adding light to your loft space depends on what they were meant to do in the first place: a window for a servant's quarters perhaps, or simply a way of getting a few shafts of light into a hayloft.

Creating a new one is a challenge. First, you will need expert advice on which style suits your house. As well as re-building the roof timbers, your builder will also be concerned about the weight of the structure: a dormer faced with stone could weigh around 500kg – half the weight of a small car. So you need careful assessment of the weight-bearing capacity of the wall and roof structure

Roof terraces

If the slope of the roof is too shallow to create any additional living space, you could consider creating a roof terrace – especially if you have a village house that lacks a sunny (or shady) area where you can while away warm evenings.

The work involved looks dramatic (hacking out a portion of the

Dormer option
If you are lucky enough to have an original dormer window (*lucarne*), it is a feature worth preserving during any roof renovation works. If you aim to create a new one, get professional advice: a stone-faced *lucarne* weighs 500kg, half the weight of a small car, while even a wooden dormer is a hefty 200kg. So check the weight-bearing capacity of the walls and roof.

ou could consider creating a roof terrace by removing a large chunk of roof and waterproofing the floor.'

roof and its timbers) but is simply a succession of straightforward building jobs, and could create for you a little private paradise with views across the rooftops to the surrounding country. It goes without saying that this should be undertaken with professional advice, and planning permission is essential.

Assuming your project has been planned, both visually and technically, the basic process starts with the removal of the tiles. The position of the roof terrace relative to the roof is usually determined by the arrangement of the roofing timbers, so the next job is to remove the rafters and battens to create the opening that is required, possibly modifying or shifting structural elements to allow access. A small section of roof could be retained over the eaves, rising to the height of the terrace wall. This means the terrace is not visible from the street level, and that the vital equivalent of a guard-rail is provided.

The next step is to build a wall between the terrace and the remaining loft space. If this loft space is to be used as a living room, it would make sense to maximise the opportunities to let the light in – using sliding doors, perhaps. The access staircase (which would be more user-friendly inside the loft) will need to be planned in with sufficient headroom, and a 'landing' area leading to the entrance to the terrace.

The whole thing will need to be watertight. This means creating a damp-proof membrane on the floor, which drains off via the system of guttering below the eaves. And above this, a lightweight floor surface, for which wooden decking is usually ideal.

A conversion job like this does not come cheap, and has so much potential for snags relating to water infiltration that it is best left to professionals who will be able to provide their 10-year guarantee for the works. If well-executed, it can add significantly to the charm of your house, and if it can be combined with a loft conversion and roof repair job, it is an investment well-made.

Terrace potential
The top floor of this house (foreground) could lose a room and gain a terrace by taking off the roof.

Chapter 9

THE CAVE

HOW TO KEEP WINE

If you are going to get yourself a place in France, one of the many reasons could be that you want to enjoy some excellent French wine while you are there. If that's the case, then you will also need to find somewhere to keep it. And ideally, you will end up in the happy situation of being able to serve a fine bottle if wine, complete with its coating of authentic dust, while telling your guests that you have a dozen more just like this down in your '*cave*'.

YOUR ROUND
If you are short of space for a wine cellar, you could create one by getting a specialist supplier to dig out a cylindrical shaft and line it with purpose-built racks with spiral stairs down the middle. At a cost of several thousand euros, this is for serious wine lovers, with a serious collection, who have a serious shortage of space!

Some old French houses will already have a perfectly serviceable wine cellar (known in French as *la cave*). Others may have a number of semi-derelict outbuildings that could do the job instead. Or you may simply need to find a space to keep wine in the basement somewhere. So what kind of conditions do you need to create?

The art of conserving wine

If you are keen to make new friends among your French neighbours, then asking them around for an aperitif, and eventually for a complete meal, can be a good start. But if you want to win them over with your respect for the fine wines of the local region (assuming you are in a wine-growing area of course) then you will need to put some thought into how, and where, you keep the stuff – especially if you propose to take them on a guided tour of your own cellar. Word could get around the village very quickly, for example, that you keep your wine – however good it tastes – in a cardboard box between the kitchen window and the radiator. Or even that your 'Kwik-eezy Magic No-Pull' corkscrew messes up the cork and leaves bits floating around in the wine.

The cave: The ideal spot for keeping wine does not have to be in a vaulted, underground cellar. You can still keep wine for many years in a much more modest *cave* (which, incidentally sounds more like 'have' than 'Dave'), provided you follow a few simple rules. The basic ones, which apply to most out-houses or storerooms attached to old houses, are these: the building should face north or east (so it is protected from the sun) and not be prone to large variations in temperature; it should be well-ventilated and away from vibrations of any kind and

The top 5% Research shows that 95% of wine is bought and then consumed within 48 hours. Much of the other 5% will be found stored in typical cellar conditions: the bottles kept on their sides, away from light, with a reasonably high level of humidity, away from fluctuations of temperature and vibration, and away from any kind of unpleasant odours. How long wine will continue to mature in these conditions varies depending on the wine. To monitor progress, the only reliable method is to open a bottle and try it. Cheers!

'Word could get round the village very quickly that you keep your wine – however good it is – in a cardboar

box between the kitchen window and the radiator.'

An expert at work
Good practice in wine cellars is passed on from one generation to another. But you don't need a vast vaulted labyrinth under your house to do it properly. Any room which remains humid and where the temperature is fresh and stable will be suitable, and you will find that many French people appear less obsessive about wine than some of their new foreign neighbours.

from any persistent odours. The walls should be thick and well insulated. And the wine should be kept in the dark.

The floor: The ideal floor is one which can 'breathe'. So a rebuilt floor, incorporating a damp proof course, such as we have been recommending for renovating the interior of your living space, is not ideal in your wine cellar. A simple floor of compressed earth – the *terre battue* – is ideal, or else gravel. If the ceiling height of the cellar is too low, the floor can be dug out, though beware undermining the foundations. You can then cover the ground with gravel, which can occasionally be watered if the place is getting dry. Alternatively, the floor could be covered with terracotta, or other basic tiles, laid onto a bed of stabilised sand or mortar.

Stocking the wine: Leaving the wine on its side is done purely to keep the corks from drying out and crumbling, so it keeps them airtight, though it also gives the impression of a well-ordered cave when all the wine is arranged on racks against the walls. Racking systems come in many materials, including lightweight concrete, stone composites, terracotta, or simple wooden boxes. Metal racks need to

'The ideal cellar floor is one which can breathe...'

Stacked up
No fancy wine racks here, but these sturdy wooden shelves do the trick, sloping back towards the wall slightly but still allowing the base of the corks to remain fully in contact with the wine.

Stacking bottles on top of each other like this saves space, but is best done if they are identical, to prevent shaking them all around each time you try to take a bottle out.

The small blackboards are useful for indicating what goes where, as well as providing a place to keep a brief note about the condition of the wine when you last tasted it.

According to some cellar keepers, there is a kind of hierarchy of shelf height when it comes to stacking bottles.

Champagnes and sparkling wines go nearest the floor, followed by dry white wines, and then sweet white wines.

Above these go the rosé, followed by young reds, with vintage bottles at the top.

be fixed to the walls for stability. Wooden racks will do the job, but over many years will suffer from the persistent humidity, particularly if a softwood prone to rot is used. If you treat the wood regularly, there's a risk the smell of the treatment agent will dominate the cave and could eventually taint the wine.

Temperature: Wine can suffer from big variations in temperature, which is why it needs to be kept away from the usual day-night or winter-summer heating and cooling patterns. The ideal temperature to store wine is somewhere between $10\text{-}15^0\,C$, which will allow it to age neither too quickly nor too slowly. The biggest challenge for most people is protecting the wine from the heat of the summer. The easiest way to do this is by insulating the walls of the cellar, and also the door, which should be robust and fit well – not forgetting also to lag any pipes for hot water or central heating that run through the cellar.

If you cannot keep the temperature below $20^0\,C$ in the summer, then the option for long-term wine storage will be to get air conditioning (at €1,500-€4,000, plus the energy consumed) or invest in a purpose-built wine fridge. Or get a friend to keep it for you.

'... so it draws humidity into the room: the opposite of what's good for your living area.'

Fully equipped
In this newly-created cellar, metal wine racking has been screwed to the back wall, and gravel laid on the floor, allowing humidity to come up from the compacted earth below. A ventilation duct is also visible on the rear wall, just below the roof level. This cellar has all the basic equipment that is required, including a manual press for inserting corks, and an old stone sink. Electrical fittings will need to be to the 'outdoor' standard because of the high level of humidity in the room. A bench and chairs are a vital part of cellar furniture. Blokes tend to hang out for hours down there.

Humidity: You will need to keep an eye on the humidity in your *cave*, with an ideal figure of around 70%-80%. If the humidity is much less than this, then the corks can dry out (look out for traces of wine seeping from the bottom of the cork), while if it is much higher than this, you will get too much mould growing everywhere, and the labels on the bottles will start to peel off. Some people who lose sleep about this kind of thing wrap clingfilm over the label. If your cellar is too humid, the best cure is to improve the ventilation. If this still does not work, then you could, for a damp underground cellar, use a special waterproof barrier paint on the walls, or invest in a special cellar lining, known as 'tanking' in English, and *cuvelage* in French.

Ventilation: Effective ventilation is essential, and a good cellar will have air ducts to bring in and take out air. Basement cellars may also have small windows – *soupiraux* – bored into the walls just above ground height. All these steps will help to avoid mould and moss invading the cellar, and a persistent musty smell, and if you can't create a natural ventilation system, invest in a small electric ventilation duct. The point about good ventilation is linked with the physical characteristics of cork: it is extremely good at capturing odours from the air and transmitting them back into the wine. For this reason it is also risky to stock other household goods near the wine – such as garden fertilisers, herbicides, creosote, paint, varnish, or even fruit and vegetables. And a smoked ham or two hanging up could add an interesting new taste to your maturing wine collection.

Lighting: If you want to play up the atmosphere in your cellar, go for subdued lighting – as long as you can read what it says on the bottles. Because of the persistent humidity in the cave, you will need to select electrical fittings designed for exterior use, which are readily available wherever you may be purchasing other electrical gear.

'A bench and chairs are a vital part of cellar furniture. Blokes tend to hang out down there.'

Laying it down
If you do have a reliable
cellar, then with a bit of
forward planning you can
enjoy very decent quality
wine at basic supermarket
prices. On the supermar-
ket shelves, many red
wines that are just three
or four years old are double the price of this year's
or last year's wines. But if
you can start planning
ahead and resist the urge
to raid your wine collec-
tion each Christmas and
New Year, it is possible to
buy now and consume
your wine, much improved,
in three years' time.
Obviously, the wine needs
to be suitable for laying
down, and your cellar
needs to be up to the task.

Traditional lines

This renovated room uses new materials but creates a traditional feel of a typically French kitchen. The floor is not actually terracotta, but made of tiles that create the look. The big kitchen range and antique style hood to the right of the picture add the most character to the room, while the rest of the elements of the kitchen are lined up alongside using unfussy joinery. The high splashback using patterned wall tiles is another very traditional touch, while the white-painted walls max-imise the light and create a simple, practical space for cooking and eating. Note the wide, double sliding doors, which are a great space saver.

Chapter 10

KITCHENS & BATHROOMS

A good kitchen or bathroom installation usually comes down to meticulous space planning and measurement, good choice of materials and installer, and having the right water heating, pressure and flow rate to suit your needs. And if you are ready to be bold, you can create something really inspirational. The good news is that more individual projects can work out to be as economical to build as factory-made fitted versions. And they could blend in even better in many rural properties.

'Creating a really 'authentic' farmhouse kitchen is a major challenge.'

It is all too easy to spoil a promising restoration project with an unlucky choice of fitted kitchen units – especially with an open-plan kitchen that is part of a carefully restored living area, perhaps with an old stone fireplace at the other end of the room.

Anyone trying to create a really 'authentic' farmhouse kitchen will be in for a challenge, unless you want to live a rather spartan existence. A typical 'antique' rural kitchen – and they can still be found today – would have a large fireplace at one end (yes, it's the original cooker), a stone sink, perhaps in a wall niche, a water pump either inside the kitchen or on an outside wall near the well, and a big multi-purpose farmhouse table for preparation of food and then dining.

Fixed below the ceiling joists, there may still be a suspended bread rack (away from rats and mice) and a wooden *garde à manger* – a ventilated box in which you can leave food, again to prevent rodents and insects snacking on your lunch. If you are lucky, the carved wooden buffet, perhaps fitted as the front of a wall cupboard, will still be in its original position.

The 20th century may have brought a rectangular 'butler'-style sink (curiously, this is referred to as a *timbre d'office* in French product catalogues) which may be mounted on metal brackets or low walls, with a cold water tap mounted in the wall above it. There may be a gas cooker with its gas canister tucked away somewhere dubious, and a few cupboards containing crockery. More modern additions will

Ancient and modern
In this kitchen, there is a fair amount of new equipment, but the overall look is traditional, thanks in part to the excellent tiled floor dating back to 1900, and which has been carefully restored. The worktop, sink, mixer tap, and oven are sleek and modern, but the steel rail attached to the front of the worktop with a simple white linen curtain attached adds a traditional feel to the whole room, as does the collection of copper cookware ranged on the back wall.
This kitchen creates superb atmosphere, but is also set up for some serious 21st century cooking.

'Don't expect you

kitchen project to go any more smoothly than it would in the UK. Delays and stress come free of charge.'

invariably include sideboards with laminate tops, or even a tired old fitted kitchen.

For many renovators, a good-looking, modern, fitted kitchen installation with good quality doors and surfaces will be enough. The profession of kitchen fitter, or *cuisiniste*, is fairly recent in France, and they cater for a broad range of tastes and budgets. They usually specialise in fitting industrially-manufactured kitchens which can be viewed at local showrooms.

Don't expect a kitchen installation to go any more smoothly than such a job would in the UK. Typically, there are delays, unforeseen expense, and stress. Problems arise because of measuring or design errors at the outset, missing or wrongly-sent components during the installation stage, or delays from one tradesman holding up the whole project.

For maximum peace of mind, and to avoid unnecessary revisions to the design, check the drawings of the proposed layouts, read the specifications, and check the measurements yourself on site to ensure everything will fit, remembering to allow for plastering and wall covering thicknesses, and the squareness and straightness of walls and floors. Natural materials such as granite, slate, and even limestone make great worktops and are much less expensive in France than in the UK, especially if you can buy direct from a quarry.

If you install a fitted kitchen along an exterior stone wall, you can provoke damp problems. As discussed in earlier chapters, stone walls 'breathe' water vapour, which can get trapped behind the kitchen units. Given their chipboard construction (often disguised by the surface finish), these units can rot and warp if the damp gets a grip. Just watch out for the wood lice scurrying about in their new habitat, created by the mix of modern industrial kitchen design and unforgiving old walls, which seem to be grumpily getting their own back on you for being boxed in.

This is also worth bearing in mind if buying a house with a fairly recently installed fitted kitchen. Open the cupboards and pull drawers right out of their housing to check for signs of damp, deterioration or musty odours.

The butler sink
A double butler sink, known in French as a *timbre d'office*, is another way to create a classic traditional look. It can be easily mounted on blockwork walls built at right angles to the back wall, usually with wooden cupboard doors across the front. The taps fixed to the back wall are an essential part of this look, for the simple practical reason that the sink may not be made with an aperture through which to mount a tap. A tiled worktop goes well with this kind of sink, and can be built over a series of blockwork walls, with simple bespoke doors created for the front. The splashback shown here is made up of a patchwork of locally sourced tiles and gives the kitchen a regional feel.

There are, of course, alternatives to the fitted kitchen. If you are employing creative professionals on your project, such as an *architect d'interieur* or designer, you could get them to include the kitchen design as part of their mission. The more bespoke kitchen, which could integrate free-standing furniture and a big stove, may sound like an expensive option but compared with a fitted kitchen, can be extremely good value for money.

Local joiners are often proud bespoke kitchen builders and they will also have colleagues who do the plumbing, electrics, and supply the 'white goods' if you want them to, sometimes from local suppliers whose prices can match those of the major retail chains. The big, flashy kitchen range (and there are some good French brands on the market) may cost more than an integrated electric oven, but will not require the chipboard worktop housing – the so-called carcass – which can be expensive to supply and fit.

Similarly, a double 'butler's sink' can be bought as a separate unit and installed on a couple of walls (built of bricks, stone, lime-rendered or tiled blockwork), perhaps with a door across the front for storage as part of the plan. This is simple and basic but can look excellent if well-executed in a rural kitchen. So above all, don't give up if catalogue kitchen photos fail to inspire you with the kitchen that you think should fit with your rural house.

Storage space in a bespoke kitchen can be created with fitted or free-standing cupboards, built by a joiner, and possibly even using reclaimed doors or shutters on the front. Note, of course, that in many rural houses there are other rooms available to install a washing machine or dishwasher, known as the *arrière cuisine* or *débarras* for more general storage. If you have this kind of space, you are not compelled to cram all your

'Local joiners are often the proud builders of bespoke kitchens, working with plumbers and electricians.'

electrical appliances into a neat row of cupboards.

In general terms, wood, stone, steel, and glass in your kitchen will harmonise well with the fabric of an old rural house, and a contemporary kitchen with modern clean lines can be appropriate too, if built to last. It's probably best to avoid the imitation rustic look. Although still very popular, it can create confusion between which features of your house are real and which are fake!

The bathroom challenge

The one room where most people renovating a home in France may be inclined to compromise on the 'authentic look' will be the bathroom. Originally, a bathroom as such may not have existed in the property you are upgrading, so there is no particular look to preserve or re-create. Antique-style sanitary-ware such as roll-top baths with claw feet are available new, and do look stunning in the middle of a large room. But they work less well in small spaces, where modern space-saving bathroom fittings look good and prevent splashes.

When creating new bathrooms, consider using existing small rooms that may previously have been dressing rooms or storage rooms, so you can avoid modifying larger rooms. Bear in mind how the house will be used – who needs access to which bathroom, and how much acoustic insulation is required? Don't forget that most plasterboard partitions will not support too much weight, and that you will need to know where existing drain runs and the water supply are routed. Re-positioning a WC, in particular, is more awkward than it first seems. Finally, what's easy to achieve downstairs, on a solid concrete floor, may not be possible upstairs on creaking (and gently moving) wooden floorboards. French builders know what they

Bath with room This vast room allows bathers to lie back in the warm suds and admire the finely renovated exposed stone walls and roof timbers. It's neat too: all the pipework and drainage is hidden behind the low false wall topped off with a useful wooden shelf. Pictured right is a finish called *tadelakt*. This is pigmented, waterproof limewash – a natural alternative to tiles – which is making a comeback in France.

Accessorized Small spaces and store rooms tucked away in your house are a first choice for conversion into bathrooms. This *ensuite* bathroom has been built into an awkward-shaped space alongside a bedroom. The design is simple and unpretentious, with basic white tiles forming a side wall and bath panel. The character of this room comes from the carefully chosen accessories, such as the ironwork coat hanger and the antique chairs.

'Go over the plans very carefully with your builders. Detail is everything.'

can do without risk of water infiltration, as they can get sued if they get it wrong. Also, they want their insurance to cover the works they have done. That is why they may not always fall in line with the plan you had in mind. A useful tip is to put plenty of time into making sure you have a clear idea of what they plan to do, and how this differs from your original plan. This could mean sitting down with your builder over a fairly detailed drawing of the proposed bathroom, sketching in where everything will go, and checking in product catalogues for how it will look. Think about the height of a washbasin as well as its position in the room, details like the colour of the tile joints, or the size, shape, colour, and power output of a radiator or heated towel rail. Detail is everything.

With mains-pressure hot water, even when reduced by a pressure reduction valve, a good shower is easy to achieve in France – though you will need to consult your plumber to make sure your hot water supply will deal with the number of guests you plan to have staying at any one time. It may be that some of the water pipes are too narrow to allow sufficient flow to several showers and baths simultaneously, even though the pressure is adequate. Ask your plumber.

When it comes to shower design, builders will very likely try to persuade you to install a free-standing shower cubicle, if you want the shower upstairs on a wooden floor. This is because cubicles are designed to be completely watertight, and so can be guaranteed against water damage to the building. The alternative is to fit a shower tray, and then tile adjacent walls or partitions, fit shower doors, and seal the joints between the wall and the shower tray with mastic. This does not comply with building regulations, though, if the floor is made of wood, as over time small movements lead to leaks down the wall and underneath the tray.

For the same reason, if you are keen to install a bath against a wall where the floor is made of timber, you could run into similar reluctance from builders. Again, they are worried about the possibility of water infiltration over the coming years (which becomes ten years if the infiltration is proved to have caused damage to the structure of the building, for which they could be held legally responsible). These periods during which their work is guaranteed (see p195) are defined by law, so builders take this seriously.

If you are putting in a new floor, you could consider a concrete slab to give you complete freedom in your choice of bathroom, and allow you to install ceramic or stone flooring too. For a large bathroom space, with a high ceiling, it could be worth fitting underfloor heating at the same time as creating a new floor.

We go into more technical detail on French plumbing systems and water heating on p183.

Rough with the smooth
This stylish bathroom allows the fabric of the building to dominate the look, with simple white bathroom elements in sharp contrast with the massive, exposed stone walls. The ironwork stair rail looks the part, but you would need something a bit safer if there are any kids around.

Chapter 11

FIREPLACES

GETTING AWAY FROM THE BIG SMOKE

Some French people think of the fireplace (or *cheminée*) as the most important piece of furniture in the house. Maybe that sounds a bit over the top to most of us, but in terms of adding character to your place in France, a fireplace is right up there with the exposed stonework, beamed ceilings, the traditional tiles, or massive heirloom-style furniture. However, a big, beautiful stone fireplace is one thing. A big, beautiful stone fireplace that actually warms your house without smoking you out? That's in a league of its own!

Fire without smoke
This is the dream: a roaring, open fire, in a fine old stone fireplace, warming the entire room, and with not a smoke particle in sight.
It can become reality, too, but not without a certain amount of careful planning and a smattering of luck. The inner surface of the chimney flue counts for a lot, as does its temperature, air circulation in the room, oxygen supply, the profile of the fireplace opening, the height of the chimney and design of the stack, the type of wood, its age and how dry it is...
Still want to try?
Bon courage!

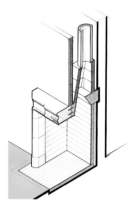

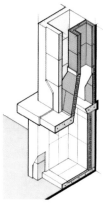

Up the chimney
Two different, but
similar, fireplace
configurations, with
a cylindrical flue liner
(top) and one built
from blocks (bottom).
Note that if you were
to use brute force to
rip out the mantle-
piece, the lower part of
the sloping flue
support structure could
just collapse.

Stone or marble have always been the materials of choice for the best fireplaces – stone for its strength and agelessness, marble for that impression of luxury. Not that stone fireplaces have ever been regarded as the 'poor relation.' Quite the opposite: centuries-old stone fireplaces can be extraordinary works of stone-masonry and are highly sought-after. In contrast, some French people regard many of the marble fireplaces from the last century as a little bit 'kitsch', and some are not all they seem – simply assemblies of thin marble panels.

Repairing a fireplace

Stone: If the fireplace is badly chipped, cracked, or has bits of moulding or decoration missing, it is worth calling in a specialist for a quote, as trying to achieve invisible repairs to carved or worked stone can be a hit-and-miss affair as a DIY job. If, however your stone fireplace has been painted – and this happens more often than you may imagine – the procedure can be fairly simple: either sandblasting, which is the quickest route, but which may blur some of the surface details; or the more laborious process of scraping and chipping off the paint, perhaps after applying paint stripper. Sand the paint first to help the chemicals penetrate.

Marble: Marble is an awkward kind of material – it absorbs all kinds of stains, picks up scratches and nicks, and many older fireplaces end up with huge cracks. It is possible to repair cracks and dents in marble using resin, which can be coloured to match the marble, sets hard and can be sanded and polished to create an almost invisible repair. The same techniques can be used to repair stone, too, by mixing the resin with stone dust. To deal with stains on marble, *savon noir* (a kind of soft soap) is the starting point, and if this does not work, move on to detergent. Avoid trying to clean marble with lemon juice – it will simply attack the marble and make it worse. If the marble is just a bit

'If it all goes wrong, changing a fireplace surround can become a DIY disaster zone.'

dull looking, you can shine it up by sanding it first with very fine paper, and then applying a creamy polish, known as *Baume des Antiquaires* which will soak into the marble before you buff it up.

Choosing and installing a new 'old' fireplace

If the fireplace you get when you buy a place in France is not ideal and you want to change it, you can either try to find one at an architectural salvage yard, or get a specialist stonemason (see p207-8) to create a new one for you – perhaps as a copy of an antique version. Some salvage yards will sell copies of antique fireplaces as well as the real thing – the main distinguishing feature being the lower price of the reproduction versions. The advantage of a good copy, of course, is that it can be made to measure, adapted to suit whatever conditions of room size, wall, and flue you happen to have.

Changing a fireplace surround (known as *le manteau*) can become a DIY disaster zone. The surround is in most cases just a façade, and need not affect the workings of the chimney itself. But it could be deeply embedded in the wall, making it difficult to remove without dislodging a good deal of masonry and possibly damaging the vital inner workings of the fireplace itself. What's more, bringing in a new surround can change the ability of the fireplace to draw air and work efficiently. Ultimately, creating a new fireplace is not an area where you can cut corners. After all, a decent looking stone fireplace is another investment in your house that will give it lasting value. And

'With older houses, it can be difficult to find a flue liner that actually fits the dimensions of your chimney.'

if you get it installed properly, by a professional fireplace fitter, there is a good chance you will get smoke-free warmth from the fireplace as well as just good looks.

Making it work

So your fireplace may look good, but will it work? For a start, there are certain basic rules of safety to observe, relating to the flue, distance from flammable materials like timber joists, the height of the chimney stack, the air supply to the room, chimney sweeping and so on. If you have it installed by professionals, these should be people who are trained and insured to do the job and carry out the required improvements to the flue.

In most old houses, the position of the flue will determine where you can install your fireplace – though you may be able to get away with a few diversions to the flue if you need to. More importantly, you could find that the chimney flue in an old house for renovation is itself going to need fixing up, including some kind of lining. A complete replacement may be the answer.

The most current specification is to install a flue-liner, in effect a metal tube (some are insulated), which ensures a completely secure conduit for the fireplace below.

The flue liner will take away all the fumes created by burning fuel, and thanks to its smooth interior, will also help the fire to draw effectively. If you do not have a metal flue liner, your existing flue will work best if it is as smooth as possible on the interior.

Flue liners are available in different sections (such as a rectangular duct, or cylindrical pipe), but it can be difficult to find one that actually fits easily into the internal shape of your existing chimney flue. Nor will you be able to get around the problem by trying to find an extra-thin flue liner, as there is a legal requirement on the dimensions too. For an open fire, the minimum section of the flue should be at least 400sq cm. This equates to a cylindrical liner of about 25cm in diameter, or a rectangular flue of, for example, 25cm by 16cm. But for a bigger open fire, these dimensions could prove inadequate. If the fireplace is closed (with a stove or something similar) you will need to check the manufacturer's instructions.

And one further dimension relates to the chimney stack. As the active part of your fireplace system that actually draws the smoke out of the fire, the stack needs to be at least 40cm higher than the top of your house (or any obstacle that could cause eddies in the wind).

If you need to divert the course of the chimney flue (to allow the creation of a chimney in another room) this is possible, but watch the angle of the flue. The ideal flue is vertical. Diagonal flues will work, but not much below 45 degrees (for a flue of 5m in height). If you don't respect this rule, the flue will give you trouble, and smoke may not get evacuated, making your fireplace inoperable. So it is essential to follow current regulations, and seek professional advice.

Ledges or shallow angles in the flue can allow soot build-up, provoking chimney fires. So you will need to get your chimney cleaned before you start using the fireplace, and again mid-way through the winter, if you are using your house regularly during the cold weather. Keep the certificate supplied by the chimney sweep, which could turn out to be a requirement by your home insurers. Roofers (*couvreurs*) usually also offer chimney sweeping services (*ramonage*).

Extra ventilation

Modern fireplaces always include some kind of air vent to help the fire to draw. You may not have this in an older house, where the solution to avoid getting smoke in the room was to leave a door or window open. Often, the kitchen window was left open all the time, which is why you sometimes find bars fitted to these windows. In any case, the fire was kept going constantly if there was daily cooking to be done in and around the fireplace itself. These days, a possible solution is to install an air vent into a wall near the fire, to allow a supply

Flue-like symptom
For an effective trouble-free fire, a good, clean flue is essential, and the smoother its interior the better. A vertical flue will work better than one at a diagonal, (though can allow torrential rain to plop straight down) and a warm flue will draw more effectively than a cold one. This can mean that if you visit a holiday home in the winter, even an efficient fireplace can still give you trouble to start with if the flue is cold and damp.

of oxygen to feed the combustion process, and enough air to allow for a good draught up the flue. If this is not possible, you could try drilling downwards, towards the cellar or *vide sanitaire*, and linking a conduit to an alternative outside wall (ideally one that is facing prevailing winds).

The so-called *insert* fireplace

For many people, there is nothing better than an open fire, and the bigger, and more open, the better – the better to see the flames, to smell the smoke, and listen to the pop and crackle of burning logs. However, if the fire is your only form of heating, there are ways of making it more efficient, and using it to heat other rooms. Hence the appearance, a few decades ago, of the *insert*.

This is a term you may have first seen in French estate agents' literature. The *insert* is like a little metal furnace that sits in your fireplace, enclosed by a glass door. They used to be fairly unsightly, with the glass quickly becoming sooted up and hiding the flames – depriving the fireplace of its crucial attraction. These days technology has moved on, with inserts that have high-tech glass that covers the entire aperture of the fireplace and is almost invisible.

Other 'closed fireplace' options exist too. You may also come across a *foyer fermé* in some more recently renovated houses, which can be situated more or less anywhere as it does not rely on an existing chimney, but has its own flue pipe, so it can even be installed in the middle of a room. Again, flames are visible behind a glass door which in modern versions is designed to stay clean thanks to internal ventilation. The system works by drawing in air, heating it up (with logs or whatever you burn) and then releasing the heat into the room, or conducting it to other rooms via a system of ducts.

Another option with an open fire is to install a *récupérateur de chaleur*, designed to catch some of the hot air that rises into the chimney and redirect it, either via ducts into other rooms, or even to pre-heat part of the water system. The major benefit here is that you don't see anything other than a classic open fire. The whole system is installed in the wall area above the aperture.

Fire wall
It may not have the allure of a spitting, smoking, open fire, but the *foyer fermé* is an efficient heater, has its own trouble-free flue, and can be situated almost anywhere in a room, including right in the centre. Critics say it's like watching a fire on TV. But at least you get a good picture.

There has been a bit of a come-back of the woodburning stove in France over recent years, mainly because manufacturers have redesigned them to become more efficient, cleaner, and better looking too. Here's a guide to help you with the brochures.

Six hot tips on woodburning stoves

1. Size matters

Stoves are sold with a rating in kW, usually somewhere between 3kW and 11kW. The mistake many people make is to think that the bigger and more powerful, the better. In fact, you will need to get a stove that matches the volume you intend to heat (though some refer to the 'floor area' rather than volume, so check what the figures refer to). However, that's not the end of the story, as this 'volume' figure is tweaked according to, for example, which way the house faces, how well insulated it is, and so on. The key thing is to make sure the stove is working somewhere at its 'cruising speed' to heat your house. If it is too powerful, but has to work on its lowest setting all the time, or if it is not powerful enough, and is going at full tilt constantly, it may use too much wood, and clog up the flue. Opt for a stove which permits relatively long logs, on the basis that the shorter the logs, the more sawing is needed.

2. Heat technique

The other choice you'll need to make is which heating system to use. The radiation stoves (known as *poêles radiants, rayonnants* or *poêles à accumulation de chaleur*) are clad in heavy material that takes several hours to heat up (some kind of stone, or tiles). It heats up gradually by burning the wood, and then, with the air supply to the fire shut off, the heat is forced out from the stove into the room, by direct radiation. The downside is that it takes a good two to three hours to get the stove hot enough for it to start radiating, and if you rely on the stove to heat your second home for just a weekend, you could struggle to heat up the walls, floors and so on by the time you are ready to go back home again. Also, the heat will remain stubbornly in the room where the stove is installed.

The other kind of stove is the *poële à convection* which allows air from the room to circulate within the stove, get hot, and then diffuse into the room via a grille at the top of the stove. This allows a more even distribution of heat, and more immediately than the radiation stoves, with warm air circulating out into other rooms.

However, these convection stoves are also built of heavy duty and thermally inert materials, which means they have a tendency to radiate when they get hot – and the potential to blast you with heat if you are sitting close by.

3. Continuous fire

This is something you might see when looking at the specification of a stove. There is a quality standard called Norme NF D 35-376 which defines *feu continu* as a stove being able, after ten hours of operation, to relight new wood from the glowing embers that remain in the stove. This matters when you want to get the stove going first thing in the morning.

4. The flue liner

Woodburning stoves generally need a metal flue liner (basically a big flexible pipe) inserted into your existing chimney flue otherwise they may not be guaranteed, and you could have problems with your insurers. This is not always a simple task, as stone or masonry flues can be the most difficult, as they tend to narrow towards the chimney stack. But in terms of the improved performance (drawing air, and security) it is worth the aggravation. Before fitting a flue liner, get the existing flue swept, as the liner will heat up and could set fire to any debris lodged around it.

5. Clear glass

If the stove is working at low capacity, this is where the glass can easily get sooted up. Hence the appeal of the 'clear glass' versions, which use a 'curtain' of air circulating next to the glass to keep the soot and tar away. If the glass does get sooted up, avoid using abrasives to clean it, as this could damage its heat-proof qualities.

6. Buying logs

Luckily, logs do, quite literally, grow on trees. However, they are not given freely, and need time to dry properly. In France, you buy wood by the *stère,* which weighs around 500kg, and is about a cubic metre of well-stacked wood, costing around €35 to €50 per stère. Check if it's ready for burning, or needs drying – which could take more than a year to 15 months. Harder woods such as oak, chestnut, hornbeam or beechwood produce the most heat.

To find out where to buy wood, check in the local paper small ads, or ask your neighbours.

In the right gear Wood-burners are best at 'cruising speed', neither straining at full tilt nor idling in low gear. So size matters.

Chapter 12

GARDENS & TERRACES

A PLACE IN THE SHADE

If you buy a rural property in France, you could end up with a good deal more land on your hands than you are used to. Some people will be content to leave it untouched. But with many regions of France enjoying a warm summer where you spend most of the day – and the evenings – outside, a bit of simple, sensible planning can help create plenty of new outdoor living spaces. And while building work goes on inside the house, now is the time to think about landscaping.

Looking out across your newly acquired 'grounds', which might actually be an overgrown and sloping field with a tangle of dry bushes, you will easily be forgiven for not knowing where to start. If you have the money in your budget, it could be worth getting in touch with a landscape gardener, or *paysagiste*, who can guide you through how you can use the space, and what it would cost to get it in shape.

As the person you choose is likely to work in your local area, you should get a chance to visit other projects they have completed. Sometimes, any jobbing gardener will describe themselves as a *paysagiste*, but may not be up to designing and project managing a more ambitious scheme. So check for experience and credentials.

We will not get too far into garden design in this chapter, as it is a subject which in itself could fill a small bookshop. But there are some design basics to think about when it comes to planning a 'blank canvas' garden for the first time.

The first step is what the professionals would call a 'site assessment.' You probably already have something in mind in terms of a garden layout, or a new terrace perhaps. However, before getting into the details, you need to go through the plot carefully to work out what's there: what you will keep, and what you will want to remove, or chop down. At the same time, think about landscaping in general terms: is a steep garden terraced, and if so, is the terracing secure and safe? Are there hills or depressions that you'd like to level, or new spaces that you want to create?

Then there is the question of drainage and, possibly, of irrigation. With water metered across the whole of France, running a sprinkler regularly can be expensive, which means that many households tend to find means of storing as much rainwater as possible during the

'Looking out over your newly acquired grounds, which are basically a sloping field and tangle of dry bushes.

you will be forgiven for not knowing where to start.'

Typical French? What is a typical French garden like? is there such a thing? Probably not, given that there are five distinct climatic zones in France. The French film with the title '*Death in a French Garden*' provided no clues: exported to the UK from France, its original title was actually '*Mort dans un jardin Anglais*', or 'Death in an English garden'! Some people believe something formally laid out with low hedges, such as you may find in the grounds of a chateau, is typically French. However, if you choose to create that look in your garden, you will be in for a lot of work. Like a short haircut, the shorter and neater the look of the hedge you are trying to create, the more frequent trimming it will need to stay in shape. The same goes for topiary (left). Conversely, French people are often quick to point to typically English gardens in France, notable for their impeccable lawns and riot of colourful blooms.

'Believe it or not, using a water diviner is not so rare in France. Many sceptics are surprised at the results.'

winter, in a tank or water butt. Alternatively, you could have a bore-hole drilled. If you are prepared to spend money on irrigating your garden by using your metered water, you will need to create a system of perforated pipes, buried in the soil within a layer of gravel. It is impossible to create a ball-park figure for how much water you may need per square metre of garden: it depends on the plants you choose, the climate, of course, and also the nature of soil and drainage on your plot of land. Many northern Europeans cultivating gardens in the south of France are keen to have an irrigated green lawn throughout the summer, which can create a kind of Californian feel to some properties.

However, there are plenty of lower-maintenance alternatives to a grass lawn during an arid summer. Hence the attraction of gravel and paving. The ideal gravel surface is actually quite firm. Think along the lines of a game of boules, where the steel balls will bounce on hitting the gravel surface, rather than sinking straight in, as they would on a beach. Think carefully too about the colour, and try to find something that will go with the façade of your house. Again, getting inspiration from neighbours and friends in the region is ideal, and larger garden centres will have samples of gravel paths installed on site to give you an instant feel for what you are buying.

If you are lucky, you may have a well on your land, or a natural water source that has not yet been discovered. Believe it or not, getting water diviners on the case is not unusual in the south of France, and you can find these talented individuals by asking at the local mairie. Many sceptics have been surprised at the results.

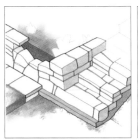  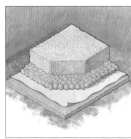

Tip: stone steps
Dry-stone steps set in a mortar bed, and a low retaining wall at the base of a sloping herbaceous border are a great way of dealing with sloping ground. Beginners beware: dry-stone walling is an art!

Tip: rustic arbour
A simple structure of wooden poles creates shade over a terrace, allowing plants to entwine the trellis overhead. A galvanised housing for the uprights screws to a concrete footing just below terrace level.

Tip: gravel terrace
10cm of topsoil is removed, a thin layer of sand is added, followed by a textile to block plant growth, then rough gravel, and finally the surface, which is levelled, watered and rolled as flat as possible.

Landscaping

The majority of major landscaping jobs in France come on the back of a swimming pool project, for obvious reasons. If the pool has been excavated, you can end up with fifty or so cubic metres of soil to distribute somewhere. Creating access for vehicles on sloping ground can also prompt a landscaping job, as this also leaves many spare cubic metres of earth hanging around.

But whatever sparks such a project off, landscaping can dramatically improve your property. It could simply be a case of creating new spaces using planting, fencing and new surfaces, or something more ambitious, moving volumes of earth around and levelling slopes, creating terraces and adding retaining walls.

Again, an experienced landscaper will understand the structural engineering elements of soil and rock (or at least will bring in an expert in this area), and will be able to guarantee and insure the work. Technology from civil engineering projects is increasingly being used in domestic landscaping – such as 'gabions', or steel wire cages in the shape of a cube, filled with boulders and used for heavy duty jobs such as retaining walls.

But what about the planting? France is a vast country, with four or five completely different climatic regions, and the best way to start out is to visit local nurseries and see the kind of plants that thrive in your region. The choice will be immense. Gardening clubs and user-groups for English-speakers are springing up, including the useful *www.mediterraneangardensociety.org*, which is actually a global organisation that offers advice on Mediterranean-type climates that exist elsewhere in the world.

When ordering plants by mail-order, there are major companies in Spain and Italy that supply across Europe, but which are virtually unknown in the UK. For many gardeners this makes the prospect of discovering new plants and a new climate in which to cultivate them all the more exciting.

choice will be immense, though gardening clubs for English-speakers in France are also growing vigorously.'

Building a terrace

First, an administrative point. Generally, if you are building a terrace you will not need planning permission (a *permis de construire)*, unless it is a construction over 60cm high and more than 20 sq m in area. However, a built terrace (on a concrete slab) of any size will require you to make a *déclaration de travaux* at the local mairie, the reason being that the terrace will add to the official gross floor area of your property, known as the SHOB, or *surface hors d'oeuvre brut* (see p201).

The most robust base for a terrace is a reinforced concrete slab. The terrace area is first excavated, levelled and flattened, with the compacted earth covered in a layer of hardcore, and then coarse sand around 10cm deep. Onto this go the reinforcement bars, and then the concrete is poured. A slab like this for external use will have a slight slope (around 2%) to allow water to drain away. It will also need expansion joints every couple of metres, and where the slab comes into contact with any walls. Concrete, like most other materials, will expand and contract with the weather.

Of course, you can avoid the trouble and expense of laying a concrete slab, and many people prefer to prepare the ground to make it level, compact and stable, and lay the terrace material onto a layer of sand, with a layer of geotextile beneath this. Alternatively, a wooden frame will support a terrace, with this frame supported on a series of small concrete footings. To avoid weeds taking hold underneath, the ground is prepared first with a layer of geotextile, which in turn is covered in around 10cm of gravel.

Terrace materials

Decking is getting as popular in France as it is in the UK, and a range of different systems are available, including basic pre-drilled boards, interlocking panels, and systems resting on screw height-adjustable pillars, like a kind of outdoor 'floating' parquet, and known in French as *caillebotis,* with square duckboard-style panels.

Wood, of course, looks great when it is newly installed, but the effects of sunlight and weather will quickly see it turn a bit on the grey side, and probably develop a few cracks too. Not that this affects its strength, provided the wood has been treated.

Expensive, but timeless, natural stone makes an excellent terrace material. The stone you choose will need to be tough and resistant to frost, and ideally from a region or climate similar to the one where it will be installed. The thickness of stone will not really be an indicator of its toughness – this is more dependent on how it is laid. Some people like to treat the surface with a waterproofing agent, which will protect the porous stone surface from moss, insects, and grease stains from a barbeque. Some months on, you may notice salty mineral deposits accumulating on the surface. This is a natural process and helps to keep a resistant 'shell' at the surface of the stone. Cobblestones may be available locally, too.

With its beautiful and varied tints and hues (coming from variations in iron oxide content, and in the firing time of different tiles during their manufacture) genuine terracotta is a good, tough material for external use in the Mediterranean climate – it is quite grippy to walk on in wet weather. One downside to using it as a terrace material is that it can easily pick up a layer of moss, and it is not guaranteed against frost.

The traditional method of putting down terracotta tiles is on a bed of lime mortar, but cement will do equally as well – or a mix of the two. Soak the tiles for an hour before installing them, as this will limit their capacity to draw water out of the mortar as it sets. Don't pack

'Terraces can give your home an additional room...'

Outdoor living

The simple low-level stone wall (left) with its stone arch is the starting point for a beautifully conceived terrace, which has a shaded roof running across the living space beyond the wall, with the window in the wall glazed to maintain the windbreak effect.

Some of the most successful terraces become an extension of the living space inside the house – which is why a terrace on its own, however ancient or beautiful the paving might be, can look a bit bare. If you have the space to make a large terrace, you can also create separate living spaces on the terrace itself, using natural trellis screens to shield an eating area from an evening breeze, or a pergola to create a room within the terrace, and to provide shade. You could simply build a framework coming down from the wall of the house, with a pull-down cotton awning to keep the sun at bay. Alternatively, wires to support a vine or roses look good, as does an overhead screen of bamboo or raffia matting. In effect you can create another room on the terrace, for eating, entertaining, or just snoozing during a hot afternoon.

'...for eating, entertaining, or just snoozing during a warm afternoon.'

them in too tightly: leave around 5 mm between each tile, and if the surface to be covered is greater than 30sq m, you will need to plan in some expansion joints for the mortar bed.

Reconstituted stone is tough and easy to install, being made of a mix of concrete and natural stone powders. Installation is straightforward: if the slabs are more than 3 cm thick, you will be able to lay them straight onto a sand bed, rather than concrete. Sourcing reclaimed stone slabs, cobblestones and bricks remains the most authentic solution of all, though.

Garden ambiance at night

Using the terrace, or indeed the garden at night, could mean investing in some garden lighting. For some gardens, exterior lighting is simply a single spotlight (or a large lantern-type lamp for more character) mounted on the wall of the house, and bathing the garden or terrace in light, broken only by the flickering of the occasional moth or circling bats. It is possible to go too far towards the other extreme, lighting up the whole garden like a late-night football stadium, which risks spoiling everyone's view of the night sky.

The best option, if you are at the garden planning stage, is to think about multiple sources of light, and invest in some outdoor-standard ducting and light fittings – ideally those offering long-life fluorescent bulbs, or low-voltage versions which can be fitted at ground level to mark out a path or set of steps.

Lighting a garden can transform it in terms of the ambiance you create – using low lighting shining up into trees, for example, or light coming down vertically close to a stone wall to pick out the contours and relief. For late night eating outside, a mix of low-voltage spotlights and more direct light on the table adds atmosphere – along with garden candles, and the indispensable citronella candle to discourage mosquitos from joining the feast.

'If you are still at the garden planning stage, think about adding outdoor-standard ducts and light fittings.'

Growing season
Many second home owners with a passion for gardening can find that it all gets a bit out of hand during the spring or summer, when everything grows incredibly fast. The easygoing weekend break in France can become a kind of gardening marathon, which is a sweaty business in summer, even if you try to rope in as many of your unsuspecting friends and family as possible.
A good solution is to find (and of course pay) local people to keep it all under control. Or better still, offer part of your plot to someone nearby who is keen to cultivate fruit and vegetables. Sharing home-grown produce with your neighbours is an excellent way to make new friends.

Pool on the hill
Built onto rocky, sloping
ground, this pool with its
relatively narrow sur-
rounds nestles discretely
in the surrounding
vegetation. Note the
overflow edge built into
the far end, where the
water flows down into
a smaller pool for chil-
dren. This pool has been
built on traditional con-
crete foundations, with
the walls built up from
formwork blocks and
lined with a marble and
quartz composite render.

Chapter 13

SWIMMING POOLS

THE WATER'S LOVELY

Sales of swimming pools in France are booming. This is partly because they seem to have become relatively more affordable these days. But also, perhaps, because of worsening traffic jams, parking problems and the general hassle associated with going to the beach in some parts of France. The swimming pool boom also means there is now plenty of choice on the market, and a surprisingly wide range of English-speaking suppliers and installers. And for anyone thinking of running a gîte business, a pool can work wonders for your order book.

The blue yonder
Think about sight-lines from the pool to the house. Some people like to screen the pool from the house using trees or bushes on the basis that during the winter it may not look at its best. People with kids, though, often like to see the pool from the house. The pool on the right, in Midi, is out of sight thanks to the steeply sloping and terraced grounds. But cutting a terrace into the rocky foundations does not come cheap.

Digging in: where it goes, style and size

It pays to create a bit of space around your pool if you can, so that there is room to walk around, and enjoy the laid-back environment that a pool in a garden in the summer so easily evokes. At the same time, you don't want your pool to be too exposed to the prevailing winds, and you may want a bit of privacy from neighbours or passers-by. Then, try to get the pool facing the sun, and facing open views. And to avoid the pool constantly filling up with leaves, try to keep it a certain distance from overhanging trees.

If you have room, you might try to hide the pool from view of the house – behind a wall or a line of shrubs. This is mainly because in the winter, the unused pool under its cover will not look brilliant. Or, if there are kids around, it could make more sense to keep the pool visible from your house. Of course, just being able to see the pool from a kitchen window is no substitute for proper security measures, or adult supervision. (For more on pool safety, see p157 and p210.)

If your land is sloping, this is not the end of your pool project – it

will just make it more expensive. In fact, building a pool on a slope can create a stunning effect, especially with an overflow, or 'infinity' pool. This creates an illusion of the water of the pool running away over the edge of the pool (which it actually does, so it's not an illusion) before flowing into a drain, or *goulotte* which runs around the edge of part of the pool (and sometimes the entire pool), and then through a filter unit which also works as a skimmer. How well such a pool looks depends in large part on what kind of view you have behind the pool. If you overlook the sea, then it is possible, sometimes, to create the impression that the pool runs straight into the ocean. In rural areas, you can get the impression that the edge of the pool is, in fact, a waterfall, cascading down into the valley below.

These pools are also very clean and hygienic, as the surface of the pool is constantly being replenished, getting rid of dust, seeds, insects and so on. They are also more expensive than a regular pool, requiring a budget starting at around €25,000.

Style and size
Some people would opt for the biggest pool they can afford, given the chance. But how big does a pool really have to be? The bigger it is, the more expensive it is to build, maintain, and run. Generally, a pool needs to be at least 4m wide, which allows two people to swim past each other without a clash of arms and legs. To create a typical rectangular pool, the width is usually doubled to create the length, with 5m by 10m and 5.5m by 11m some of the most common sizes.

Apart from rectangular pools, people often opt for the *forme libre*, in other words ovals, circular pools, and so on. These don't always look as good as people imagine on paper, and getting advice from an

'Some people will opt for the biggest pool possible.'

Reinforced concrete is the key when building an in-ground swimming pool. Whether it's poured into a hollow block structure, or between formwork panels which define its eventual shape, or is simply sprayed

Still waters
A simple in-ground pool of 10m by 5m will cost around €20,000 in its finished form (fully equipped and ready for a swim). This figure does not include excavation. Count on two to three days' digging, at €500 per day in trouble-free ground, plus €500 per day to remove the earth. In rocky ground, excavation costs are likely to be €1,000 per day. An exceptional terrace, (such as the one pictured left) will add a few thousand more to your bill.

'Paving around the pool can push up your costs.'

architect or a landscape specialist could be money well spent at the start.

Another element you will need to choose at the outset is what kind of material will form the paving, or the *plage* around the pool. Some people will try to integrate it with the look and feel of the house by using stone flagstones around the pool, for example, if they have an old stone house. The choice is wide, and very often the best solutions are the least conspicuous. Moulded edging is the most common, made of concrete or reconstituted stone, and with a variety of finishes and anti-slip surfaces. The only downside is that some of these can be a bit dull – which can spoil a bit of the charm of your pool – and can look out of place with local stone buildings if you can't get materials to match. Stone, terracotta, or wood can look a good deal better, but get slippery when wet. They are not always resistant to frost either, and can encourage moss and fungus growth.

Whatever material you choose, the paving can add significantly to your costs, as the quantity required is considerable. A 10m by 5m pool with 1.5m of edging will need more than 45 sq m of materials, so if you are paying €30 per sq m for materials, the costs for the pool surround alone will reach more than €1,300.

echnology works

against the pool walls, it is highly resilient and allows the creation of all kinds of pool shapes. The process starts with excavation, after which the concrete base slab of the pool is poured in over a frame-work of reinforcement mesh. After that, there are several effective ways of building up the pool walls. Here's a guide to get you discussing the various options with your builder.

Formwork (Coffrage)

Wooden panels define the two faces of the eventual concrete wall. Reinforcement bars are inserted between the panels, and the concrete poured into the cavity. Waterproof render is then applied. The formwork pool pictured left is perched on a tight space on sloping ground – with just a small 4 sq m terrace

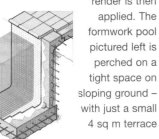

Formwork blocks (Blocs à bancher)

The pool walls are built of concrete blocks with cavities to take reinforcement bars. Apart from the first layer (which goes onto a mortar bed) subsequent layers just stack together dry, after which concrete is pour into the cavity. This pool, in a sloping Provenç garden, is lined with 2cm x 2cm mosaics.

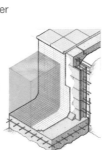

Spray-forming (Gunitage)

This involves spraying concrete directly onto the excavated walls of the pool, prepared with reinforcement bars. This 'gunite' pool (left) has two hidden drains, one for the pool and one for water running off the terrace. On the left side, the pool drain is neatly hidden below the level of the lawn, to stunning effect.

Concrete panels (Reveline technique)

Reveline's modular concrete panels fit together to create a formwork frame with a concrete inner face. Reinforcement bars are slotted in, and the concrete is poured. Note how this pool floor (right) follows the contours of the sloping ground, limiting the excavation required.

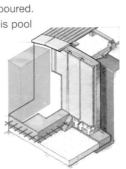

What the pool is made of

As for the construction of the pool itself, concrete remains king for most of the larger, excavated pools (see box on pp152-153), and also for any pool that needs to be built on tricky hilly terrain. If you get a concrete pool installed on flat ground that is free of rocks, then you could pay less than €20,000 for the complete installation. Where foundation work and landscaping become more demanding, this price could rise by several thousand euros.

There are cheaper self-build options. Kit pools made of wood are becoming increasingly popular, and suit all kinds of configurations, from the traditional (not dug-in) to semi-excavated and completely excavated. You can put them up in just a few days, and they come in decent sizes too – up to 8m long – and in a variety of shapes, often complete with a decked terrace. A complete pool of this sort is likely to cost between €4,500 and €10,000.

Polyester is universally popular for cheaper pools, starting at around €5,000 for the complete installation including filters. There are three main types. The monocoque pool is a large basin made of polyester or epoxy resin, moulded in a factory, and simply inserted into your excavation. You finish off with a 'gel coat' which protects the polyester and provides the finish. Slatted pools use interlocking slats propped up from behind, and allow a number of different shapes to be created. A flexible pool liner finishes the job. Similarly, pools can be built from PVC-coated panels which slot together to create the form of the pool, which is then fitted with a flexible liner.

The pool lining

What you choose to line the pool with, and how good the water filtration system is, will in large part determine how easy, or how

'A 5m by 10m concrete pool built into flat ground that is free of rocks could cost less than €20,000 for the

Maintenance costs If you have a pool at a holiday home which is not occupied all-year round, a maintenance contract could be the best solution. For a typical pool of say 10m by 5m, this could cost in the region of €2,500 per year, not including chemicals. Such a contract would include weekly visits to the pool during the summer months, to check the water level and top it up if necessary, check the water quality, remove any leaves or debris, and clean the filters (which operate daily on automatic timers). In peak season, when the water is warm, filters may have to run for eight hours per day, though can be programmed to do so at night. Outside the summer season, as the water cools down, fewer daily filtering hours are required, so maintenance visits are scaled back to once a month.

expensive, your pool is to look after. **Flexible pool liners** are by far the cheapest and most commonly used option and account for around one in four pools in France. The liner is a supple but strong sheet of PVC, cut to fit the dimensions of a range of fairly standard-shaped pools, and then stuck or clipped to the edges of the pool – in effect a DIY job if you are careful. These liners are available in several different colours, including the usual turquoise. While they are fine for a budget pool, their main drawback is that they can get creased, especially after emptying and then re-filling the pool.

The **reinforced liner** is thicker than the simple liners, so is more durable, and also more expensive. They are cut to fit the exact shape of your pool, so can run over steps or curves without problems. A reinforced liner needs to be fitted by an expert, who cuts out panels of material (which is about 1.5mm thick) to fit your pool dimensions, and then solders them together, before heating the entire liner to make it fit tightly to the contours of the pool. These liners are available in a variety of plain colours or mosaic-style patterns.

Resin liners are a throwback to public swimming pools of old. The resin is applied in liquid form with a roller, after which it hardens to create a watertight shell. It then needs to be sanded, and fin-

complete installation. Building on awkward or sharply sloping ground will add a few thousand euros more.'

ished with a gel coat. This is only suitable for rigid pools built of blocks or concrete, and needs to be applied by a specialist.

Waterproof renders are another option, and are good for a kind of brutal, minimalist finish, as they mix resin directly with the concrete and create a waterproof layer that is more or less invisible. They are applied (again, by a specialist) with a roller or a plastering float and can be tinted with pigment if required. Note that you cannot use this finish if you want to treat the water with an electrolysis-based system.

An attractive option are the **powdered marble** or **silicon-based mortar renders**, applied with a trowel. A weak point can be that various algae can attack this surface, and if the pH value of your water is on the low side (acidic), the marble will also be eroded. Seek specialist advice on this one.

Mosaics remain the classic finish: 2.5cm by 2.5cm square glass mosaics are available on sheets, and give you maximum choice in terms of creating a very individual pool, or recreating an ancient Roman bath if you so wish. You will need a specialist for this job.

Water treatment

In France, people who use their pools regularly generally change the water only every 2-3 years – thanks to the efficiency of water treatment systems. With water being metered, it would typically cost around €80 to refill an average swimming pool of 50 cu m. This may not seem an enormous cost, but emptying a pool can be a problem, especially if you are not on mains drains. And with water rationing a possibility after some of the driest summers on record, a good treatment system that conserves your water is essential.

There are plenty of home water-testing kits available today to allow you to find out more about your pool water. Generally, you take a

'Small glass mosaics remain one of the classics for a pool lining...'

Sense of proportion
Ideally, a pool should be at least 4m wide to allow two swimmers to pass each other in comfort.
Beyond this, the proportions depend on how you will use it. Serious swimmers often go for longer, narrower pools, deep enough to execute a flashy 'tumble turn' at the shallow end.
Families prefer a very shallow end and a gentle slope, or a linked paddling pool. As a 'rule of thumb', plan in at least 15-20 cu m of water per pool user.

water sample, add a chemical, and then check the colour change against a chart. This process is essential so that you know which kind of treatment you need, since the choice depends on acidity, and on the level of minerals – calcium and magnesium carbonates and bicarbonates. During the summer, this test for acidity should be carried out once or twice a week, and the result should be somewhere between pH 7.2 and pH 7.6 (very slightly alkaline). Alternatively, you could invest in a system of automatic acidity regulation.

There is a wide range of disinfectant treatments and filtration systems available on the market. Many specialist pool suppliers in France will be able to explain (in English) the various options available.

Paperwork, maintenance and security

Like any construction project, a pool will involve a certain amount of official paperwork. Check at the mairie that what you are planning to do is permitted in your local area. You will have to make a *déclaration de travaux* or (more rarely) get planning permission – a *permis de construire,* depending on the size of the pool you want to build, and if there is a building next to it. Finally, you need to remember that a pool will be liable for local taxes if it is a permanent masonry structure, which is considered for tax purposes to be an outbuilding.

It will also have to be insured, and meet safety the latest safety regulations. Until recently, it was up to the property-owner to decide how careful to be about pool security. However, as pools have become more popular in France, so too has the number of tragic accidents increased, often involving young children. In response to this, the French government introduced a new law on 3 January 2003, which now means that every pool – whether open to the public or in a private garden – must have a certain minimum level of security to

'... allowing you to go for that Roman bath look.'

prevent accidents. The aim is to ensure that a pool can be effectively shut off from those to whom it could present a hazard. You can also find various kinds of alarms now – such as infra-red beams, or floating movement sensors – which will detect when someone enters the pool. For more on the pool safety law, see p210.

During the winter, the best security is provided by a rigid pool cover, consisting of interconnected slats which can be rolled across the pool. They should be strong enough to support the weight of a child who ventures across.

Access to the water itself also has safety implications. There are two options: the straightforward aluminium ladder (which is starting to come back into fashion thanks to improvements in the way they are fixed to the wall of the pool); and the steps integrated into the form of the pool itself, allowing bathers to get into the water gradually. Ladders are generally not suitable for young children to use, so the steps are the better all-round solution, and can create a good-looking addition to one end of the pool. You can also play extra safe and cover the steps with an anti-slip material.

Getting a pool ready for winter
Known as wintering, this is often left to a pool servicing contractor (*piscinier*), and it is easy to see why, as it is the time for extensive cleaning and servicing of the equipment. Note that in most parts of France, a pool is not generally emptied over the winter. Instead the water level is reduced by around 10cm, and the water left in place, both to protect the walls of the pool against frost, and to let the weight of the water reinforce the rigidity of the base and walls of the pool against the pressure exerted by the mass of earth and rock surrounding it. It also helps protect against damage from any rise in the surrounding water table. The water left in the pool is then given

a hefty sterilisation dose, followed by chemicals designed to inhibit algae and scale formation.

At the same time, access ladders, diving boards and other accessories should be removed and stored indoors, the filters serviced and cleaned, and the water treated against the growth of algae and other bugs. The pool walls and floor should be cleaned carefully, with extra attention paid to the water line. The surface should, of course, be covered, and the more robust the pool cover, the better. Note that a light-proof cover will cut down on the growth of algae.

Pool house and shower

This is a rather anglo-saxon tradition – to the point that there is not even a term for this in the French language. The pool house is used to house the filtration and pumping equipment for the pool, as well as poolside furniture, towels, and, in some of the larger ones, a WC, showers – even a kitchen. This can be ideal for pool parties where the pool is some distance from the main house.

Outbuildings can be used if they are close enough to the pool. If you need to build a bespoke pool house, then think about selecting building materials to harmonise with the rest of your property, or at least to blend in with the materials chosen for the terrace around the pool. A cheap pool house in PVC or in metal will certainly do the job in terms of providing a place to store your equipment, but it won't do much to help create another useful living space.

An outdoor shower is a great decorative addition to your pool area too, and brings something of the holiday mood to your garden. And taking a shower before taking a dip will also help the whole pool filtration system to work better – you will be removing many of the pollutants such as suncream, perspiration, and dust that will otherwise end up in the water, and eventually clog up the filters.

Stepping down
Curving steps across the corner of a pool add a touch of glamour, and make it easier for small children to make their way into the water. Note that planning a safety enclosure for a pool close to a house needs careful thought.

Leak alert!

If you notice that your pool water level is consistently dropping, then it's more likely to be a leak than evaporation. Finding and fixing a leak in a pool is no easy task. It could be a problem with the liner, or the structure itself, or a failure in the pipework leading to the filtration system. Luckily, technology exists to make this job easier. Leaks can be pinpointed by applying a small electric charge to the water, and then searching for the point at which it makes contact with the earth. This only works, though, with liners made of an electrically insulating material, such as PVC. Otherwise, the technique for finding a leak is rather more basic – a fingertip search, plus listening for the sound of water escaping. Not everyone's ideal way to spend a weekend by the pool.

 We hope this first part of the book has given you a few ideas, and also taken some of the **uncertainty** out of how these old houses can be renovated. In the end, **the fun part** of your project will be turning the property you buy into your own unique home in France, which is all down to **your own style**, and of course **your budget**. To make your project even more enjoyable, we thought we would devote some space to trying to unravel some of the mysteries of those **everyday tasks** that accompany getting a renovation job in France off the ground – like sorting out your electricity or water supplies, getting planning permission, organising the builders, and all the rest. In **The Basics**, over the next 50-odd pages, some of the questions you have on these **tecky and admin matters** will be answered.

THE BASICS

The Basics: The Contents

Finding out how other people have done a job, and more importantly, how much they had to pay, is a quick way of trying to work out how difficult your own project will be. Here, we look at two contrasting projects – one large, and one small. The Farmhouse Renovation in Gascony was a large scale job, taking over a partly-renovated farmhouse (but which was virtually uninhabitable as almost every-thing had been ripped out!). The couple used an ex-pat project manager who lived locally and spoke fluent French. The Town House Renovation in Normandy is a small, compact job, which takes a completely derelict building (that cost just €25,000) and turns it into a cosy two-bedroom house.

For more real life projects from people renovating in France, take a look at our website: www.renovationfrance.net and click on 'Project Diaries'.

Real Projects: 1. Farmhouse renovation in Gascony

This story shows how it is possible to get a big, complex project in France completed 'at arms length' – in this case using an ex-pat English project manager to run the site.

This is a large house in spacious grounds, and the costs of getting the outside space sorted out were considerable – at around €15,000. The gravel area in front of the house cost around €4,500, and landscaping and site clearance added further large bills. The upside: an exceptional and tranquil site.

In search of perfect calm

Ian and Mary Roberts wanted to find a house that would provide a peaceful environment where people could come and find perfect calm – a place of relaxation for friends, and, during part of the season, for paying guests too. An estate agent suggested the couple should start searching in Gascony – which proved to be sound advice. Soon after, on a wet day in March, they were fortunate enough to find just what they were looking for.

The house, called Le Mouret, is a traditional farmhouse with medieval origins which had remained unoccupied for the last fifteen years. While it had recently been partially renovated, with new windows and some new interior partitions upstairs, it was otherwise uninhabitable. However, the location was perfect, with 25 acres of land surrounding the farm, and the nearest country road more than 100m away across a field planted with sunflowers. The nearest town is a few kilometres away. What's more, it was spacious, with room for expansion: 270 sq m of living space in the house, plus a further 750 sq m of outbuildings.

The couple bought the house in July 2002 for €253,000 (including legal and estate agents' fees of €27,000). The price also included a sum of around €33,000 for some of the renovation work already completed – new windows, some partitioning and rewiring, plus baths, basins and a central heating system, all of which had yet to be installed.

However, the main work was about to begin. The couple had a budget of around €70,000 to make the house habitable, install a pool, and get the exterior tidied up – although they had also set aside a substantial overrun fund.

Finding the right builder

With the owners based in the UK, it was essential to find a builder who would act as the site manager and get the whole job completed in around six months – in time for the summer letting season. Their first attempts to find someone came to nothing: a British builder considered the job but lived two hours' drive from the site and so was reluctant to take on the job. A local architect thought the budget inadequate and also turned down the job. (As it turned out, his instinct about the budget proved correct.)

Finally, it was a Briton based in Gascony who took the job on: Tim Badgett – who had already completed a renovation project nearby, and spoke fluent French. He also had a team of competent builders that he had worked with before, and began the Roberts' project at the start of 2003.

The need for speed

The work on this house illustrates how a large number of moderate-sized jobs can add up to a hefty renovation bill.

Several jobs remained half-finished after the partial renovation that the previous owner had started – such as the electrical refit – and even though the central heating system was already on site when the house was bought, it cost a further €8,700 to install. There were also some major works required, the most expensive being the swimming pool. This was a fairly standard 11m by 5m pool on level ground, constructed by a local supplier, at a cost of around €21,000.

A new septic tank, with the capacity to deal with a dozen people staying in the house at the same time, was also needed, at a cost of €5,100.

Within the house itself, the major works involved digging up the dirt floors under the old tiles to install a damp-proof membrane and concrete slab to enable complete re-tiling downstairs. Re-pointing and plastering were fairly straightforward but time-consuming (and therefore expensive in labour). While new windows were already in place, new shutters had to be made to order, at a cost of €6,500 for 17 sets of wooden shutters in pine.

The long list of other jobs – such as fitting out new bath and shower rooms, security measures, general repairs and sand-blasting, as well as decorating throughout the house and renovating some of the original features including beams, fireplaces, medieval stone walls, and floorboards accounted for well over €40,000. This cost could have been reduced,

but the plan was to preserve the rustic charm of the house by renovating and repairing, rather than ripping out and replacing with new fittings. This is almost always the more expensive option, as it tends to be labour intensive – unless you are committed to putting the time in yourself to make the repairs (such as filling cracks and sanding down old wooden doors). This is virtually impossible for property owners based in the UK who do not have time on their side.

This wooden farmhouse fireplace was eventually shortened to extend the old cupboard doors down to floor level.

Double the budget

The original budget for the whole renovation project proved insufficient – not surprisingly because of the amount of unforeseen work that was eventually revealed as the renovation work took shape. One drill-bit alone, needed to get through some of the metre-thick walls, cost a tidy €170. By the end of the project, the total renovation bill came in at over

€140,000 – double the original estimate. The owners decided not to compromise on quality where it mattered. 'The house needs to be comfortable, and needs to look right,' says Ian. 'You decide on certain things that will help to create the look that you want, but they tend to be more expensive than you first imagine.' Crushed stone around the house, for example, looks absolutely right, but cost about €2.20 per square metre – which over 2,000 square metres really adds up.

Value for money?

And then there was the timescale, with the whole job being completed in around six months, starting in January and ready in time to take bookings for the summer season. 'If you want the job done at speed, it costs money. But there are benefits. If the job drags on over two years, your enjoyment of the place is compromised,' Ian says.

Thanks to the relentless pace of the work, Le Mouret was completed six months after the site opened, and has been transformed into a beautiful and welcoming home. 'To some extent, going over budget has been a concern,' admits Mary. 'But at the same time, it looks as though the house in its completed state is now worth rather more than the total of what we have spent on it and, most importantly, we have been fortunate enough to create a haven not just for us but for many others who will spend time there.'

The house (just visible, left) includes 750 sq m of outbuildings. The pool cost just over €20,000 including paving, which had not been installed at the time this picture was taken.

FACT FILE

Gascony farmhouse with four double bedrooms, 270 sq m habitable space, plus 750 sq m of outbuildings. Property includes 25 acres of farmland, part of which is managed by a local farmer.

Property Cost*	**€253,000**
Renovation budget	**€71,500**
Actual renovation costs	**€148,730**
Total (property & work)	**€401,730**
Approximate market value**	**€500,000**
Projected timescale	**6 months**
Actual build time	**6 months**

Project route
The owners, who live in England, hired an English expat site manager (with fluent French) living locally to run the project. He hired local French builders, some of whom he had used on a previous project. The site manager's fee was based on a percentage of the overall build costs, and is included in the totals listed.

Project cost breakdown

Floors: tiling downstairs, sanding/polishing upstairs	€10,870
New pine shutters for 17 windows, plus door	€7,720
Joinery: kitchen fitting, interior doors, skirting	€4,580
Sanitation: septic tank	€5,150
Walls: sandblasting, re-pointing, plastering	€13,440
Plasterboard ceilings and partitions	€6,300
Finish bathroom & showers	€2,720
Finish electrical installation	€10,720
Finish plumbing	€6,580
Central heating installation	€8,723
Decorating	€15,730
Masonry work	€5,005
General labour and materials	€14,870
External repairs and landscaping	€14,443
Swimming pool (including paving)	€21,879
Total:	**€148,730**

*Property bought in July 2002. Includes taxes and fees and €32,900 of plumbing/central heating materials and pre-sale ren-

Real Projects: 2. Town house renovation in Normandy

This derelict house and barn in the middle of a small market town cost the owner just €25,000. The next step was to convert it into a cosy two-bedroom house, with a modern twist.

The roof comes off, in readiness for the new wall and windows (see sketch, next page). For step-by-step shots showing how this job progressed, visit our website, www.renovationfrance.net and click on Project Diaries.

A village house for a busy midwife

Jane Pelham[1], a qualified midwife, was looking for a village house to renovate in northern France, which would eventually become her permanent home. She began searching for property with a fairly open mind about the amount of work needed to get it in shape, though she was aiming for a good quality of finish throughout. Her basic requirement was for a property with two bedrooms, and which would fall within her overall budget of about €130,000. Eventually, Jane found what looked like an extraordinary bargain, but at the same time, a major challenge. Based in a beautiful market town which was high on her list of favourites (as it was close to her work), she found a completely derelict property that was on sale for just €25,000.

Unoccupied for 100 years

The property was within the old centre itself, with a total of 300 sq m of floor space in a group of buildings around a courtyard. It had a water supply, but no electricity or mains drainage, although as it was in a village, getting connection would not pose a problem. At the back (on the other side of the buildings pictured above), there is also a charming walled garden.

So what was the catch? Well, the main village house (pictured left) had remained unoccupied for around 100 years. Another part of the building – a small barn (on the right-hand picture) – had been used as an abattoir for the butcher, who lived nearby, while the central parts (pictured with roof removed, centre) had been used as cellars to smoke meat, and still had smoke-blackened walls and timbers providing a lasting reminder. More recently, they had been used as holding pens for livestock.

A mix of new-build and traditional

Jane's plan was adventurous. The obvious route was to convert the existing derelict house. But after looking at various options drawn up by her architects, she chose to convert the abattoir and cellar area, which are at right angles to each other. To make the most of the space, she decided to extend upwards the single-story cellar areas, to create new living space at first floor level, with the upper part of the existing wall glazed with 11 new windows (visible on the sketch, next page). This would create a two-bedroom house with living room, kitchen/dining room, bathroom, a downstairs WC, and laundry room (in the stone-floored cellar) covering around 120 sq m in total. It would also leave untouched the existing house, on the left of the courtyard, as a potential later project or as an asset that she could sell on at a later date.

Jane decide to get advice from design professionals right from the start, and hired one of the authors of this book, David Ackers, to run the project.

Get in the professionals

The project was scheduled to take about seven months to complete. The work would involve a new roof, new floors on the ground and upper levels, repairs to the masonry throughout, plumbing, electricity, a new kitchen and bathroom, and a new section built to connect the two separate buildings, and which would house the living room, bedroom and bathroom. The project started at the end of January, with a temporary electricity supply laid on for the builders. A part of the roof was first removed, to allow masons to prepare the tops of the walls for the new timbers, and to repair the stonework – including modifying window openings. In the same phase, the ground floors were dug out, and a damp-proof course and concrete sub-floor cast – ready for installing electric under-floor heating below a flagstone floor later.

The upper floors were also created – using a concrete 'pot and beam' technique (similar to the floor shown on p80), but using concrete rather than insulated inserts between the beams). Before these floors were created, the plumber and electrician (which in this project was one and the same man) put in the ducting required for feeding through cables and pipes later.

With the roof removed, and the masonry made good throughout, the roof carpenter returned to fit the new roof timbers, followed quickly by the roofer, who fitted roofing felt and new Spanish slates on black tinted slate hooks. This took place in April, about ten weeks after the project began.

Eighteen new windows

The new roof incorporated one dormer window, and all the other windows in the house were also brand new – built by a regional joinery company. A total of 18 windows and two new doors were required.

With the roof complete, and the new windows in place, the house was now weatherproof, allowing the next stage of works to continue. Masons had already worked to consolidate the interior walls with a rough-coat of 'mortier-batard' – a mix of sand, cement and lime (as pictured on p84). Most of the interior walls were then lined with plasterboard fixed to a metal frame – with a layer of insulation between the rough-coated stone wall and the panels. It's worth noting that the 'plasterer' is becoming more of a rarity in France, as it is a trade that's transforming itself into 'plaquiste' – in other words, a specialist in putting up 'dry lining': plasterboard, or some of the blockwork alternatives. Some interior walls were lime-rendered and any worthwhile

stone features conserved. Further partition walls in the house were built using the same plasterboard on metal rails technique. During the course of this work on the walls, the electrician made a number of visits to fit ducts and outlets for sockets and lighting.

Compact and economical

With underfloor heating on the ground floor, the floor covering chosen was a limestone tile. Upstairs, where the heating method would be electric radiant panels, the flooring was created in economical seagrass throughout.

The kitchen and bathroom were among the final parts of the job, with the painter starting preparation of the external joinery while this was being completed – before returning when all the dust had settled to finish the paintwork inside. Part of the success of this project is down to the speed and coordination with which the work was done. In this project, the builders (who all lived locally) agreed a written schedule beforehand with the project manager.

But the other secret is its small size. Although the L-shaped ground plan was complex to design, this was a compact property, which lent itself to a complete refit but which did not cost a fortune to complete.

FACT FILE

A derelict village house, adjoining a disused abattoir and barn, with a total of 300 sq m of floor space. The conversion leaves the original house and another outbuilding undeveloped as a potential future project, but converts the two other buildings into a 120 sq m two-bedroom house.

Property Cost*	€25,000
Renovation budget	€110,000
Actual renovation costs	€111,919
Total (property & work)	€136,919
Projected timescale	7 months
Actual build time	7 months

Project route:

The owner hired a partnership of architect and interior architect (David Ackers – Design Associates) to design the conversion and run the project.

*Property bought in autumn 2003. Includes taxes and fees.

Project cost breakdown

New roof (110 sq m) including 3 Velux and one dormer window, and zinc guttering	€11,772
Roofing timbers, and interior doors etc	€13,683
18 new windows, and 2 exterior doors	€10,533
Ceilings, dry lining, interior partitions	€3,927
Masonry and stonework, pointing and rendering (interior & exterior) concrete floors, and some groundworks	€35,354
Wall and floor tiling, including stone	€7,663
Plumbing and bathroom	€4,058
Rewiring, plus ground floor electric underfloor heating	€10,000
Painting and decorating, incl. seagrass	€9,929
Kitchen: bespoke twin run of worktops (not including appliances)	€5,000
Total:	**€111,919**

ETUDES DE NIVEAUX
20/01/04

The traditional house (left) is not renovated, so remains as a potential future project. The cellars (centre) are extended upwards to create a new upper level (with 'gallery-look' glazing), and which links with the former abattoir (right) in an L-shape layout.

Buying property: Introduction, estate agents

Buying a place in France does not have to be worrying, difficult or complex, but for many people it is all of those things. Here we give you a run-down of the buying process, which will give you an idea of what to expect. For many people, a friendly English-speaking estate agent can be a great support during the first stage of the process, and a good English-speaking notaire will prove vital if you are to avoid sleepless nights. So find the right people to help you, approach this with the same caution that you would if buying in the UK, and don't sign anything that you don't understand!

200 years of estate agents!
French property law is based on the 200-year-old *Code Napoléon,* introduced in 1804, and at first sight looks fundamentally different from that of many other European countries, including the UK. In fact, though, it is pretty close to the system practised in Scotland. In a nutshell, when the buyer's offer is accepted by the vendor, the contracts are exchanged. Then there follows a 2–3 month period of land registry searches and so on, before completion (see box, p171). What is more of a struggle to understand are the inheritance laws, which you also need to think about when you buy property. More of that later.

Bring on the experts
What follows is a guide to the things you need to consider when you set out to purchase French property, and it is no substitute for the advice of legal professionals. If you are buying real estate in France, ideally you should consult a bilingual solicitor who is a specialist in the complexities of French property law, and keep them involved at all stages of the process. Even if you are fluent in French and confident about understanding legal nuances of meaning, it is sensible to employ a specialist to read over and explain to you any contracts before you sign, as much to check what might have been left out of the document as what it contains.

All the information given here refers specifically to the purchase of stand-alone older properties – that is, buildings more than five years old. Different regulations and types of contract apply when buying properties under construction or less than five years old, or when purchas-ing an apartment in a block. We do not have the space in this book to go into these other kinds of properties in detail, so again the best bet is to talk to the experts.

Estate agents
Estate agents (*agents immo-biliers*) handle the majority of house sales in France, but are not as numerous as their British counterparts and are more closely controlled. Agents are, however, much more likely to be involved in sales to overseas buyers, and many have reciprocal agreements with British agents. It is rare for French estate agents to get sole agency on properties they are offering for sale. *Notaires* (see below) are also entitled to develop a limited estate agent activity, practised within their own offices. They increasingly fulfil both functions, particularly in rural areas. Agents and notaires usually close for lunch and some begin the weekend at Saturday lunchtime. Many do not open on Mondays.

How to spot the pros
The main trade federation for estate agents – which lays down quality standards for how its members should operate – is the FNAIM. Non-members of this organisation, however, can also provide you with excellent services too.
Any agent you deal with

should be professionally qualified, with a current permit – a *carte professionelle* – issued by the *Préfecture* and, if they are to accept deposits from clients, insurance to indemnify them against loss. The amount guaranteed (*pièce de garantie*) should be displayed in their office and on their letterhead. Do not deal with an agent who cannot show you these qualifications.

Pro forma contracts

An estate agent may offer to speed up a sale by presenting you with a pre-printed or pro forma purchase contract to sign. These almost always require a good deal of modification, and you should never sign one without first seeking legal advice confirming if amendments need to be made. Agents or vendors should grant you a few days' grace to do this. If they do

not, it is best to walk away from the sale.

Payments

Never pay a vendor any money directly. Payments should be made to the agent or the notaire. You don't always need a French account to pay agents. Deposit payments – cheques on British banks denominated in the sterling equivalent of the euro price are sometimes accepted by estate agents. However, the notaire's client's account is lodged with a branch of the French inland revenue, which will *not* accept a cheque or draft from a non French-based bank. Electronic transfers, or a banker's draft – *un virement* – are other options. Payments should only be made to the notaire who draws up the purchase contract, or to the estate agent.

L'ABER-WRAC'H
◄ Le Port

Fees

French estate agents charge a larger commission than their British counterparts, usually 5–8% of the purchase price: the lowest rates are paid on the highest value properties. A list of fees should be displayed in the agent's office. Agents' commission is usually paid by the seller. Sometimes, though, a contract will specify that the buyer pays, so check this before signing. A notaire acting as an estate agent will usually charge a lower rate of commission than an estate agent (2.5–5%), but this commission is always paid by the purchaser. All agents' or notaires' fees are subject to VAT (*TVA*), currently at 19.6%.

Private sales

As in Britain, it is perfectly possible for buyer and seller to negotiate a sale between themselves, without the benefit of an estate agent. A notaire should, though, be brought into the deal as quickly as possible to draw up the contract and act as a stakeholder for the deposit, if needed. You should never hand over any cash directly to the vendor at all – as this can be viewed as attempted tax evasion (ie to disguise the 'official' price of the house), and is illegal. Similarly, it is not advisable to pay the vendor until all the relevant checks have been made: they may not be the owner!

The notaire

Notaires are public officials responsible for overseeing property transactions in France. There are about 7,500 notaires in France, working from around 5,000 chambers (known as *études*). A notaire's ultimate responsibility is to the French Ministry of Justice. He or she does not act for the buyer or the seller – although in rural areas a notaire often serves as an estate agent, too. Notaires do not 'take sides' for their clients, as do British solicitors. They are supposed to remain neutral.

Two notaires

Even though the buyer is responsible for paying the notaire's fees, the notaire is usually chosen by the vendor.

However, purchasers are entitled to bring a notaire of their choice into the process, and this happens in around half of all property sales. In such cases, the two lawyers generally share the work and the fees. Employing a second notaire may be advisable when the first is also acting as an estate agent for the vendor, or used to act as the vendor's notaire. Notaires are customarily addressed by the courtesy title *Maître*.

Contracts and searches

The notaire will not necessarily be responsible for drawing up the purchase

Buying a property: Contracts, searches and surveys

contract (the *compromis de vente*, of which more shortly) but will always draft the final deed of sale, or *acte de vente*. Once the former is signed and the deposit paid, the notaire undertakes the various searches usually carried out in Britain by solicitors after an offer has been accepted, and before exchange of contracts. These include checking the seller's title to the land at the local registry, finding out if there are any outstanding charges on the property, and looking for any planned developments that will directly affect the property. He is not responsible for checking anything that indirectly affects a property – the building of a motorway within earshot, for example. For this kind of knowledge, you could make enquiries at the mairie.

Surveys

A seller does not have a legal responsibility to point out any problems with the property being sold, as the property is sold 'as seen'. The principle of 'buyer beware' applies, and any structural defects that come to light after the contract is signed are the responsibility of the buyer. It therefore makes sense to check the condition of plumbing, heating, electrical and sewerage systems (where applicable) as well as getting a profes-

sional to evaluate the soundness of a building before signing a contract.

Structural surveys

Potential lenders do not always insist on a full structural survey of a property as they do in Britain, and a surveyor and valuer (*expert immobilier en bâtiment*) on the British model can be hard to find in France. Having said that, a growing number of good British surveyors, specialising in inspecting French property, are starting to establish themselves in France. Their French counterparts, *experts immobiliers*, tend to specialise in one type of property – commercial, housing, industrial or agricultural – so if you use a French surveyor, check you have the right kind of expert.

Surveys by builders

Often, surveys of buildings in rural areas are undertaken by a local builder (ideally one familiar with all the relevant trades who has worked as a site manager, or *maître d'oeuvre*) or an architect familiar with the building methods and materials used in the region. If they are quoting for any work that needs doing, try to get a binding written quote (*un dévis*). Solicitors specialising in French property law, or the local notaire or estate agent will usually be able to recommend someone to provide *une expertise* – a general summary of the state of the building based on a visual inspection – or *un bilan de santé*, a more expensive full structural survey. A surveyor's fees will depend on the scope of the work, the value of the property and the distance he has to travel.

The géomètre

The *géomètre* is a land sur-

veyor, whose speciality is in mapping property boundaries which might help settle disputes. You will need to employ a *géomètre* if you are buying a property that does not seem to conform to the boundaries recorded on the land registry map.

The cadastre

The *cadastre* is part of the French inland revenue, responsible for defining and recording the boundaries of the commune and all the individual properties it contains. Local offices keep detailed plans of all the plots, or *parcels* of land in the district, each with a unique reference number. If you plan to buy part of an existing parcel of land which would need to be divided – for example, a house plus a little piece of an adjoining field for a septic tank – you will have to employ a géomètre to find and fix the new boundaries for registration at the cadastre so that they can be included in the final deed of sale.

THE COMPROMIS DE VENTE

After you agree a price with a vendor, the next step is for an estate agent, a notaire or a solicitor to draw up a preliminary purchase contract. In effect, this puts into writing the fact that your offer has been accepted. One of the most important parts of this

Buying a property: Compromis de vente, conditions suspensives

will be the conditions of purchase and sale (the *conditions suspensives*, or get-out clauses, of which more below). It will also contain a description of the property with its *cadastre* reference (see above), the price and how it is to be paid, the amount of the deposit, the date of completion and the name of the notaire who will draw up the final deed of sale. The amount of commissions due to interested parties and the names of those responsible for paying them, the legal rights and obligations of both parties, and their personal particulars including date and place of birth and precise marital status will also be set out. This contract will form the basis of the final deed of sale. Make sure that any agreements you have made with the seller about fixtures and fittings, boundaries, vacant possession, and so on are spelled out in the contract. An inventory might also be useful.

Two-stage process

Contractually, buying a house is a two-stage process. First, you sign a preliminary contract, the *compromis de vente*, which is binding on both parties, and you pay a deposit. This is like exchanging contracts, but is subject to certain get-out clauses. It helps keep the two parties committed to the deal while the various legal and

administrative processes are completed, and during which time the buyer gets the funds together for the purchase proper. Then, the final contract – the *acte de vente* is signed.

At this point, the buyer gets the keys, the seller gets the money, the notaire and agents get their fees, and the state collects its various taxes.

Promesse d'achat and promesse de vente

While the most common form of preliminary purchase contract is the *compromis de vente*, there are two other forms: the *promesse d'achat*, binding only on the buyer, and the *promesse de vente*, binding only on the seller. These are far less commonly used than the *compromis*.

If the seller insists on a *promesse*, rather than a *compromis*, extra care should be taken in checking the

contract before signing. There are no statutory fixed penalties for breaking a contract: these are, therefore, set out in the body of the document itself.

Who will own the property?

Generally, before the contract is drawn up, the purchaser has to decide who will own the property and how, as this information is included in the contract. This decision is particularly important, both for tax reasons and because of the operation of French laws on inheritance (see below), which apply to all real estate in France, no matter where its owner is domiciled. The exception is if you buy the property through a company, and remain domiciled in the UK (again, more on this later). There are radically different consequences if you purchase in a single name, joint names or the name of a

company set up for the purpose. It makes sense to consult your legal adviser about this before you begin to look for properties in France, as making the wrong decision can be costly.

If all this is too much to take in and you can't decide under which name to purchase the property when you sign the contract, don't panic. You can include a 'substitution clause' which will allow you to substitute any person or company when you eventually complete the sale.

Married couples

You will need to provide the notaire with details of your 'civil status' (*état civil*), which should be included in the contract. This includes the occupation, nationality, birth dates, marital status and 'matrimonial regime' of each individual involved in the purchase. In French law, couples can adopt one of several régimes in their marriage contract, depending on whether they wish to hold property in common (*communauté de biens*), with all property bought after the marriage by either partner belonging to both, or separately (*séparation de biens*). If you have been married under UK law, without specifiying which *régime* applies, the notaire will usually state in the contract that you are married under the *séparation de biens* regime. Changing your actual marital

NOT SO COMPLEX

The French system is not so complicated if you compare what is happening with buying a house in, say, England.

In England, when the buyer's offer is accepted by the vendor, all the background conveyancing work starts (land registry search etc). No contract is signed, though, until the end of this period, when all the various queries have been answered, at which point contracts are exchanged and the sale completed.

In France, when the offer is accepted, contracts are exchanged right away (and a 10% deposit paid) but the contract (compromis de vente) includes various get-out clauses (the conditions suspensives). Just as in the UK, it takes a couple of months to do all the relevant conveyancing work, and if everything is OK, the sale is then completed: with the 'acte de vente'.

Buying a property: Signing the 'compromis'

regime and adopting one available under French law may have legal and tax advantages, if you feel up to doing all the paperwork!

Conditions suspensives

As the generalised notion of 'sale subject to contract' is unknown in France, property contracts contain *conditions suspensives*. Sometimes known as 'parachute clauses', these are agreed by both parties and set out the specific circumstances under which the contract can be broken without penalty. These could make the sale dependent on, for example, the property proving free of planning restrictions, easements (rights of way or access for adjoining properties), covenants, pre-emptive rights of purchase or claims from local or national government. If works such as the addition of a water supply or septic tank are needed to make the property habitable, the practicability and cost of such schemes should be the subject of a *condition suspensive*. In practice, anything agreed between the buyer and seller can be included. Nothing so vague as 'subject to satisfactory survey ' is acceptable, but if you are worried about a particular aspect of the building (say the condition of the roof timbers), a survey of this can be made the subject of a *condition suspensive* – if the vendor agrees. *Conditions suspensives* are also included to make the sale dependent on the property receiving a clean bill of health from lead, asbestos or termite infestation. These surveys, compulsory in some parts of France, are the seller's responsibility.

The gap of around two months between signing the *compromis de vente* and the final sale going through will provide time to check out the various questions raised in the *conditions suspensives*.

Subject to finance

If you are applying for a mortgage, a *condition suspensive* should make the contract subject to finance being granted. You will,

however, have to apply for a loan and fail to secure it within a specified period to have the benefit of this clause.

Compromis de vente: What are you signing?

Signing the contract binds both parties to the sale. On or before signing, the buyer lodges a deposit with the notaire or estate agent. No interest is payable on this amount, which the buyers will lose if they withdraw from the sale for any reason not covered by the *conditions suspensives* (see above) in the contract. If vendors cancel a sale without a valid reason they must return the purchaser's deposit, and might have to pay a similar amount on top of that in compensation (depending on the contract). Penalties for non-completion, and what triggers them, should always be spelled out in the contract. Signing such a contract without taking legal advice on its contents can prove costly.

Paying the deposit

The deposit, customarily 10% of the purchase price, is usually lodged through the notaire's or agent's account before the contract is signed. The simplest way to do this is by bank transfer to the relevant account. This can be a quicker process if you have set up a bank account in France in advance; if not, electronic payments to overseas accounts are also rapid, though they incur extra fees. You will be given a receipt for the deposit.

Setting a date for completion

The contract will usually include a suggested date for the formal signing of the deed of sale (*l'acte de vente*) usually 60 days in the future to give time for the necessary searches to be made. In practice the signing day is a moveable feast, subject to the vagaries of the bureaucratic system. You can, however, be confident that it will not be brought forward. There will not be interest penalties for delayed completion.

The cooling-off period

Buyers can withdraw from a contract without penalty (that is, without losing their deposit) within seven days of receiving notice that the contract has been signed by both parties. You should send any such cancellation by recorded delivery or appoint a bailiff to give notice to the vendor of your withdrawal.

BETWEEN COMPROMIS AND ACTE DE VENTE

Once the contract has been signed, the notaire has to undertake a series of legal checks. These take anything from five or six weeks to three months to complete.

The SAFER option

Depending on the surface area of your land, the notaire has a duty to inform the French Rural Development Agency, the *Fédération Nationale des Sociétés d'Aménagement Foncier et d'Etablissement Rural* (SAFER). This is a body controlled by an offshoot of the Ministry of Agriculture and set up to preserve farmers' interests. SAFER has the right to pre-empt any sale of land over a certain area, generally 2,500 sq m. Although this right is rarely exercised in the sale of relatively small domestic properties, it can take SAFER up to two months to come to

a decision, though you can pay a fee for a fast-track service. If SAFER does take up its option, you will lose your purchase, your deposit will be returned, and your contract cancelled.

Legal searches

The notaire must check with the *Bureau de Conservation des Hypothéques* (the equivalent of the Land Registry) that there are no restrictions on the vendor's title, nor any outstanding financial charges on the property. If you request it and have a project in mind, the notaire will apply for a *certificat d'urbanisme*, which outlines the planning status and potential of the property. This is a step up from the *note d'urbanisme* which you will get anyway, and which just indicates planning zones and rights of way.

Planning applications

When applying for a *certificat d'urbanisme*, it is worth giving the mairie an outline of any proposed development you have in mind for the property – such as conversion of outbuildings – and provide a draft plan. The vital information to give at this stage is the extra floor area to be created, as well as any change of use, such as from agricultural to residential.

Personal identification

The notaire has a duty to check all the personal details given in the contract, and will require proof of identity. The precise documentation requested may vary, but potential purchasers will generally have to provide copies of documents such as birth and marriage certificates, divorce decrees and passports. Those who have been widowed will need to show their spouse's death certificate. You will have to provide documentary proof – a utilities bill will usually do – of your residential address. If you have a marriage contract, the notaire may want to see this too. All these checks must be completed before the final deed of sale is signed.

Property insurance

You must arrange insurance cover on the property to take effect as soon as you sign the final contract. A minimum of third party civil liability insurance (*assurance à responsabilité civile*) and fire cover are required by law. It makes sense to take out a comprehensive householder's policy (*assurance multi-risques habitation*) to cover damage to or loss of property as well as risks to neighbours and third parties. It may be possible to take over the existing property insurance – in which case you must check precisely what is covered – or to arrange cover with an English firm specialising in insuring French property. Remember that premiums, particularly on a comprehensive policy, are likely to be higher if the property is used as a holiday home, or is otherwise left uninhabited for portions of the year.
(For more information on insurance, see pp196-197.)

'QUOTE UNQUOTE'

'The weird thing about French estate agents is that they often don't seem to have much in the way of property details to hand out. We asked about properties, and beyond being told how many rooms they had, and how many square metres of living space and outside grounds, that was more or less it. The next stage was a viewing. That was all good fun, but the agents don't always understand why you turn various places down. If they had more info to give you at the beginning, it could mean fewer wasted journeys for them, and for us!'
(Mike V, Tarn)

Buying a property: Final paperwork

COMPLETION: THE ACTE DE VENTE

When the searches are done, the notaire will invite all the interested parties to gather in the notaire's office for the signing of the *acte de vente* (deed of sale). This marks the transfer of title to the property. Be prepared for postponements, often at short notice. To provide for the possibility that you cannot be present, you can give someone on the scene the power of attorney to sign on your behalf.

Draft contract

The notaire will send you an account of all the money that will have to be paid on the day of completion – the balance of the purchase price, fees, taxes and commissions – along with a draft (*projét*) of the *acte de vente*. If the draft is not included with the accounts, request a copy to look through. The draft should be shown to your legal adviser and checked against the *compromis de vente*. Look out for any changes.
The amount of money requested by the notaire for taxes and fees is usually set a little high to cover possible unforeseen costs. The purchaser often receives a small rebate from the notaire afterwards – sometimes a while later – once the final calculations have been made.

Arranging for payment

The balance of the purchase price plus any legal fees and duties must be in the notaire's hands before the *acte* can be signed. Going to the signing with a banker's draft is probably the best and simplest method of doing this. Bank transfers and clearance of funds between British and French bank accounts can take a week or more. Opening a French account can help, and may be a requirement in some cases.

Power of attorney

The notaire will, on request, draw up a Power of Attorney (*procuration*) for you to sign, allowing a friend or relative resident in France (or, often, someone working in the notaire's office) to sign the *acte de vente* on your behalf. Even if you are planning to attend the signing in person, it may be worth setting up a power of attorney in case problems arise that prevent you travelling at the last moment, or delay the signing beyond your intended stay. It is not something that can be arranged on the spot in an emergency.

Final checks of the property

Before completion, you should check the property – preferably accompanied by an agent or legal adviser – to make sure it has not significantly deteriorated since the preliminary contract was signed, that the vendor has not removed anything that was included in the price, and that any special conditions in the contract have been met. If there is a problem, you must inform the notaire, who may keep back some of the purchase price to pay for repairs or replacements. If you are not satisfied with these arrangements, you should not sign the *acte de vente*, as it is virtually impossible to obtain any redress after signing.

Registration of the sale

Once the *acte de vente* has been signed, the notaire will keep it in his or her archive (for 100 years!) and will send you a certified copy, once it has been registered at the *Bureau de Conservation des Hypothèques*.
Sending you this official copy (*expédition*) can take anything up to six months after the signing of the deeds of sale. So if, in the meantime, you require proof of purchase – to take out property insurance, import furniture or have utilities connected, for example – the notaire will supply a certificate called an *une attestation d'acquisition* to serve this purpose.

Legal fees, duties and taxes

The buyer is responsible for paying the notaire's fees and all legal costs and expenses, including stamp duty, which usually adds around 6.5% to the price of the property. These fees must be included in the payment made to the notaire when the *acte de vente* is signed. If the notaire has arranged a mortgage for the property, you will have to pay an additional fee for this.

The notaire's fees

Notaires are paid on the basis

of a fixed fee plus a sliding scale from 0.825% to 5% of the value of the transaction. In practice, most deals are charged at the lower rate. Notaires will charge extra for advice or any additional work requested, such as arranging a mortgage. All the fees are subject to Value Added Tax (*TVA*), currently at 19.6%.

Duties
Stamp duty currently stands at 4.89% of the cost of the property. Three quarters of this goes to the département and the rest to the commune. There is also a registration fee of 0.75% of the purchase price payable to the *Bureau de Conservation des Hypothéques*.

INHERITANCE LAWS

In France, the laws of inheritance are very different to those in England. Fixed percentages of the estate are mandated by law for the deceased's surviving children and other descendants or parents and grandparents. A will can affect only what is left after the heir(s) have taken what is due to them under French law.

Main residence in France
If you move your main residence to France, all your assets, anywhere in the world, will be subject to French inheritance rights and death duties (see below). The excep-

tion is properties in the UK (and some other countries) which would remain subject to UK law. Even if your main residence is outside France, any *immeubles* – unmoveable property, or land and buildings – that you own in France will still be subject to French inheritance law. There are ways to circumvent the unwelcome effects of these laws, but if you plan to implement them, they should be included in the original contract. If you try to amend the title later, it could be expensive and may not succeed.

Leaving it to the children
What happens to your property when you die is laid down by law. You can't get round it, even if you make a will! So if a deceased had one child, that child receives half the estate by statutory inheritance right. Two children take one-third of the estate

each, while three or more take equal shares of 75% of it. If there are no living children, the deceased's parents have a mandated share. If children die before a parent, their share of the legacy is split between their own children. If there are no living descendants, then parents and grandparents inherit the shares. The deceased's spouse has mandated rights only in remote circumstances, where there are no children or no parents still alive.

If there is no will
If the owner of a French property dies without making a will (*intestate*), his property in France will be divided among his heirs in a different way to Britain, where a surviving spouse will inherit the bulk of an estate. In France, the spouse of anyone who dies intestate (if there are children from the marriage) gets two options. They can have a 'life interest' in the whole estate (they can use it, or take rental income from it, but can't own it). Or they can own a quarter of the value of the estate. The children and parents (if still alive) of the deceased take the greater share.

Family complications
The inheritance rules will not suit everyone, particularly those in a second marriage, with children from a previous relationship. Even if a couple

have bought a house together, when one of them dies a portion of the house will be shared between his or her children, and the surviving partner will be left sharing a house with strangers.
In English law, children under 18 cannot own property. Inherited property is usually held in trust for them. But French law does not provide for trusts. So under-18s who inherit property assume full rights directly. This can cause problems when attempting to sell a property. For example, French law will recognise a child or teenager living in England as part-owner of a property, whose permission is needed to sell – but no-one in England is authorised to give that permission on his or her behalf except the Family Division of the UK High Court.

Joint ownership
There are usually three ways in which individuals can jointly own a French property; either *en indivision*, *en tontine*, or as part of a marriage contract.
a) Separate ownership
Owning a property *en indivision* means you have shares in the whole property according to your financial contribution. This means any of the owners may be able to force the sale of the property, or sell their share of it, although co-owners usually have a pre-emptive right to

Buying a property: Fees, taxes, and CGT

buy out a partner willing to sell. When one of the co-owners dies, their share is portioned among their own relatives according to French inheritance law.

b) En tontine

The insertion of a *clause tontine* in the original contract means that when one owner dies, their share of the property goes to the other (assuming there are only two owners). Only when the second owner dies do the usual inheritance laws apply. However, while both joint owners are alive, one of the two cannot force the other to sell (in the event of a divorce, for example.)

c) Marriage contract

By signing a nuptial agreement and setting up a community fund (*communauté universelle avec clause d'attribution au survivant*) the spouses would purchase in joint tenancy. On the first death, the fund in which the property (or other assets) is included will pass to the survivor, free of French inheritance tax. It also overrides the effect of French statutory inheritance tax, until the second spouse dies.

SCIs

By purchasing and holding property through a civil property company (*société civile immobilière*) set up for the purpose, non-resident owners of French property can override the French inheri-

tance laws, as shares in a property company are a moveable asset and so fall outside the scope of French law. Note, however, that although the non-resident owner of shares in an SCI can leave them to whomever he or she likes, the one who inherits must pay French death duties which, in the case of a legacy to an unrelated individual, could be as much as 60%. The other drawback to setting up an SCI is that it has tax implications in the UK and in France. Seek advice from legal and financial experts in this field. An SCI, as a civil company, should not trade except within specific limits or it will attract corporation tax, so this option is generally not available to those who wish to use their French property commercially.

Usufruct

Another possibility is to give the property to those children or others to whom you wish to bequeath it while you are still alive, while retaining, with your partner, a usufruct (*usufruit*), or life interest in it. When both of you are dead full property rights will revert to the owners.

This can save large amounts of French inheritance tax if you get the paperwork right, as well as getting around the inheritance laws, but does have disadvantages, largely that you are no longer the

owner of the house, and are not free to sell without the permission of your 'heirs'.

French tax law as a whole is a complex subject outside the scope of this guide. Here we will just look at those taxes relating to the purchase, ownership and sale of land and buildings. The rates quoted here were correct at the time of publication.

Sales Tax and Stamp Duty

French VAT (*TVA*) currently stands at 19.6% and is chargeable on all fees and commissions, but not on the property itself if it is more than five years old. Stamp duty (*droits d'enregistrement*) on any property over five years old is 4.89% of the purchase price, and is payable when the *acte de vente* is signed.

Inheritance Tax

French death duties (*droits de succession*) apply to the whole worldwide estate of anyone who is domiciled in France. Property in France owned by a non-resident is also subject to *droits de succession*. The taxes fall due to the beneficiaries of the estate, wherever they live, rather than to the estate as a whole, as in Britain. Beneficiaries unrelated to the deceased by blood or marriage might pay 60% on the

whole amount of their legacy. Others can inherit a certain sum, based on the degree of their relationship to the deceased, tax-free. The surplus is then taxed on a sliding scale from 5% to 40%.

Local taxes

There are two local taxes on property, both paid annually and falling due at the beginning of January. You will be registered to pay these at the local branch of the inland revenue (*la recette des impots*) soon after you take over title to the property.

Taxe foncière: This is a land tax payable by the owner of the land on 1 January. When you buy a property, you will usually have to pay the seller pro rata for the remainder of the year; this is generally covered in the contract.

Taxe d'habitation: The equivalent to British council tax, this is charged to the person occupying the house on 1 January. You will not have to pay anything until the 1 January after you move in. Note that you do not have to be physically present to be considered to be 'occupying' the house, though a completely empty property might be exempt.

Taxes assimilés: Some parts of France levy special taxes to deal with local problems such as clearing snow in upland areas. The buyer and seller should agree who pays what share of this tax.

So you have finally signed the Acte de Vente, and the house is yours! Congratulations! But what happens next? Here, we run through some of the basic utilities: water, electricity and gas supply. How to get connected, and what you may have to do next.

WATER SUPPLY

Pay as you go
Water supplies in France are metered. Tap water quality is usually fine, although many French people prefer to drink bottled water (which is cheaper than in the UK).

Getting connected
If you plan to buy a property with no mains water, and the nearest water main is more than 10m from your own land, then you will need to find out from the mairie if the local commune will agree for mains water to be brought to your property. If the only route is to lay a pipe through someone else's land, this will create major administrative, legal and financial headaches, and you will not be guaranteed to win your case to get a supply.
In some extreme cases, people have had to buy a strip of land from a neighbour, through which the pipe is laid (which could be at your expense as it is on your own land). The cost of all this can run into thousands of euros. The water company's fee for installing a pipe will only cover the supply of water to your domestic water meter (and you may also have to pay for the trench to be dug). Running pipes from the meter (at the edge of your property) to the house, and any domestic plumbing, will not usually be the responsibility of the water company. Water pipes located outside will need to be at least 80cm deep, to avoid frost.

Water meters
The water supply is metered, so you pay for what you use. Meters are typically fixed just inside the boundary of your property, as near to the mains as possible. There is a small charge for fitting a new meter.

Billing
There are wide local variations in the cost of water, but it is never cheap: an average would be around €2 per cubic metre (1,000 litres) with prices lower in small villages, higher in big cities. It is always difficult to estimate water usage costs, but as a rough guide, a typical family of four people would probably use around 120–150 cubic metres per year. Water bills are issued once or twice a year. Consumers usually contract to use a certain amount of water, paying extra if this amount is exceeded. Charges are significantly lower if your property has a septic tank rather than mains drainage.

Hot water
Hot water is heated and stored at the same pressure as the cold water entering your domestic plumbing system – in other words, at mains pressure, or slightly below if your cold water supply is fitted with a pressure reduction valve. Always use taps designed for this higher pressure (which could be up to 4 bar) and make sure also that pipes are well secured to cope with the higher pressures.
(See plumbing, p183.)

Natural water
Rural properties may have a well (*un puits*) or access to a spring (*une source*). Wells and springs can of course dry up and fail, particularly in dry summers in the south, but the water quality can be very good and it is free – although you may have to pay for a pump to raise the well-water. Before you start using water from springs, streams or wells on your property. it must be analysed for purity by the local water authority or the *Département de l'Action Sanitaire et Sociale*. It should be checked periodically after this. One way to purify water is to use an ultraviolet water steriliser.
If your property is wholly dependent on wells or springs for its water supply, be absolutely sure before buying that you own the water source and have the right to use it, so that it cannot legally be diverted or intercepted by anyone else. Equally, you should check the condition of this water supply during the summer months. If the well is deeper than 7m, your water company may have the right to restrict its use.

Electricity: Connections, tariffs

Saving water

Where water supplies may be interrupted, you can get a storage tank installed for emergencies. Butts can store water for the garden, and it makes sense to recycle bath water on the garden too. Dual function cisterns, with long or short flush, help save water, while showers are far more economical than baths.

ELECTRICITY SUPPLY

Mains electricity in France is supplied by *Electricité de France* (EDF), a state-owned company. Three-quarters of French electricity comes from nuclear power stations, the rest from hydro-electric schemes.

Taking over

If your house already has an electricity supply, it is your responsibility to request a meter reading (*relève spécial*) from your local EDF service centre before you take over. You will need to pay a small connection (*mise en service*) fee. Check the meter to see the power setting. If the supply is insufficient or too high for your purposes (see below), you will need to contact EDF to have it altered, which is free of charge. If you have an internet connection, then the EDF website (see the link on p220) has information on what you need to do,

with a few useful pages in English, too.

Getting connected

If there is no mains electricity nearby, you will have to seek permission from the mairie to get a connection if you are some distance from the nearest power lines and the connection will mean putting a trench across someone else's land. However, if your house is within 30m of the nearest EDF pole, you will not have to get the approval of the mairie. EDF will connect you – for a fee.

Anyone planning to buy a property in rural France with the idea of bringing in mains electricity should get an estimate of the cost from EDF before completing a purchase, as it can run to several thousand euros (see box, left). Electric cables now tend to be laid underground, replacing the much cheaper, but unsightly networks of overhead wires previously used in rural areas.

When applying for an electricity supply you will need to

specify the level of supply and tariff you require (see below), and produce proof of ownership of the property, known as an *attestation* (see p174 'Registering the sale').

Power supply

Domestic power is supplied in multiples of 3kW to a maximum of 36kW (note that in France kW are often referred to as kVA). The higher the rating you choose, the higher will be the standing charge. To discover the optimum power supply for your household, add the consumption of all the appliances you have or wish to install that you are likely to run simultaneously, and then round up.

The 9kW rating is usually just about enough for a three-bedroom house, though 18kw is needed if you have electric water heating.If you attempt to draw electricity above your supply rating, the trip switch (*le disjoncteur*) on your meter will automatically turn the power off.

Tariffs

Electricity consumers can choose one of three tariffs:

Basic rate (l'Option Base):

A simple base rate charged at all times. The standing charge is lower than the other options, though this tariff is only available for installations up to 18kW.

Off peak
(l'Option Heures Creuses):

This option will give you eight hours (usually 10pm to 6am) of off-peak power per day at a lower rate, and basic rate tariffs at other times, and is available for supplies of up to 36kW. The standing charge is slightly higher than that of the basic rate option. It is recommended if you have electric central heating and water heating, and a programmable washing machine (that can operate during the night).

Tempo (l'Option Tempo):

Available only for power supplies of 9kW and higher, and with a standing charge somewhere between those of the basic and off-peak options, Tempo is designed to dampen demand during very cold weather. The year is divided into 300 blue days, (when the tariff is cheapest), 43 white and 22 red (when the tariff is most expensive). The days are selected by EDF

CONNECTION CHARGE

An example
A property owner in the Manche département wanted to get electricity connected for a barn conversion in early 2004. She was quoted €1,100 plus TVA (French VAT at 19.6%) to get a supply put in. The nearest electricity pole was 25 metres away, and the client had to dig the trench and lay the conduit for the cable.

according to temperature, with prices higher during colder weather.

Billing

Bills are usually sent every two months. A standing charge (*l'abonnement*), based on the level of power supply, and national and local taxes, is included in the bill. Accounts can be settled by cheque, direct debit (*virement automatique*) or standing order (*prélèvement automatique*), so you will need a French bank account. In the case of a standing order, use is estimated for the year and a monthly payment set. At the end of the year the actual use is calculated and the user gets a bill or rebate accordingly.

Generators

A diesel or petrol generator (*une groupe électrique*) provides a ready alternative if mains electricity is not

available. A 5kW generator will provide enough juice for light and hot water in a two-bedroom house. Diesel generators are considerably more expensive to buy than those run by petrol, but are easier and cheaper to maintain and run. As well as being not too close to your house (because of noise) generators should be housed in secure premises, particularly if you are not living in the house all year-round, as there is a market for stolen ones.

Wiring

Most French homes will have power supplied by two cables at 220–240V. The cables are known as *phase* (live) and *neutre* (neutral). Wiring colours follow EU standards: yellow and green for earth, blue for neutral, and red, black, brown or white for live.

Current French standards for domestic wiring are very

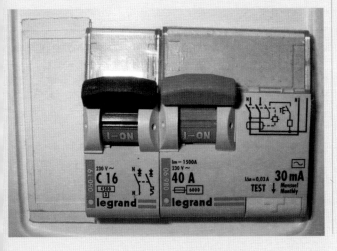

strict and provide an extremely safe system. Protection is provided by overload trip switches, and by what are known in English as residual current devices, or RCDs, and in French as *disjoncteurs differentiels*, or *un dispositif differentiel à courant residuel*).

These protect against the risk of electrocution by detecting sudden changes in the current between the live and neutral, indicating a short circuit, or a current leak to earth. This can be caused by deteriorating insulation, a faulty appliance, or an electric lawn mower cutting through its own cable, for example.

However, many rural properties in France fall well short of such modern standards, simply because of the age of their electrical installations.

There are a number of tell-tale signs to look out for which will give you an instant indication of the state of the electrical system that comes with your house.

The current safety norms in France were introduced in 1974 (though are regularly updated), so installations carried out before the 1970s and left unchanged since then will almost certainly not be up to the standard. Rubber rather than plastic-coated flex is a dead giveaway that the wiring is at least 30 years old, as is a

circuit board with porcelain insulators. If this is the case, you should get an electrician to review the system and install a modern 'consumer board' with circuit breakers to protect against power overload, and RCDs, which also protect against electrocution.

Getting your wiring checked

If you are unsure whether your system conforms or not, you can get an expert from the non-profit organisation Promotélec to inspect it. They offer a service called *Diagnostique Confiance Sécurité*, which will give you a 53-point check and a written report on what might need to be improved. The price of the survey depends on the size of your house. Rewiring a three-bedroom house could cost around €3,000–€5,000, and should be carried out by a qualified electrician: French safety regulations and protocols are different from those in many other countries.

New connections

In the case of a new EDF connection (where there was no electricity supply before) the new wiring must be certified by the electrical quality standards organisation *Consuel* before EDF will start supplies. So if your electrician gets it wrong,

Electricity: Installations and the French norm

you will have make changes to your system, which could get expensive as you will have to pay to get a Consuel official to return to check the new work you have had done. Once satisfied, Consuel will issue a document called *un attestation de conformité* (a certificate of compliance).

Existing connections
If you are renovating a house that has older wiring, and you take over an existing electricity supply, you will not need to get it checked by Consuel. Even if you get an electrician to run new circuits to, say, a loft conversion or a new bathroom, you will not need to get any outside organisation to check the job. However, an electrician will certainly want to protect you from any problems that may arise from the condition of the older wiring in your home: so the older circuits, as well as the new ones, will be protected with a new RCD.

ELECTRICAL INSTALLATIONS

Use a qualified electrician
We strongly recommend that all electrical installations are carried out by a qualified electrician. What follows is a selection of points which are covered by the current French safety norm. It should help you to understand the

kind of system that your electrician will propose for you, as well as give you an idea of how far your existing system meets, or fails to meet, the recommended quality standards.

Getting your electrical system to comply with the law
The French norm, known as NF C 15-100, is the gold standard in terms of safety and technical requirements for domestic electrical installations. Despite the lightweight appearance of French plugs and sockets compared with those in some other countries, the French system is in fact extremely safe and logically thought out.

Trip switches and circuits
The French system is very different to the 'ring main' set-up of the UK. In France, a radial system is used, with a number of separate circuits

looping out to serve different parts of the house, each with up to eight electrical outlets, and each circuit is protected by a fuse or miniature circuit breaker.
There are three types: the main trip switch is on the EDF installation, and will cut out if you attempt to draw more current than you have allowed for in your contract, or if there is a short circuit. Then there is the standard circuit-breaker or trip switch on each circuit, (sometimes called an MCB, or miniature circuit breaker) which will shut off power in the event of a short circuit or if you attempt to plug in too many appliances on that circuit. And for added security there is the residual current device which protects against electrocution.
The norm stipulates how many of these devices must be used to protect circuits, with larger properties needing

more safety devices.
The consumer board must be between 1 m to 1.8 m from the ground. It should not be placed in a cupboard, near water supplies (depending on its IP rating) or close to heating appliances.

Check out Promotélec
For a complete guide to the rules governing domestic electrical installations, you can contact Promotélec, the quality standards organisation. English versions of this are hard to come by, so what follows is a brief run-down of some of the main points of the norm. Don't forget, meeting these conditions is an obligation for a new house or for a new connection to the electricity supply, as opposed to just taking over someone else's connection. If you are renovating, you are not legally bound to follow this norm, but it is worth comparing what you have with what is seen as an ideal system.

A GUIDE TO THE FRENCH NORM NF C 15-100

1) Circuits
The main consumer board will have a number of circuits running to various parts of the house, each protected by their own circuit breakers and RCDs. The thickness of the wiring and the capacity of the circuit breakers depend on what a circuit is used for. And there are maximum numbers

of electrical outlets that can be connected to each circuit. This is how it works:

1) 16A wall sockets (typical wall sockets)
a) If wiring is 2.5 mm²:
This will need a circuit breaker of 16/20A, allowing up to eight power outlets per circuit. (A double socket counts as two power outlets) There is also a minimum number of sockets per room: three per bedroom; at least five in the living room; six in the kitchen, of which four are at worktop height, but not over the cooking elements or the sink; and one socket per 4 sq m of floorspace, except in WCs.

2) Sockets operated by a wall switch (for lamps, say)
Wiring should be at least 2.5 mm², protected by a 10A circuit breaker or fuse. One wall switch can operate up to two sockets. Remote switching devices can operate more than two sockets.

3) Special purpose sockets (for large kitchen appliances)
Wiring should be 2.5 mm², protected by a 20A circuit breaker. In a property of more than 35 sq m, at least three circuits are recommended, for washing machine, dishwasher, tumble dryer and the like.

4) Electric hobs or stand-alone cooker
Wiring should be at least 2.5 mm² (depending on the kW rating of the appliance)

for tri-phase, with 20A circuit breaker or fuse.
Wiring of 6 mm² is required for a mono-phase supply, with a 32A circuit breaker or fuse.

5) Lighting
Wiring should be at least 2.5 mm², with a 10A circuit breaker or a 10A fuse. A maximum of eight lighting points per circuit, and at least two circuits should be provided in a property of more than 35 sq m. Each room must have a lighting point. A special, separate circuit is required for exterior lighting. It is recommended that wiring that serves lighting appliances should be terminated in a box set into the wall, into which the connection with the light fitting is then made.

6) Water heater
Wiring should be 2.5 mm², protected by a 20A circuit breaker.

2) Embedded conduits
In general, a duct or a conduit must cover all wires. Ducts and cables can be put in the spaces between partitions or wall linings and so on, if they are sufficiently insulated and cannot be damaged. However, take care over how they are routed. You cannot run embedded cable across the diagonal of a wall. Cables running vertically in a wall (rising up to wall lights, for example) must be at least 1.5 m apart and at least 20 cm from any corner. Cables running horizontally on a wall (to a light switch, for example) can be no further than 50 cm from a corner. Electrical equipment such as switches and sockets must be mounted in boxes.

3) Wall sockets
Wall sockets must all be earthed, and should be covered with a blanking plate or cap (security for children). Each wall socket circuit must have its own circuit breaker (16A, 20A or 32A depending on its use). Indoors, a 16A socket is mounted 5cm from ground level, and a 32A socket at least 12 cm from the ground. Outside, sockets must be at least 1 m from the ground and meet the IP55 protection rating.

4) Multiple circuits in ducts
A circuit is a set of wires supplied by the same source

and protected by the same security device (circuit-breaker or fuse). You can insert several circuits in one duct, but only if:
a) All wires are insulated.
b) All circuits are connected to the same RCD.
c) The conduit is not overloaded with cables. (There is a formula to work out whether the conduit is the right size for the cables running through it. Larger cables tend to have their own conduit.)
d) Each circuit must be protected by an overload circuit-breaker.

5) Connection boxes
All connections must be made in special boxes (*boîtes de dérivation*) and be permanently accessible for maintenance and inspection. British cabling, sockets and some switches do not conform to French regulations, and may render your house insurance void in the event of a catastrophe. If you try using UK equipment in a new rewiring job, Consuel will not approve the connection.

6) Lightning protection
Installing a lightning-protector is compulsory in areas prone to thunder – indicated by a measure known as the *niveau kéronique*. A lightning-protector must be installed directly after the EDF circuit-breaker and

FIRST TIME CONNECTION

Temporary supply
If there is no mains electricity, EDF will provide a temporary supply at 3kW, but only via a temporary meter box, which can be supplied by an electrician, and is attached to the nearest EDF pole. Some temporary circuits can run from this box for power tools on site. EDF will not connect a proper supply until a certificate of compliance is issued by Consuel.

Gas: Supply, billing and installations

must be connected to the earth terminal of the installation, which should have a connection resistance of no more than 30 ohms. Check with your local mairie to find out if your house is in a département where this is required. It is also a good idea to protect all sensitive appliances (computers, video-recorder etc) with a 10A or 16A socket with integrated surge protection.

6) Earthing connections

The earth takes all the earth connections of the various appliances to a single point (known in French as *la borne de terre*) which is a kind of metal spike or plate embedded in the earth outside your property. The connection to the earth point should be made of copper or galvanised steel, up to 25 mm² if the connection is exposed to corrosion, and 16 mm² if not. The earth connection will need a test point where an electrician can measure the resistance – which should be no more than 100 ohms.

As in the UK, the earth lead insulation is green and yellow. It should be protected from any potential damage, and ideally inserted in the same conduits as the live and neutral wires that it protects. The cross-section of the earth lead should be at least equal to that of the live wire it is protecting.

It is strictly forbidden to use metal conduits such as water or gas pipes as earthing systems. Note that every metal element of your house which could carry current (such as water pipes, steel beams etc) must be connected to the earth at all times (this earthing bond is known in French as the *liaison equipotentielle principale*).

7) The neutral conductor

The neutral wire must be at least as big in cross-section as the corresponding live wire.

Warning: Even when the live wire is not supplying electricity for an appliance (because a light switch is turned off, for example), the neutral wire can still carry current. The only way to cut the power is to turn off the circuit breaker for the lighting circuit (or whatever you are working on). If you are not sure which circuit to turn off, switch off all the power by the mains switch.

8) Bathrooms

The norm contains very specific rules about electrical installations in the bathroom. It divides the room in four zones, or 'Volumes' with separate rules for each:

Volume 0 (Inside bathtubs or shower cubicles):
Specialist low voltage lighting only in this area.

Volume 1 (Up to 2.25 m above the base of the bath or shower tray):
Only low voltage lighting, provided the transformer is outside Volume 2.

Volume 2 (Within 60 cm of the edge of the bath or shower tray):
An electric water heater can be installed, protected by an RCD, and 'Class II' light fittings (suitable for bathroom use).

Volume 3 (Anywhere else)
Beyond this 60 cm zone, you can install normal light fittings, and 230V power sockets protected by an RCD of 30 mA maximum.

Mains gas is rarely available in France outside town boundaries. It is supplied by *Gaz de France* (GDF), part of the same organisation as EDF. Outside urban centres, bottled gas – butane and propane – is widely used for heating and, especially, cooking.

Getting connected

If your property is already connected to mains gas, it is your responsibility to advise GDF and have the meter read and the account transferred into your name. GDF charges a small start-up fee (*la mise en service*). If there is mains gas in the area, GDF will connect you at a fee that varies according to the distance and tariff; those choosing the B1 tariff pay roughly half of those on the base or B0 tariffs (see below) for connection.

Billing and tariffs

Bills are issued every two months, although meters are read just two or three times a year. Tariffs depend on the amount of gas you expect to use. Base rate (*le tarif Base*) is for those using using less than 1,000kWh per year (roughly corresponding to cooking only). Next up is B0 for 1,000–6,000kWh per year (gas used for cooking and hot water) and B1 for a consumption of 6,000-30,000kWh (to use this amount of gas, you would need to have gas central heating).

Bottled gas
Bottled gas, propane or butane, is widely used in rural France, particularly for cooking, but also for water heating. Competing firms supply gas in 35kg and 13kg bottles – which are standard but for their colours – which are sold in most filling stations and large stores, as well as village shops. Bottles of butane can be stored outside if protected from frost, but propane can withstand much lower temperatures and is generally stored outside without problem.
The typical arrangement is to have two bottles, with a tap that shifts supply seamlessly from one bottle to the other when one empties. The feed to the house should be a copper pipe.

Gas central heating
Where there is no mains gas, gas central heating systems can still be installed and fuelled from a storage tank (*une citerne*) on your property. This can be hired by the year, or comes free from a supplier – provided you contract to use them exclusively for a specified time.

Gas installations
These should be carried out by a qualified gas fitter, and we do not recommend any DIY activity in this area.

Qualigaz, which is the gas equivalent of the Consuel, will check new installations before the connection is approved.

Main features
In general terms, you will need a metal gas pipe running from the gas main (or your gas bottle) to the central heating or hot water boiler, and to a shut-off valve for each gas appliance.

Vissogaz fittings versus rubber hose
From the shut-off tap to the appliance, the recommended system is a '*Vissogaz*' flexible tube which screws onto the supply pipe at one end and the appliance at the other. Vissogaz fittings are also fitted with an automatic shut-off should the pipe ever become severed.
All gas appliances sold in France since the mid-1970s have a fitting which will accept the Vissogaz tube, though the tube itself may have a limited life – five or ten years, depending on the type. The year of replacement should be printed on the pipe.
If you stick with an existing old installation, you can continue to use a rubber hose, but check its condition carefully (see box, p184). However, if you renew your appliance, you should install a new Vissogaz connection. It is much safer.

Plumbing & heating: Water pressure

Water pressure is generally good across France – and with domestic hot water at mains pressure, or close to it, getting a good hot shower without the use of electric pumps is usually simple. Here's a short guide to how it all fits together.

WATER PRESSURE

Water pressure is generally pretty good across France – and in domestic installations, British holidaymakers are often surprised at the high pressure hot water that is available – without any kind of electric pump or power shower installations. This is simply because domestic hot water is heated up and stored at mains pressure (or slightly below it) all the time – with mains pressure often guaranteed by keeping the water in those slightly sci-fi-looking concrete water towers that loom over the French countryside.
Contrast this with the UK, where cold water is provided by a feed and expansion cistern, usually at the highest point possible in the building, and is heated in the hot water cylinder. If the cistern is not particularly high, the pressure, provided by gravity alone, is also not very high. Generally in France, domestic plumbing installations keep the water pressure no higher than 3 bar (which is

plenty). Any higher than this, and you will find taps wearing out quickly, frequent leaks between various joints, and the chance of vibrating pipes all round the house if a tap (or even a washing machine valve) is shut off too quickly.
To avoid the risk of this, it is worth making sure pipework is not fixed solidly into masonry. Most plumbers use pipe clips on a slightly flexible mount. What's more common, though, is to install a pressure reduction valve (*détendeur*) just after the water meter, which keeps the water pressure within a set limit.
Obviously, lack of water pressure will cause trouble. In France, low water pressure problems are often caused by pipes that are too skinny (or which are too scaled up) to bring enough water to the taps.

Water pipe dimensions
The underground pipe that brings water to your meter will probably be around 25 mm in diameter. Within your

Plumbing & heating: Pipes, pressure and flow

house, though, the main water pipe that serves the various rooms should be 16/18 mm (this notation simply means 16 mm internal diameter, 18 mm external), though is slightly larger for longer runs. The dimension of pipes running off this will depend on the rate of flow that you need for various purposes. These are the recommended dimensions:
Bath and water heater: 14/16 mm
Shower, kitchen sink, dishwasher, washing machine: 12/14 mm (though powerful showers could need a wider pipe)
Washbasins, WC, garden hosepipe: 10/12 mm
Washing machines are often fed by their own pipes that run all the way back to the cold or hot water source, to avoid scalding in the shower when the machine comes on.
Waste pipes: The WC and the general drain taking waste from the house will be 100 mm in diameter. The bath, shower, kitchen sink, washing machine and dishwasher will need a waste pipe of 40-50 mm in diameter, depending on the distance from the main drain and the fall (the slope) of the waste pipe. A wash basin will get away with a 32 mm waste pipe, generally available in PVC. But watch out for the noise of gushing water as they drain out: it is best to insulate and hide

them behind plasterboard if you can.
The pipe fall should be around 2 cm per metre, and slightly steeper for a shower. However, if the the fall is too steep, not only will this be noisy, it could also lead to the water rushing down so fast it leaves the waste material behind and sucks water out of the syphon (the U-bend under a wash basin for example). This will mean odours from the drains can waft back into your bathroom.

Pipe materials

For hot or cold water supply, you have a choice between copper pipes or PVC. Copper is better looking (it is thinner in diameter than its PVC counterparts, especially when it comes to the joints, which in PVC can be very bulky) but is less easy for the DIY-er as joints need to be soldered.

There are two types: rigid copper pipe (*cuivre écroui*) or the more supple annealed copper pipe (*cuivre récuit*) which can be bent without heat. Both are available in lengths of up to 5 m.
Rigid pipe is harder than in the UK, and should be annealed before bending. There are two ways of soldering the pipes. Soft-soldering with tin solder is fairly simple, but less long-lasting than brazing, or hard-soldering, which requires intense heat from an oxyacetylene flame. Non-soldered joints are also possible, using various types of compression fittings.
PVC pipe systems can be cemented together with glue, so are popular for DIY plumbing installations. However, this requires careful planning, as once the glue has set it will be hard to rethink the layout without cutting it all up and starting again. Note that

solvent weld pipe diameters are not compatible with push fittings.

Basics on showers
A high-performance shower with multiple jets could use 30 litres of water per minute, and will need 16/18 mm pipework for hot and cold water supplies. A factory-made cubicle housing a single shower is unlikely to use much beyond 20 litres of water per minute. For either of these, you will need to keep the hot water in a tank (*un ballon de stockage*), which is maintained at the domestic water pressure (2-3 bar). An 'instant' heater that heats the water as it is drawn through may not be able to keep up with the volume of water the shower uses.
The drain pipe diameter needs to be around 40 mm, with a wider pipe being used if the shower is more than a metre away from the main drain. The minimum fall of the waste pipe should be 2 cm per metre. If this is hard to achieve, you should opt for a raised shower tray (*un receveur de douche surélevé*).

A WC with a pump
If you want to install a new WC in a position too far from the main waste pipe, or you want your new WC to operate below the level of the outside drainage (for example in a basement or cellar) the

solution is a WC which pulverises and pumps out the waste – known as a WC *à broyeur*. These can generally pump waste vertically 3–4 m, and horizontally up to 50m! The waste pipe needs to be around 40mm in diameter (compared with the usual 100mm for a WC) and there are two types of system: a pump which is stand-alone, and deals with all the waste-water from the bathroom, or a pump integrated into the WC only.

WATER HEATING

Oil-fired heating
Oil fired heating accounts for the majority of sales in France, with the oil (*le fioul*) contained in a tank outside the house. The central heating unit will be either wall or floor mounted, and versions are available using condensing technology for energy savings of up to 20% over a standard boiler design.
Generally, oil-fired boilers can be pretty big, and will need plenty of space for installation. But since a bigger boiler heats up and cools down more slowly, it is usually seen as more suitable for large stone houses when combined with cast iron radiators or underfloor heating.

Electric water heating
For a second home where central heating is not installed, an electric immersion water heater is a simple and practical solution, with no worries about a flue or duct to take away fumes (as is needed for gas heating). Tanks are available in a range of sizes from about 50 litres right up to 300 litres, with the larger tanks capable of being fitted horizontally or vertically. If a powerful shower will draw 20 litres per minute, mixed 50-50 with cold water, you can get an idea of how many five-minute showers you will get out of one tank-full of hot water. Most tanks contain a device to prevent rust – either a piece of magnesium (which can be used up after about five years) or an electronic anode, which lasts the life of the heater.

Gas water heating
There are two main options here. One is the gas-fired

heater specifically for water supply – the *chauffe-bain* or *chauffe-eau* – while the other is the gas-fired central heating boiler that supplies heating and hot water for the whole house. Whichever option you choose, you will need to have the equipment serviced annually, as a condition of your household insurance.

The water heater
The *chauffe-eau* will generally be available with a tank of 75 to 200 litres capacity, and is similar to the electric immersion heater, except that the heating system is fuelled by gas. If you run one of these from propane, it will cost you roughly the same as an electric immersion heater operating at the cheaper night-time tariff. If you run your heater with natural gas from the gas main it will be cheaper than an electric one.

The on-demand water heater
Known as a *chauffe-bain*, this is the kind of instant heater that comes on when you turn on the hot water tap, and goes off immediately afterwards, heating the water as it is drawn through the tap. Check the flow rate, as this will be crucial. Five litres per minute will be OK for a sink or a fairly weak shower. 10 litres per minute will supply a shower, sink and wash-basin, while beyond this, 13 to 16 litres will fill a bath in a reasonable time, given enough heating power.

Heat pumps
Still in its infancy for domestic applications, heat pump technology is becoming more popular for its environmental credentials. Typically, a heat pump can extract 4kw of heat from the air for every 1kw of electricity used. Fluid-based systems are even better, as the heat is pumped from a grid buried in the ground to a heat exchanger inside, and the warmer water thus produced feeds the conventional system. The installation costs are high, but the savings in running costs make it an appealing choice.

Solar panels
Grants are available for fitting solar panels, which can can provide all the hot water for a typical household during the summer months, and a useful contribution the rest of the year. The wet systems use a non-freezing mix in the panels, and a heat exchanger inside the house.

Central heating boilers
While most people would like a quick formula to work out how big a central heating boiler (*une chaudière*) they need, this can only be done from a consideration of the size of the house and the level of insulation – or lack of it – to calculate the heat loss.

WINTER PIPES

If your house is in a region that experiences cold winters, make sure any pipes on exposed areas of the house are well insulated, and the water turned off at the mains when you are away during the winter.

Plumbing & heating: Room heating systems

FROM STONE-COLD TO A WARM HOUSE

Some people are quickly disappointed with the performance of their central heating system in a traditional stone house. The reason goes back to a point we talked about in Chapter 3 (see p47). Stone takes a relatively long time to warm up (compared with warming up the air in a room) and can also 'breathe' cool and damp air into your house. The only way to ensure your house warms up quickly when you turn on the heating is to insulate generously, which means lining some of the walls with insulated panels, plasterboard or blockwork. Not the most charming and rustic solution, but it's effective.

Obviously, the number of bathrooms, showers, and so on come into the equation. If you are replacing a boiler, don't assume you need to bring in a similar boiler of the same size or power rating. Technology is moving on quickly, and it is likely you will be able to get away with a less powerful – but probably much more efficient – boiler than was installed there before. There is a wide range of size and performance features available when buying a gas central heating boiler, and they are available as wall or floor-mounted units. Other options: an integrated hot-water tank of up to 80 litres; a separate water tank of up to 150 litres that can be situated nearer the bathrooms; a mini hot-water tank of around 6 litres, which will mean the boiler does not have to fire up if you just want to wash your hands; a stainless steel heat exchanger, which is less prone to scale. And condensing versions, which use a super-efficient technology to save energy (see p189).

Hot water tank safety

As hot water is stored at close to mains pressure, the pressure inside a hot water tank will be somewhere above 2 bar even when the water has not been heated. When the water is hot, it expands, so the pressure on the water tank becomes more intense, and can rise to 7 bar. For this reason, a pressure release valve is always fitted on hot water tanks, which makes sure the pressure does not exceed a safe level. This safety valve will usually release drops of water when the tank is heating up, which helps to keep the pressure of the water in the tank under control, and is not a sign of a fault. The valve needs to be checked or replaced every few years.

Underfloor heating

Underfloor heating is increasingly popular in new homes, and can also be included in renovation projects – especially where new concrete floors are part of the plan. They operate on low temperature heating, with the temperature of the floor not exceeding that of the soles of your feet – in effect 28°C. Typically, though, the temperature of the floor is about 20–25°C, which will maintain the room at about 19°C, depending on how well insulated it is.

There are two main versions: the most common uses **water circulating** in thin tubes beneath the floor, and is sometimes known as a 'wet' system, or *un plancher chauffant à l'eau chaude*. The other uses **electrical heating elements** beneath the floor – commonly seen as a system for heating tiles in a bathroom, but suitable for heating other rooms too. This is the *plancher rayonnant électrique*.

If you are creating a new floor as part of an overall renovation job, it is a good time to think about underfloor heating. Laying it over an existing floor is possible, but it will raise the floor level by several centimetres. Expect to pay around €100 per sq m for the supply and installation of the floor and heating system (not including the eventual tiling or parquet, or the water heater).

One added advantage is peace and quiet – not only because there is no water gurgling through the radiators, but because the added insulation has acoustic qualities too. Tiling must be installed with a slightly flexible grout to allow for greater expansion as the floor heats up.

'Wet' underfloor heating

A typical 'wet' system comprises a network of thin tubes which circulate warm water, laid on an insulated sheet which provides channels for the tubing, and which is covered with a self-levelling liquid screed *(une chape autonivelante)*, on which you can lay tiles or a laminate floor. It is possible to get specially designed screed for the purpose, which does not need to be much more than about 2–4 cm in thickness, and which takes around seven days to set properly (compared with three weeks for older-style screed. As a heating system, it is quiet, does not create draughts, does not occupy wall space, and allows you a free choice between oil or gas to heat the water.

This kind of heating is not instant, and may take two days to reach working temperature. These systems work best when they are permanently on, and combined with an additional source of heat, such as a wood stove. However, you can install a water chiller with change-over valves in the summer, and enjoy a cool house in the heat of the summer.

Electric underfloor heating

The electric version can be appealing if it means not having to invest in a new central heating boiler. Running costs depend on the size of the room being heated and how well insulated it is, so it is always difficult to make a comparison between electric underfloor and 'wet' underfloor heating. Electric underfloor heating looks more expensive on paper, but does not incur annual maintenance costs associated with a gas or oil-fired boiler. So the upfront costs could be lower, but the running costs higher. The most effective way of operating is to equip each room with its own heating circuit and controller. A grant is usually available for all types of electrical heating systems which are newly-installed.

Internet control

One advantage of electric underfloor heating (and in fact any electric heating system) is that the manufacturers are developing remote control systems which will be an ideal solution for second homes. In effect, you will be able to control your heating by an internet connection – in theory allowing you to put the heating on a few days in advance before you arrive at your holiday home for a winter break!

OTHER ELECTRIC SYSTEMS

Heated ceiling panels

Electric room heating is also possible via heated ceiling panels, 8–12 cm thick, made up of a sandwich of plasterboard and insulation, and an electrically heated film. The floor surface reflects back the heat, so will also need to be well insulated. This kind of heating works best in rooms with a high ceiling – around 3 m. Make sure anything that has to go behind the false ceiling (such as light fitments) are in place before the installation is finished. Expect to pay 70–85 euros per sq m for supply and fit.

Electric radiators

Known as *radiateurs électriques à inertie*, these are simply stand-alone radiators filled with fluid, which circulates when warmed up by an electric heating element inside the radiator body. They are relatively cheap to buy, but expensive if they are your sole form of heating.

Heated panels

These *panneaux rayonnants* are electrically heated panels, usually fixed to a wall, which heat by a mix of radiation (with a heated panel at the front) and convection (via a heating element at the top). They can be useful in a room with high ceilings, as the radiating heat allows you to warm up by standing right in front of the panel, rather than waiting for the air in the whole room to warm up. They are generally more expensive than a standard warm air convector heater.

SPECIAL FEATURES

Low emission boilers

These are generally viewed as being a clean technology. Look out for the especially environmentally friendly versions, known as *Bas NOx*, which have reduced emissions of NOx, or nitrogen oxides, known in French as *oxydes d'azote*. There is no legal requirement, yet, to limit these emissions.

Condensing boilers

Available in both gas-fueled and oil-fired versions, these recapture heat from the boiler's flue gases, and use this to help heat up the water in your heating system. They are generally better suited to underfloor heating systems or low-temperature radiators (*radiateurs chaleur douce*). The reason for this is that the hot gases heat most effectively water that is not too hot – in fact it must be under 53°C. Water in an underfloor heating system is usually only around 22–28°C in the room being heated, and by the time it circulates back to the boiler, it is even cooler. At this point, the pipes run through a heat exchanger where they are warmed by the hot flue gases, which transfer heat to the water in the pipes, while water vapour in the cooled flue gas condenses and is drained away. These systems use around 20% less fuel than standard modern heating boilers.

Low temperature radiators

The low-temperature radiator (*radiateur chaleur douce*) uses water circulating at around 50°C, which is 25–30° cooler than traditional systems. They work best in well-insulated houses, and create a more even heat around the various rooms, with fewer draughts. They are better suited for use with condensing boilers than conventional higher-temperature radiators.

High efficiency

These high efficiency (*haut rendement*) oil-fired burners allow virtually 100% of the fuel to be turned into heat, compared with older models, dating back to the 1970s, which only offered about 70% efficiency.

TIP SOFTENING UP HARD WATER

Parts of France suffer from hard water, and if you are installing a new plumbing system, you could think about water softening to protect new equipment and make cleaning easier. Hard water in France is measured by a TH factor (le titre hydrotimetrique) expressed in degrees. If the TH is higher than around 25°, then you should consider getting a water softener, especially if you have an electric immersion heater. There are several systems available: filters, using disposable cartridges; scale preventers (antitartres), which could be electronic systems that wrap a cable around the pipe as it enters the system, setting up a weak electromagnetic field, or magnet-based systems, or an electrolysis-based device (known as a salamander in the UK) to stop the water dumping scale. They do not however, soften the water, but they do prevent the damaging effects of scale formation.

To enjoy soft water, you will need a water softener proper (un adoucisseur), which usually employ some kind of a resinous-like substance to take the calcium out of the water.

Septic tanks: How they work

If your house is in a village, or on its outskirts, you may find you have a connection to the mains drainage system. Most rural properties, though, use a septic tank (*fosse septique*), which generally works very effectively, if you keep it properly maintained.

How it works

A septic tank is a system of interconnected chambers which work as a unit to degrease waste water (for example from the kitchen sink drain), to capture and degrade solids from the WC, and treat the remaining liquid. This is then allowed to leach out into the surrounding earth, via a long network of perforated pipes laid in fairly shallow trenches, and known as a soakaway or run-off.

The treatment process is biological, which is why you should not use bleach to clean the WC, the sink or washbasin in a house that uses a septic tank.

Even someone in the household who is using antibiotics can accidentally kill off the bugs in the septic tank simply by using the WC.

If by mistake you do damage the bugs, this is just a temporary problem. You can buy replacement packs and reactivate the system (see box opposite).

A typical modern system
There is, of course, a French norm for septic tanks, which is called NF P 16-603, and any new system should conform to this standard. According to this norm, water from the kitchen sink will run first to a **degreasing tank**, which separates grease by allowing it to float to the surface. This tank needs to be at least 200 litres in capacity if it is dealing only with kitchen waste, and 300 litres if it takes waste from the entire house. It must be installed no further than 2 m from the house.

From the degreasing tank, waste flows to the main *fosse*, or **septic tank**, where the waste waters go through a fermentation process. No air is allowed to come in contact with the contents of this tank. When the contents eventually flow out of the tank, they go through a **filter unit**. After this, the waste is channelled off to the **soak-away pipes** (there will be an inspection hatch at this stage, and also at the far end of the soakaway system.)

An **extractor vent**, usually situated on the roof, will draw up odours from the exit end of the septic tank itself.

The tank will be made of concrete or tough PVC. Sometimes there will be local regulations about which material to use. It is best to check at the mairie first, or consult your local builder.

Assessing the condition of an old septic tank

It is difficult to check the condition of an existing septic tank, as it is buried underground, and you would need to excavate the whole thing to find leaks or other problems. Lifting a few inspection covers won't tell you much either, though a specialist will know what to look out for.

When dealing with an old house that has remained unrenovated for the last 20 or 30 years, it is possible the existing septic tank is just too small. A generation ago, the septic tank was designed only to treat waste from the WC, and everything else, from the baths, kitchen sink, or washing machines, would just be allowed to drain away into the surrounding groundwater. Today this is unacceptable, and local authorities in rural France are increasingly concerned by the ecological impact of domestic drainage systems. In some cases this will eventually oblige property owners to upgrade their septic tank if the existing one is seen as damaging to the environment: check with the mairie (see box, p191).

Finding it by accident

A problem with a renovation project is that it is often not clear where the septic tank is located. Some people first find the network of drainage pipes when a delivery truck accidentally drives over them – and sinks into the trench. For this reason it is a good idea not to work on the septic tank system until much of the heavy building work has been completed. Furthermore, unless your vendor can show you proof of when the septic tank was installed, and what kind of system it is, you could be

---

PAPER-FREE ZONE?

If you have a septic tank, you should be careful what you flush down the loo. The tank uses bacteria to break down the waste, so using bleach to clean the WC is not an option. You will also need to avoid blocking the system with any paper or other sanitary products (other than toilet paper, of course). That said, we have heard of one gîte owner who had a sign asking guests not to flush '*les papiers*' down the loo. Bemused holidaymakers took this literally, disposing of their little packages of used loo paper in the waste bins outside the house.

totally in the dark about whether it will work or not. Installing a new one could cost €3,000 to €6,000, which for many people is the price to pay for peace of mind.

First-time installations
For renovations of properties which have never had a septic tank – such as a barn – the feasibility of the project depends on the nature of the land available.

Rocky or impermeable soil
If the ground is rocky or impermeable (clay, for example), the soakaway will either send waste through the rocky substrata and straight into the groundwater, which is illegal, or the waste water will just hang around in the clay and fail to soak away at all. In fact, as you

needed planning permission for a barn conversion, part of the documentation required would be proof that the ground was suitable for septic tank installation. If it is not, there are alternatives, such as a filter bed system. This is an underground pit, about the size of a small swimming pool, full of sand. It filters waste before releasing it to the groundwater.

Siting the tank
You will also need enough space. The law is fairly clear on siting a septic tank: it must not be closer than 35 m to a well or watercourse, no less than 5 m from your house (though the degreasing tank is closer to your house), and no less than 3 m from the boundary of your land, or any tree. It should be

at least 20 cm under the surface, and away from anywhere that may get driven over by a car or truck.

The soakaway or run-off
The various chambers themselves do not take up much space – but the soakaway needs around 45 linear metres for a typical 3-bedroom house, with an additional 15m or so for each further bedroom.
The soakaway is a series of perforated pipes laid in shallow trenches, typically at least 50 cm deep and about 50 cm wide, bedded with gravel above and below so the pipes are about 20 cm from the surface.
It is better to have a series of trenches in parallel, rather than one very long one.
In some properties with sloping grounds, there is space for the septic tank, but the only space for a soakaway is uphill from the tank itself. This is not an impossible situation: the solution is a pump which takes the liquids from the tank up to the soakaway zone.
This could add €1,500 to the cost of the project, though.

How big should the tank be?
Tanks range in capacity from between 1,000 and 5,000 litres, with 3,000 being enough for a 3-bedroom property. But If you are planning to entertain regularly,

you may need to design a system with a greater capacity. The penalty for having a unit that is too small is a complete breakdown of the system, usually when all your special friends and family have come over to see you. If the system backs up (ie waste is flowing into the tank faster than it can get treated and drained away) then the level of water in the tank will rise, and solids (including lumps of detergent, soap and all the predictable nasties) will rise with it, blocking the filter unit, so that waste will start to hang around in the pipes running from the tank and back to your house.
One solution, rather than buying an extra-large tank, is to use two tanks, both feeding the same soakaway.

Pumping out and cleaning
A tank should be pumped out every two to three years, and usually the contractor that does this will be able to rinse it out with clean water – the truck usually has a water tank as well as an effluent tank. The de-greasing tank should be checked and cleaned every four to six months, as should the filter.

Bad smells
The most obvious problems with a septic tank are ones you can smell. Septic tanks use a ventilation duct which

TIP There is an increasing tendency now among local communes to put in the infrastructure for mains drainage for properties close to the village, while more isolated properties will be expected to upgrade their septic tanks to new versions that satisfy all the current norms. This will be a gradual process, and it could mean that as planning permission requests are received at the mairie over coming years, home owners who are planning building work will also be required to invest in a new fosse septique, if their existing one is not up to scratch, as a condition of getting planning permission. This has two implications for home owners. First, if you move into a rural area, it is worth finding out if there is a plan to bring mains drainage into your area in the near future. Secondly, if there is no such plan on the cards, you may have to buy a new septic tank system when you apply for planning permission for something else. It's a good, environmentally friendly idea, but quite how many people will actually be rushing to comply remains to be seen.

Project planning: DIY versus the pros

A successful renovation project is always a challenge, even if it is in your own country where everyone speaks your mother tongue. Not surprisingly, then, horror stories abound from French projects, with 'troublesome builders' and sites grinding to a halt. Don't be too worried, though. The route to success comes down to plenty of planning, communication, and teamwork. Over the next few pages, we show how you can do well at all three.

is linked to the main 100 mm pipe stack that rises up the wall of the house to roof height, releasing what could be politely called 'marsh gas.' Marsh gas, though, is heavier than air, so can waft down the walls and into open windows.

Another source of unpleasantness can be caused by the syphon (or U-bend) of a wash basin or even a WC, which, if the house has been unoccupied during a long warm period, could dry out, turning the waste pipe into a rather too effective air duct coming straight up from the contents of the septic tank and into your house. This problem is solved once you refill the U-bend simply by flushing the WC or running a tap for a few seconds.

Mains drains

If your house is on mains drains, then count yourself lucky, as this will make life simple. The only complication, if you are renovating, is to check the height of the mains drainage system in relation to your various plumbing outlets.

Some people putting a bathroom into a basement conversion find that the outflows are actually below the level of the drains.

The solution to this is a WC that pulverises waste and then pumps it out, while you will need pumps too for the bath and basin wastes.

DIY versus builders

Getting stuck into a project yourself, learning new skills as you go along, is a rewarding and fun experience, and if all goes to plan, it is deeply satisfying. An enormous number of people embark on DIY renovation for second homes in France, with brilliant results. This is something that is within reach of everyone. The way to make sure things do not go wrong is to just take an honest look at your own skills, the time you have available for the project, and the kind of finish you are aiming for.

What to avoid

For obvious safety reasons, most DIY-ers should steer clear of any structural work, roofing jobs, boiler or fireplace installations, gas installations, and electrical work. And if it matters that you have a professional finish to joinery or plasterwork, for example, you will of course need to hire professional joiners and plasterers. If you are doing a renovation job that involves more than one skill (such as a new plumbing layout, a concrete floor, plus new partition walls) then planning and the sequence of works are as important as the building skills needed to carry out the jobs. Yes, we know, it all sounds obvious and easy!

Huge tax break for builders

In France, if you buy materials for your DIY jobs, you pay VAT (TVA, in French) at the standard 19.6%. However, if you hire a builder to do the work, the builder charges you only 5.5% TVA, because of a tax-break on upgrading existing buildings. This is effectively a hefty state subsidy which encourages people to use the building trade rather than try to go it alone. This arrangement tends to be renewed or changed by the Government every few years.

How much to DIY

Most people mix hiring builders for the difficult stuff and doing the rest themselves. Getting the balance right can save you time and money. A lot of backbreaking manual jobs can be done more quickly by a builder with the right equipment. In return for the money you pay them, you not only get the job done, but give yourself a few days to do something else. You are buying time to recharge your batteries. In fact, if you try to put a money value on your own time – your own kind of daily wage rate – you will be less likely to get drawn into mind-numbing tasks that never seem to get finished. Some people decide to give up a job in the UK and go out to France to get on with a renovation project. The trick is not to go out there too early. If you decide to 'help' your builder by going around the site with a wheelbarrow, you might save yourself the daily rate of a labourer. But if you were still at work, back in Britain or wherever, you could be earning enough money to pay for the labourer, and for a project manager, and still have change left in your pocket.

Finding the builders

But we are jumping ahead here. For many people embarking on a project in France, the most pressing question is 'Where can I find a good builder to do the job for me?'

The language problem

France is full of good builders who can do great renovation work. Unfortunately for most people renovating in France, the majority of these builders don't speak English. What could be useful is someone who can speak both English and French who can help you with the language problem. This could be a neighbour or friend in the vicinity with time to join you when you meet your builders, and help to overcome those communication barriers. Once works starts, your translator could also send you photographs of progress on the site, and keep you updated of any problems. This is a useful arrangement. However, (as discussed on p33), there are risks if you try to take this too far, and start to devolve day-to-day responsibility on this person to manage the site. If there is a misunderstanding, and the builders make an expensive mistake, who is responsible? Of course, many people are willing to take the risk, and just keep fingers crossed that there are no mishaps.

The best bet is to find yourself a translator, but stay very much in the driving seat of the project yourself, or hand over project management to a professional builder, and use your translator only for language problems.

Managing the project

Someone has to be in charge. You have a number of options. If you use a **building company**, (*une*

entreprise générale) they will run the site for you, and hire subcontractors. The downside of this is that you will lose some control over the finished result: you will be further away from the day-to-day decisions that are made on site. Questions about replace-or-repair will probably favour the replacement option, as it is more cost-effective for the builder. Alternatively, you may be working with an **architect or designer** (and by law you have to use an architect if your property, after the building work is finished, exceeds 170 sq m of living space). If so, they could run the project for you (and see below 'How the pros do it' for a fuller explanation of the process). Or you could **run it yourself**, co-ordinating the schedule and spelling out the work required. Many home owners try to employ a team of tradesmen who don't know each other, but expect them to work together like a well-oiled machine. This is unlikely to happen unless you are able to get them to stick to the plans and the schedule. And there is a lot that can go wrong.

A worst-case scenario

Projects that run into trouble usually fail because of lack of planning, lack of anything written down, and a failure of communications. It is not unusual for people to invite builders to their property to try to get an estimate, showing them the site but with nothing written down and often no attempt to make any drawings or plans. This may be repeated with another builder, perhaps a day later. Both builders will probably have a different interpretation of what you want, so when their quotes come in later, they are each rather different in terms of price and the work specified. When the work eventually progresses, a builder could be some way through a job, having bought materials and committed labour to it, before you realise this is not what you wanted at all. Who is to blame? If there is no detailed plan, and a language handicap, it would have been due to luck alone if the builder had interpreted what you wanted exactly. No wonder some builders storm

HOW TO AVOID THE COWBOYS

Make sure the builders you hire are legal. Their letterhead should show the company registration (SIRET) number. It will also show what they actually do as a trade, and any registrations with a trade body. You can also ask to see their professional insurance documents. These cover the trades which they practise – and are the basis of the various guarantees (see p196). This insurance tends to stop a builder becoming a jack-of-all-trades, but can make tradesmen seem a bit inflexible at times. The other insurance to ask for is third party liability insurance (*responsabilité civile*). There are also general trade associations, such as Qualibat, a network of qualified builders of a wide variety of trades. However, don't turn down a builder just because he is not registered with such a group.

Project planning: How to learn from the professionals

off a site never to return, and in some cases never to work with foreigners again.

The sequence of work

An understanding of the sequence of works helps. Think about a typical renovation job. First, the site will need water and electricity for the various tradesmen's use. The walls must be made safe and secure, then the roof. This simple sequence involves close cooperation between the roofer (*couvreur*) and the carpenter (*charpentier*). When the roof cover is removed by the roofer, the masons will come in to check the soundness of the chimney stack, and possibly to consolidate the tops of the walls (which will be housing various timber beams). The carpenter works on the roof structure, and then the roofer returns to finish the job. The masons could then return to work on the wall rendering. The aim is to avoid delays, and having to hire scaffolding twice for the same part of the house.

Meanwhile on the ground floor, if a new concrete floor is planned then all the service runs for electrical and plumbing ducts must be planned and installed first. The same goes for any new floors and also for partition walling. So the number of electrical sockets and their position is one of the earliest things to be decided. Bathroom and kitchen installation come later in the project, but are planned from the outset. Last of all comes painting and decorating, carried out when all the dust has settled.

How the pros do it

Let's look at how the professionals run a building project. Even if you don't want to hire an architect or project manager, you can steal some of their common sense techniques to make life easier.

Architects will start out by **discussing the project** with the client, to find out how much money is available, what the client is trying to achieve, and find out if it is technically possible to do. The next stage will be careful **measurement of the site**, with detailed scale drawings made before the creative bit starts.

The proposals (say of an extension, or a barn conversion) will then get discussed with the client, and kicked around a bit until the client is happy with the design, and the architect is happy that it will work. The architect will then go on to seek **planning permission**.

Once this is granted, the large-scale plans are fleshed out to create a more **detailed plan, plus a separate job description for each trade**

(plumbers, electricians, carpenters and so on) that will be required. This pack of information is known as the DCE, or *Dossier de consultation des Entreprises*.

It puts the whole project down in writing – with a detailed plan of what goes where, cross-sections, plan views, and the list of what each trade must do. It allows the people working on site to get on with the job without constantly having to ask the client exactly what is needed. The architect – or whoever will run the project from this stage on – will then **pick the team of tradesmen**, either by an open tender or by using trusted people known already.

The next phase is to draw up the **schedule of works** between the various tradesmen. This basically means getting everyone together with their diaries out so that people will agree to come on site when they are needed. There is nothing binding about such a schedule, and builders can still let each other down because of commitments on other sites. But at least this initial look at diaries will highlight potential clashes early, and if the builders agree between them the schedule of work, you will be in with a chance of keeping to it. Major commercial projects impose **penalty clauses**. This is unlikely to stick on privately-run jobs, though. If builders doubt the project will be well run, they will never agree to a penalty clause if they think there is a risk that delays will be out of their control.

Planning permission: Permis de construire

A 'lite' version of the above

You don't need to hire an architect and go through the whole process described above. But there are some vital parts anyone can do. The first is to make a reasonable drawing, roughly to scale, on graph paper, of what you want to do. Measure the rooms, and measure furniture and fittings to make sure there is room to move in the new spaces you want to create.

Write down as much of the project as you can, describing the jobs you want done in as much detail as possible. You can also add sketches where necessary. Be precise. Don't say: 'Install the wash basin by the door.' Do say: 'Install the wash basin with its top at a height of 75 cm from the floor, with the right hand side 25 cm from the door, as shown in the sketch. Put the hot tap on the left hand side.'

If there are things you are not sure about, leave that out of the description and ask the builders you invite to show you solutions and give you an estimate.

Whether you are using one builder or numerous different trades, get them to agree dates collectively, allowing you to create a schedule of works.

This will not be foolproof. But it will at least give you the best chance of keeping the work moving along.

PLANNING PERMISSION

Local planning guidelines

Before you seek planning permission, you should first take a look at the local planning rules, which are contained in the PLU, or **Plan Local d'Urbanisme**. In some areas, this will be called the POS, or the **Plan d'Occupation des Sols**. This is a vital planning document, setting out the ground rules of what you can and cannot do. It will define all kinds of detailed things like how close your house can be to the nearest road, or to the edge of your land; the permitted colour of the facade, the shape of windows, the materials you can or cannot use; and plenty more besides. Getting on top of this body of information will save you time and money: it will stop you going down the blind alley of working up a detailed plan that would simply be rejected out of hand by the local planning authorities.

Planning permission, or Le permis de construire

You will not need to get planning permission for every kind of building job – but the law stipulates that it is required if you are planning a change of use (such as a barn or loft conversion), or you plan to change its exterior appearance or its interior habitable surface area, or to add extra storeys of accom-

modation. Work on *inscrit* listed buildings also requires planning permission.

Paperwork needed

The paperwork that you have to hand to the mairie is fairly comprehensive: a map of the vicinity showing where your property is situated (*le plan de situation*); a more detailed plan showing your plot of land, its immediate neighbours, access roads and services (*le plan de masse*); scale drawings (around 1:100 will be OK) of each level of the building, all the external facades of the building – before and after – and sectional drawings where relevant; and some photographs. Within two weeks of filing your application, you should receive an acknowledgement of receipt (*un accusé de reception*) giving an idea of how long it will take for the application to be dealt with. This is usually within a couple of months. It will be

longer if your property is a listed building, or – a surprise to many people – if your property is within a radius of 500 m of a listed building, or in a special conservation zone called a ZPPAUP (see p203). In these cases, the application is referred to the office of the *Architecte des Bâtiments de France* – which can take between three to five months. Include an extra copy of the dossier in the pack, just in case.

Approval or rejection

If your application is successful, you will receive your *permis de construire*. Alternatively, you may hear back from the mairie with amendments to your original plan, or the plan may be rejected – setting out the reasons for this. This gives you the chance to have another go, taking into account what was ruled out the first time around.

It could simply be a case of repositioning a window, or it may concern a roof modification that looks incongruous, or the wrong choice of render. Many of these problems can be avoided by careful scrutiny (with your builder or architect) of the local regulations contained in the PLU and local practice.

Rejected dossiers

If you have forgotten something, your application will be

THREE KINDS OF PLANNING PERMIT

1: The Certificat d'Urbanisme

Known as the Cd'U, (pronounced 'say-dew'), this is outline planning permission. It may state that a change-of-use, say, from barn to living accommodation will be allowed, or that you may build on a spare plot of land within your property.

2: The Permis de Construire

Full planning permission, where you submit full details of your proposal, with drawings at 1:100, and photographs. Required for all new builds, change of use, changes to external appearance, creation of new floor area, and additional storeys.

3: The Déclaration de Travaux

Notification by the householder to the mairie for certain kind of works that do not need planning permission – for example, many kinds of swimming pool, or perhaps a new roof or a 'facelift' to your property.

Planning permission: Permis de construire

returned to you, with the message *Dossier Incomplèt*. If you have applied for the wrong kind of planning permission (for example, you ask for a *déclaration de travaux* when you should be seeking a *permis de construire*, the dossier will be returned marked *Dossier Irreçevable*.

Neighbours get their say
However, even if you have been granted permission, that is not the end of the story. Third parties – your neighbours, basically – then have two months to throw in their comments. They can apply to the mairie to look at your application, look at any advice given, and read the terms of the permit being granted. This is one reason why you must put up the obligatory *Panneau de Chantier* (the site notice board with your planning permission reference), once you receive permission, to alert third parties and allow them to scrutinise the documents and lodge an objection if they wish.

The Déclaration de Travaux
This is the 'lightweight' version of the *permis* and relates to renovation work that does not significantly alter the external appearance of the building.
This could include a new roof, or a 'facelift' of the outside of your property, such

as applying a new coat of render.
You make a *déclaration* to alert local planning authorities that you have a project underway. Building an open-air swimming pool also comes under this category, as does any construction that is less than 20 sq m in surface area.
You will need to hand in your declaration form a month before you plan to start the work, and then you may receive a letter back indicating when you can start work, or sometimes no reply, indicating tacit approval.
Check with the mairie if you hear nothing and are unsure of the outcome.

Once work begins
Once you have the necessary permissions, the work can begin. If you sought planning permission or made a *déclaration de travaux* you need to inform your mairie once you start, with a *declaration d'ouverture de chantier* – in effect a notice pinned up in the mairie to say that your building site has started work. When the work is completed, you will again need to inform the mairie, and within the next three months, possibly following an inspection, you may receive a certificate to confirm the work conforms with the details of planning permission originally granted.

GETTING CLOSE TO THE NEIGHBOURS

There are strict rules about changes you may make to your house – including adding windows or a terrace – that create a view that overlooks your neighbours' property. If a window looks out straight into your neighbours' home or garden, this window must be at least 1.9 m from the edge of your land. If the window is at an angle to the neighbour's land (so you would have to turn your head 90 degrees to overlook them) the minimum distance comes down to just 60 cm.
These rules get complex, and are written into French law in the Code Civil (section on Servitude Légale de Vue), which covers windows close to boundaries. These rules can be over-ridden by strict local planning laws too, so it is essential to get expert advice. The authors have heard of a case where an English couple knocked a new window opening in their house, only to set off a bitter dispute with their neighbour who claimed that their action was breaking the law.
The conflict spoiled their enjoyment of their French home for some time.

When you get work done by professional builders in France, the work will be guaranteed. The length of the guarantee depends on what is involved, with work that has an impact on the structure and weatherproofing of the building itself carrying a 10-year guarantee. There are one-year and two-year guarantees operating too, giving you a quite reasonable amount of protection if things go wrong.

BUILDERS' GUARANTEES

The hand-over process once work is completed

As the person who owns the property, you are what's known as the *maître d'ouvrage* or the head of works – and so it is your role to accept formally the completed work at the final hand-over, known as *la réception des travaux*. At this stage you can either accept the work as complete, or accept it on the proviso that certain things are put right or properly finished. The various guarantees (described below) run from the date of acceptance of the finished work, so if you don't go through this hand-over ceremony, you could find it difficult to prove at what stage the guarantees came into force.

Before hand-over

You will need to go over the work with a fine-tooth comb, checking against the original plans, estimates and so on. If you fail to point out some anomaly on hand-over day, it will be judged to be correct, and the obligatory guarantee period starts. If you have been working with just one large building firm, then an authorised representative of that builder should be there. If you have been working with a number of different tradesmen, you should get them all to come to the site at the same time for the hand-over.

Tie down the dodgy builders

Some dodgy builders may try to avoid the hand-over day. Don't let them get away with this. You should send them an invitation to the hand-over day appointment, by registered post to make sure they receive it. However, if they don't come, you can still write down an account of what remains to be fixed, if there are still problems, and send this to the builder by registered post.

If everything is OK

If you are happy with the quality of the work, then you sign a document recording what has been discussed – *un procès-verbal de réception des travaux*, which is literally the 'minutes' of your meeting with the builders. You will then pay the builders whatever is left owing, if you have not already done so.

If it is not OK

If there are things that need to be fixed, you can postpone the hand-over until they are fixed, or you can accept the hand-over, but stipulating the things that need to be put right. If you do this, the builder or builders must then sort out the problems, however insignificant they may be, under the terms of the one-year guarantee (described below). Generally, you should work out your

---

MAITRE D'OUVRAGE VERSUS THE MAITRE D'OEUVRE:

Maître d'ouvrage
This is the 'contracting authority' which is probably the owner of the property: it could be you!
Maître d'oeuvre
This is the 'master of works', which could be your architect, your architecte-d'intérieur or designer, or project manager – if you have contracted such a professional to manage your project.

Builders' guarantees: 1, 2 and 10-years

contract with the builder so that you do not pay the whole amount until all the remedial works are completed, but without using financial blackmail!

In case of dispute

If the builder does not agree that there are problems, and refuses to come back and finish the work, then you will need to get legal advice in a bid to force the builder to complete the work.

GUARANTEES

There are three main kinds of guarantee of work:

The 1-Year Guarantee

This is known as *la garantie de 'parfait achèvement'*, and under its terms you can draw attention to any faults in the work as soon as they are completed, or any other faults which arise over the following 12 months, excluding damage from wear and tear. It's a fairly legal operation. You will need to contact the builder in writing (by registered mail) and then agree a time scale for the work to be put right.

The 2-Year Guarantee

This is known as *la garantie de 'bon fonctionnement'* and applies to anything installed in your building, rather than the fabric of the building itself – though including doors and windows. It could include a shower unit, or floor tiling, for example. Again, you need to contact the builder by registered mail. The builder can get off the hook only by showing that the defect is caused by your own misuse, by someone else's, or by some external factor such as a lightning strike and so on. If he cannot do so, and is liable to pay but doesn't, you could try to pursue the matter in court.

The 10-Year Guarantee

This is the celebrated *garantie décennale*, under which builders, architects and other project managers are held responsible for faults in a building as a result of their work for a period of 10 years. The kind of damage that comes under this guarantee is something that would put at risk the structure of the house itself or make it uninhabitable. This includes certain kinds of leaks, damp, and damage to parts of the house that cannot be removed (windows and doors do not come into this category). Most renovation and building work will come under this kind of guarantee, but bear in mind that it only relates to serious damage that can affect the structure of your house.

The 'assurance dommages-ouvrages'

This is covered in more detail in the section on new houses (see p201). Basically, it is an insurance policy that allows work to go on, even if the various trades that you are hiring are in a frenzy of finger-pointing litigation and want to 'down tools' until the dispute is settled – which could take years. This insurance allows the project to be completed, with the litigation running on in parallel, perhaps being settled months or even years later.

INSURANCE AND HOME SECURITY

Insuring a second home in France is not too complex, though if you find an insurer used to dealing with foreign owners, and who speaks English, you will find it all a good deal easier. Here's a rough guide.

Buildings and contents combined

Most insurance policies will combine the building insurance with the contents insurance. Building insurance only will however be available if you intend to let out the property completely unfurnished (in which case the tenant will insure their own contents).

Insuring unrestored or derelict buildings

There is a general concept called *dévaluation* which takes a bit of understanding. Generally, if your house is completely destroyed, the insurance policy will replace on a 'new for old' basis. However, this does not mean that if you own a derelict barn which is destroyed by fire, the insurance company will pay you to rebuild it as a luxury gîte with en suite bathrooms and a sauna. In fact, there is a neat formula to work out how much you will get if a dilapidated building is damaged.

An illustration

Suppose you own a tumble-down farmhouse that is unrenovated, and which gets damaged in a fire. To rebuild the farmhouse as new would cost €100,000. However, you did not own a new farmhouse to start with.

The insurance company will therefore assess what condition the building was in before the fire damage happened. If they reckon it would have cost you, say, €60,000 to renovate the house to something like a 'new' condition, then they will say the building before the damage was only worth €40,000. It is subject to what they call a 'devaluation' of 60%. However, in the event of a successful claim, insurers will not just pay you this figure of €40,000. They will also pay you a further 25% of the 'new' value if you rebuild: in this case a further €25,000. So the total payout will be €65,000. You would have to fund the rest of the building

INSURANCE: THE PERSONAL TOUCH

No-one travelling in France can fail to spot the enormous number of insurance company agencies. In a town of just 7,500 people, for example, it would not be uncommon to find ten insurers competing for your business. The trend towards call centres, phone and internet services is starting slowly, but the French like to have that personal touch – and it can be reassuring for holiday home owners too.

work yourself to rebuild the house as new.

Depends on its condition

You will spot from this that if your house would have cost, say, just €25,000 to get into its 'new' condition, then insurers will pay you €75,000 for the value of the house (a 25% devaluation), plus the additional 25% of the 'new house' value if you rebuild – a further €25,000, giving you the whole value of rebuilding the house to its new condition.

So if the insurers reckon your house has a devaluation of less than 25% of its 'rebuild new value', then in the case of your house being totally destroyed you would receive the whole amount required to rebuild as new. (However, your insurers will not give you more than the value needed to rebuild as new.) And note also that if the 'devaluation' is greater than 25% of the rebuild new value, you will find that the payment from the insurers will not completely cover the rebuild cost.

Quotations by number of rooms

Your insurance premium will be based on the number of rooms, which include living rooms, bedrooms and so on, but excludes bathrooms, kitchens, and utility rooms. For the purposes of a quote, the maximum room size is 40 sq m. So a room of 50 sq m will count as two rooms. A typical insurance premium, around 2004, was €50 per room per year.

Public liability insurance

This is known as *responsabilité civile* and is a valuable insurance against personal injury.

Insurers may not automatically offer you this option, and it is not a legal requirement. However, it will cover you for any accident that may happen to third parties – to friends, or anyone coming onto your property, or to anyone injured by you or your family wherever you may be. Typical accidents could include someone being hit by a falling slate, or bitten by a dog, or slipping on your steps. This kind of policy could cost from €40 per year.

Holiday home insurance

If you are absent from your

property for more than 90 days in a year, it will be classified as a holiday home for insurance purposes, and you will pay a slightly higher premium (perhaps 15% higher). You will need to satisfy certain conditions for home security: a two-point lock on the front door, and wooden shutters or bars on all ground floor windows. If you are unsure if your home complies with the conditions, you could ask an insurance agent to visit. Otherwise, you make a declaration that you have the relevant security in place (and you must use it, too).

Alarms

With rural properties, alarms are not terribly useful, as there may be nobody around to do anything about it. However, if you have contents worth more than €80,000, your insurer may ask you to install an alarm linked to a control centre, whose staff will visit the property immediately if the alarm goes off.

Absent owners making a claim

You generally have between 2–5 days to make a claim after discovering the damage. However, if you live abroad, don't panic. The key word is 'discovering' the damage, rather than the date the damage actually took place. So if you arrive at a holiday home to find that a storm six weeks ago has lifted the roof and the house has become rain-damaged, then you make your claim within 2–5 days and the damage will be covered. Obviously, for peace of mind, you could ask a neighbour to check on your property. When they alert you to a problem, you will need to take action promptly. Note that to claim for storm damage, wind speed (recorded by Météo France) must exceed 100km/h.

How to make the claim

Your insurance claim could be accepted by the insurer without any discussion, and paid in due course. If the claim is particularly large, you may need to provide receipts of items lost or missing. For any crime, you must report it to the gendarmerie, and quote the reference number for your case to the insurer.

WARNING! NO INSURANCE FOR DIY BUILDERS

If you get friends or relations around to your house to help you out with building work, you will not be able to include them in your public liability insurance, and they will not be covered for helping you with your DIY renovation. In effect, if your friend is injured when helping you with your building job and claims damages from you, there will be no insurance policy to fall back on. If a professional builder has an accident, he is covered by his own insurance. However, as the maitre d'ouvrage (the owner of the property), you usually have an obligation to appoint a health and safety coordinator (Coordinateur SPS) for your site – they are listed in the phone book. In reality, few people bother to do this because of the costs involved, but risk serious legal issues in the event of a bad accident on their site.

Building a new home: Finding the plot

If you are up for a challenge, you could consider buying a plot of land and building a new house in France. This is something that thousands of French people do every year, with a home created on a small development of houses grouped together, known as a 'lotissement.' Alternatively, you can go it alone: if you find the right plot, you could end up creating a stunning individual home. Surprisingly, it could turn out to be cheaper and quicker than a major renovation project.

BUILDING A NEW HOUSE

Unrenovated getting scarce
Property prices in some of the most popular regions of France are rising quickly. Overseas investors are flooding in to snap up second homes, while better motorway links are extending the range of rural second homes that are appealing to French city dwellers. In some regions, estate agents report that getting hold of an unrenovated country property is becoming more and more challenging, and expensive, with buyers from the US, Japan and even Australia arriving on the scene.

The alternative: build new
Against this backdrop, finding a decent building plot, (*un terrain à bâtir*) in a great location, and building a new house from scratch can be a viable alternative. Although the idea of building a new house abroad sounds daunting, in some ways it can hold a lot less uncertainty than a major renovation project. Renovations can be full of surprises, and the project timetable, and budget, can easily be thrown off course by unforseen problems. A new-build can also go wrong. But on the whole, a carefully planned and well-executed build project can be completed to a predictable timescale, and the use of modern building systems and technology creates a comfortable, secure home. And yes, it can also look good!

Prices for a plot of land suitable for building vary enormously across France, influenced by very local factors. In terms of euros per square metre, you could be looking at €10-€15/sq m for a fairly remote plot in central France, to €15-€25/sq m within easy reach of the Atlantic, and perhaps as much as €75/sq m down on the Côte d'Azur or on the borders of a big city.

Three kinds of building plot
There are three main kinds of building plot generally advertised in estate agents.

1) The lotissement
The most common will be on a *lotissement*, which will effectively become a housing estate once all the plots are

TIP What if you find the perfect plot of land, with open views across the countryside, and decide to build a house there: how can you find out if the neighbouring fields will soon become another new housing estate? The answer lies in the Plan Local d'Urbanism, which will show which 'parcels' of land are zoned for further housing development.

developed. Typically, this starts out as a field, which is then often sold to a developer (or to the local council). The developer carves up the land into individual plots of varying sizes – with the smallest around 600 sq m (enough space for a 3-bedroom house where the walls are about 10m from the edge of the plot,) with larger plots of around 2,000 sq m. Water,

drainage, electricity and sometimes gas are supplied to the boundary of each plot (where the meters are located) and the access road, pavements, and so on are also developed.

The plot buyer will then either choose a house layout 'off plan' – from a selection of options provided by the site developer, or create something a bit more individual from their own house builder (who may also simply offer a choice of off-plan houses, or a mix of off-plan with bespoke touches, or completely design your house to your requirements. However, there may be a whole set of rules about what kind of house you build, designed to create a certain uniformity between all the houses on the lotissement.

A no-frills new house, with three bedrooms and an economical choice of interior finish, could cost from as little as €80,000 to build.

2) The 'hors lotissement' plot

Some people are attracted by the community atmosphere that can thrive from having neighbours close-by. Others are appalled at the idea, or simply want to go it alone and find a one-off plot in an interesting location. Any plot that is not part of a collective group of houses is described in French as a terrain 'hors lotissement' (ie, not on a lotissement) or some-

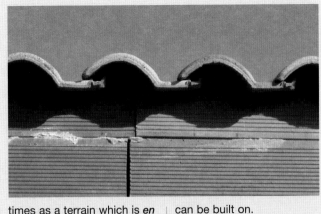

times as a terrain which is *en diffus*. These could be a spare plot that is adjacent to someone else's house, or a small field divided into a couple of plots of land, or just a piece of land tucked away somewhere that is now up for sale.

The key word: viabilisé

The key word to look for with these plots of land is *viabilisé* or *non-viabilisé*.

Viabilisé means the essential services are already in place – water and electricity. You may not have mains drainage in a rural location, and similarly there may not be any mains gas supply. Neither of these are a problem. But the absence of electricity or mains water (on a terrain non-viabilisé) is a potential problem, and getting them laid on can cost several thousand euros on top of what you are already paying for the site.

If a plot of land is *viabilisé* it means that the land has electricity, water, vehicle access, and what's more,

can be built on.

3) Land for a horse, not for a house

Another kind of plot of land is on the market: the *terrain de loisirs* which is much cheaper than a building plot for the simple reason that you cannot build on it. Some people buy these as a speculative punt, hoping that one day local land-use laws will change. It is best to avoid these, though, if you seriously want to build a place in France anytime soon.

Buy a ruin, knock it down?

The alternative to buying a building plot is to buy a ruin, knock it down, and build the house that you really want. Unfortunately, you cannot assume that you will always get planning permission, as that all depends on the local planning authorities. A couple who bought a ruined farmhouse on an agricultural zone found that they were prohibited from demolishing the house. However, they were allowed to extend the house to a maximum of three

times its initial floorspace, which is the route they took – in effect 'cloning' the house by building a short terrace of replicas right alongside it.

The first place to check what might be allowed is the local mairie, though they may not have the complete picture. You should also refer to the departement planning office, which is the *Direction Departementale de l'Equipement.* Getting a French-speaking architect or builder to help you through this process is a good idea.

The local planning laws

The key document you need to see is the local PLU, the *Plan Local d'Urbanisme,* which is replacing the POS, or the *Plan de l'Occupation du Sol*. The PLU is available in the mairie, and will include a large scale map of the entire commune (the area under the jurisdiction of the mairie) outlining the boundaries of the various properties. This will also show zones according to land use: agricultural, residential, commercial, mixed and so on. This will be valuable, not only to check that a plot of land can be built on, but also to see what is going to happen to land nearby.

A view across open fields could turn into a view across a new lotissement if the adjacent land is zoned for development.

Building a new home: Who to work with

RURAL FRANCE'S LOVE OF THE NEW

Driving through rural France, Brits are often amazed at the dull uniformity of some of the small beige bungalows with brown shutters that seem to pop up everywhere. However, for older people living in villages, these houses are seen as highly economical and convenient. Typically, pensioners will eventually sell their traditional stone houses, which they find expensive to heat and maintain, and have a new house built, within or close to the village. It will often incorporate wide doorways and ramps for potential wheelchair access as they get older. These properties may not have the charm of an ancient *fermette*, but for older people who want to remain independent in their own homes for as long as possible, they are the ideal place to live: cheap to build, low maintenance, and economical to run.

planning issues. This will be very broad brush, relating to such issues as how high you can build, rules about exterior finishes and colours, or typical forms of windows.

How big can you build?
The PLU will also include a stipulation about how large a property can be built on a given size of building plot. This is known as the COS, or the *Coefficient d'occupation des sols*. It is usually expressed as a decimal figure such as 0.1 – which means that for a building plot of 1,000 sq m, you can build a house with a total of 0.1 times 1,000 sq m, or 100 sq m. In cases where your commune does not have a PLU or a POS, then you will need to take a look at the RNU, or *Règlement National d'Urbanisme*, which will apply instead.

Building a new house on an individual building plot
You may decide to go it alone and build on an individual plot of land. If so, you will have to go through all the administative hoops of buying the plot (which is the same as the conveyancing process of buying a house, see p168) and then getting the planning permissions (see p193). Here's how the process works.

1) Outline permission
First, you need a certificate to show that you have per-

mission to build something on the land – the *certificat d'urbanisme* or outline planning permission. To get one of these, you fill out a form and follow instructions about providing ground plans and drawings, and drop it in to the mairie, and you should get a response within two months.

2) Apply for the 'permis'
If the answer is positive, the certificate is valid for 24 months, so during this time you should get your dossier together to seek the *permis de construire*, or planning permission. If the 24 months period elapses, you can apply to renew the *certificat d'urbanisme*. One reason your renewal might get refused would be if there had been a change in policy relating to the PLU.
The application for planning permission can only be

drawn up by an architect for projects of over 170 sq m (SHON – see box opposite). For projects under this limit your builder can draw up the application. It will involve plans and elevations at a scale of around 1:100, location plans, a ground plan and a graphic to show how the proposed building blends into the existing landscape. Later on, when the contrac-

> **TIP** There is a trend in new houses in France to create a living room, or 'salon-séjour', with 50 sq m or more of floor area. Is this a good idea? If you tile the floor (which is common practice in France) the acoustics can be pretty 'bathroomy' in such a large room. Creating flexible living space (say, with sliding room dividers) is an effective alternative.

tors are being briefed, more detailed drawings at a scale of 1:50 or 1:20 will be needed. These form part of the specifications of the whole project, otherwise known as 'The book of specifications' (*Dossier de consultation des entreprises*).

Who do you work with?
There are plenty of different ways to run a new-build project, and which you choose will depend on your level of skills and experience, the time at your disposal, your budget, and your ability to speak French!
You don't have to work with an **architect** unless the living space you plan to end up with is greater than 170 sq m. But if you do get an architect involved, he or she can design the house that you want, and run the project for you. Fees may be around 10% of the cost of the building works, though an architect may not take on a very low-cost build project as the fee income could be too small (or he may simply increase the percentage).

Here are some of the ways it could work:

1) Architect designs the house, builder runs project
You could get the architect to design the house and create the detailed specification, which you take to a general building company which will build the house for you.

2) Architect designs the house and runs project

The architect handles the planning permission phase and runs the construction project, including overseeing all the various trades required. Assuming you do not have the time or skills to oversee a building project, it is worth getting the architect to do this for you – down to choosing the various tradesmen and companies, and planning and monitoring all stages of the work

3) Architect designs house, subcontracts build to a general house-builder

In this arrangement, once the design is approved, a general house-building company – *une entreprise générale* – is appointed as main contractor, and sub-contracts work to the various trades involved as necessary. This will cut down on how many operators you, or your architect, have to deal with, though ultimately giving you less control over the finished result.

The paperwork here involves a *contrat de construction* where the building enterprise does not supply the plans for the house – *sans fourniture de plans* – because these have been drawn up by the architect.

The contract will give you a guarantee that your house will be completed, or your money back.

4) House-builder designs the house and builds it: buying 'off-plan'

The other way of getting a new house built *hors lotissement* is to use a specialist house-building company that will give you a choice of house types from a catalogue, which can usually be tweaked slightly to your own specifications. To see better what you are getting, you could visit a *village expo* which is a collection of show houses from various house-building companies. The contract here is the *Contrat de construction de maison individuelle* or CCMI, with plans included, or *avec fourniture de plans*. You should study this carefully, particularly when it comes to the description of the materials being used. If you get time to view examples of, say, flooring, and find the quality too low, try to seek an upgrade. Note that the price on your contract is the price you pay, even if the building work takes longer and costs more than anticipated. The contract should also include penalty clauses which the developer must pay in the case of delays.

You pay for the house in stages as the work progresses. The CCMI is similar to getting a house built on a *lotissement* in the sense that you do not have to get drawn into monitoring the building process yourself.

Insuring the building project

If you are the client for a new-build house you are in French law the *maître d'ouvrage* and in this capacity it is a requirement to take out insurance against things going wrong on the project.

Peace of mind: l'assurance dommages-ouvrages

All the various trades working on the project will have their own professional insurance policies. But imagine a scenario where a mason completes a wall, the roof goes on, and then a crack appears in the wall. Who is to blame? Insurers will send inspectors to look at the foundations, the work of the mason, and the roof trusses. This will take time. During this time all work on the site will stop.

Unblocking the process

The *assurance dommages-ouvrages* is designed to unblock the process. Insurance inspectors need to scrutinise the work completed to date, but once their reports have been written, work can continue, and the property can be completed. Any litigation that follows may continue long after this, but at least by then your house will be built, and the technical problem put right. This kind of insurance policy is not cheap – typically costing €5,000 to €8,000, perhaps more. However, if something goes wrong and you are not insured, your project could be held up indefinitely.

ALSO AVAILABLE IN BEIGE: WHY ARE NEW HOUSES ALL THE SAME COLOUR?

Local planning regulations vary from one local area to another, but very often the stipulation will be that new houses must be finished in a beige or sand-coloured render. Some will prohibit the cladding of a house in stone facings, or the use of other natural materials. In a sense, this looks like the French 'good taste police' making sure a brand new 'lookalike' country cottage does not clash or confuse the appearance of the real thing. However, exceptions will be made to this rule – for instance if the house is of particular architectural interest. The message here is that new houses bought off-plan are likely to be compelled to use the familiar beige finish. But if you decide to hire an architect and create something more individual, you could find that the architect can argue a route around these strict planning rules.

MEASURING SURFACE AREA: 'SHON' AND 'SHOB'

Living space for tax and admin purposes is often referred to as so many square metres SHON, which stands for Surface Hors Oeuvres Net. It basically refers to the interior living areas of your house, and is calculated as follows: first, you measure the overall surface area defined by the external walls, adding up each storey, and adding any outbuildings. This is the SHOB, or Surface Hors Oeuvres Brut. Then you deduct certain parts (like your garage, rooms with ceilings below 1.8m, a covered terrace), to arrive at the SHON. This is commonly referred to as 'surface habitable.'

Listed buildings: aka Monuments Historiques

If you are looking for a house in France that is just oozing with history, you may find yourself tempted by a listed building. Grants are available for restoration work, but be warned: this is no cash cow. The work required can be expensive, and is sometimes tightly controlled by the authorities. It also involves an incredible amount of paperwork!

LISTED BUILDINGS

In France there are two categories of classification. **Monuments Historiques Classés** are the most interesting properties, designated because of their historical or artistic merits by the Minister of Cultural Affairs. At the next level down, you have **Monuments Historiques Inscrits**. These are properties registered on a so-called supplementary list of buildings, by order of the regional authorities.

Why classé, why inscrit?
Classé Here, a building is seen as being of public interest from an artistic and historical point of view. It is classified either entirely or in part, by the minister of cultural affairs.
Inscrit These are buildings or parts of buildings, either public or privately owned, which are of sufficient artistic or historical interest to justify preservation. They are registered on the supplementary list of *Monuments Historiques*.

How buildings are chosen
Numerous people or bodies can initiate the preservation process. **The state** can conclude, having assessed the merits of the building (looking at the history surrounding it, and where it is located) that it should be protected. Alternatively, its **owner** can apply for its protection, as can a **third party** (such as a village/town council, a local association or even a history buff who takes an interest in the property).

Requests for a protection order are submitted to the DRAC, or the *Direction Régionale des Affaires Culturelles*. The dossier required is then compiled by researchers from the CRMH, which is the *Conservation Régionale des Monuments Historiques*, and sent for approval to the *Commission Régionale du Patrimoine et des Sites* (the CRPS), which meets about twice a year. The CRPS will reject the request if it thinks the building is not interesting enough. If the request is accepted, the building is registered as protected on the supplementary list of historical monuments (the ISMH, or *Inventaire Supplémentaire des Monuments Historiques)*. The building is then said to be *inscrit*.

When the CRPS considers that the building could merit being *classé*, they send the dossier for the opinion of the higher commission of *Monuments Historiques*. If the full *classement* protection order is considered justified, the owner of the property will be invited to confirm their view of the matter in writing. In some instances a combined protection order can be established, with different parts of the same property being either *inscrit* or *classé*.

If the owner is not keen
If the property's owner rejects the *classement* order, the commission will again be called on to make a judgement, with the minister ratifying the decision.

If the owner digs their heels in, a protection order can be imposed by decree by a *Conseil d'Etat*. An *inscrit* protection order can also be made against the owner's wishes. If a building is considered to be under imminent threat, emergency procedures can be adopted by the minister, instructing the regional authorities to notify the owner. On receipt of this notification the protection order applies, running for a year, during which time the decision will be ratified or made permanent.

When a building is listed
Once registered as *classé* or *inscrit*, a considerable degree of protection and control over its destiny becomes inevitable. For example, it cannot be destroyed or modified, or receive works to restore or repair it without the prior consent of the Ministry of Culture. Similarly, it cannot be transferred, sold or altered without the minister being informed. Any works authorised to be undertaken on a *monument historique classé* must be done so under the administration's control. If the building is *inscrit*, however, you can still choose your own builders and craftsmen. Of particular interest is the fact that maintenance, repairs and restoration works can receive a state grant (see p203).

Planning constraints
Around both categories of *monuments historiques*, there is a protection zone of 500m

radius within which all new building, demolition, restoration or renovation, whoever proposes it, must be submitted for approval by the official *Architecte des Bâtiments de France (ABF)*. Even if they fall outside this zone, developments could still need permission if they are within the 'field of view' of the monument. There can, however, be exceptions to this rule, if the local council decides to draw up a '*zone de protection du patrimoine architectural urbain et paysage*' (a ZPPAUP in French jargon). This is basically what's known in the UK as a conservation area.

The conservation area (the ZPPAUP)

The locally derived ZPPAUPs were created by the law of January 7th 1983, modified ten years later, under which the local commune and state bodies redefine the blanket 500m zone into a specifically planned *zone de protection du patrimoine architectural urbain et paysage*. Drawing up the ZPPAUP is the work of the mairie, along with the ABF. Different zones are established, each with its own set of regulations. Following a public inquiry and approval by the CRPS, the ZPPAUP is integrated into the urban planning scheme (the PLU, or *Plan Local d'Urbanisme*). Once it

has been set up the ABF checks that each project meets the requirements of the local ZPPAUP.

Grants

The state may help to finance works needed for conservation, and the owner can also get tax relief to soften the impact of the building costs they face. For monuments historiques *classés*, grants of up to 50% might be authorised, but expect a maximum 20% upper limit for grants relating to buildings *inscrits*. However, these figures are the maximum. In practice, grants are unlikely to exceed 40% for *monuments classés* and 15% for *inscrits*. What's more, the cost of work is likely to be high, as owners are under tight control in terms of using original materials and craft skills. There is another source of funding. If works are approved that will be undertaken by young volunteer groups, state aid can be granted for the purchase of building materials and equipment. This could represent up to 50% of the costs for *monuments historiques*, *classé*, or 25% for *inscrits*.

Tax benefits

These can be applied for by the owner of a *monument historique classé* if they are deprived of its use. The starting point is to contact

the DRSF, or *Direction Régionale des Services Fiscaux*. There are a number of advantages available. Deductions from income tax can be made for the cost of works not covered by a state grant. A varying percentage of restoration work, management costs, and so on can be set against income tax. The amount you get depends in part on whether the building is open to the public or not, but the running costs of opening to the public can also be claimed against tax. Other benefits to the owner can be negotiated concerning, for example, maintenance of furniture, décor and contents in the event of guided visits, loan of premises for cultural events and so on.
Remember, though, that the owner of the protected building is responsible for its conservation. And you will not necessarily be able to get the maximum grants available to help you.

Getting works approved
1) Monuments Historiques Classés:

Although restoration works are exempt from planning permission, they do need to be declared in advance at the mairie, and need the authorisation of the Minister of Culture. The owner or the state administration can take the lead in scheduling necessary works. If state aid is paid, the work

will always be undertaken under the control of the Architecte en Chef des Monuments Historiques (ACMH) in charge regionally. Works will be scheduled according to an analysis of priorities (established annually) with the property owner agreeing in principle to finance their share of the cost. The DRAC then puts this to the *Préfet de Région* for approval. The technical and architectural aspects of the works schedule are the responsibility of the ACMH, but require the approval of the *Inspecteur Général des Monuments Historiques*.

Getting work under way

A contract signed by the state and by the owner is prepared, defining who is paying what. This requires the owner to pay his or her share within six months of the financial package being made available.
As soon as the finance is in place the ACMH can allow works to start, with the owner being the contracting body. However, the owner has to sign a contract with the ACMH and sign an agreement with the state, as well as signing a contract with the builder. The state takes control of ensuring the works undertaken match those contracted.
The state provides documentary evidence of the grant being made

Listed buildings: Restoration work

available before works start, and those funds will be transferred to the owner's account either during the works or at the finish. This means the owners can find themselves obliged to pay for the full works up front before receiving the grant. The maximum amount of grant aid is not predetermined by law, but will reflect the priority given to the building and the owner's commitment. There is nothing to stop owners seeking grants from other organisations in addition, the most common source being the département's *Conseil Général*.

Works approval: 'Inscrits':
Works are subject to planning permission (*permis de construire*) no matter how great or small the proposed works are. Approval of the usual bodies is needed but in addition the application dossier will be sent to the DRAC for the subsequent approval of the Minister of Culture. If approved, works will be executed under the owner's authority, under the control of a competent architect (preferably one specialised in restoration). The law fixes an upper limit of 40% grant aid, and the DRAC handles applications, approved at regional level. Works should not begin before the owner receives the grant. Once under way

the works will be checked for conformity by the department's *Architecte des Bâtiments de France* and certified on completion.

Archaeology: digging in
Any building that is either *classé* or *inscrit*, is considered to be an 'archaeological site'. Any works such as digging are therefore subject to a strict set of regulations. The law forbids anyone undertaking ground-works on their own land with the object of searching for edifices or objects of pre-historical, historical, artistic or archaeological interest without prior authorisation. A more recent law introduced in 1980 stipulates that anyone who intentionally destroys, damages or causes the deterioration of archaeological finds discovered during earthworks, or the land containing archaeological remains, faces a prison sentence of up to two years, and a hefty fine. A later law

extended this to limit use of unauthorised metal detectors too.

The organisation in charge of applying these rules and regulations, and of granting authorisations and control of 'digs' is the Service Régional de l'Archéologie (SRA).
As any work below ground level can endanger the various archaeological layers, considerable forward planning is necessary. Works such as re-excavating a ditch or moat, removing debris piled up over time, or looking for original floor levels, all require permission starting with an application (in the preceding year!) to the SRA. The SRA may instigate its own archaeological dig before any decision, negative or positive, is made, for the work that you intend to carry out on the site.
A similar approach applies to structures above ground level, again requiring SRA permission, following in some cases a comprehensive survey of the walls and the materials used in their construction.
The discovery of any objects or structures (while authorised works are under way) must immediately be notified to the SRA or alternatively the local mairie. This situation eventually leads to the Ministry of Culture bringing in the archaeologists to take a look at what you have found.

Still interested?
For many, the appeal of owning a listed building, of living in a place oozing with history is strong. However, what you should not believe is that a *monument historique* will in some way open the door to a wealth of grants and tax concessions to help you complete a renovation. For one thing, tax relief will only help you if you pay tax in France (that is, if you are a resident earning your living). But also the various grants that are available may not compensate you for the extra costs involved in the restoration work.
With *classé* buildings, you start to give up control over the programming and quality of the work required to the ABF, which will insist on very high standards, and big budgets to match.
This is less the case with *inscrit* buildings, where you will have more scope to choose your own builders and craftsmen.
The other crucial factor is that while the grant structure is well-established, and you may indeed be eligible for a grant, you may not get any funding at all simply because there is no money in the budget.
All this is a major challenge, then, and is as much about dealing with the multi-layered French bureaucracy as it is about creating an exciting restoration project.

THE GRANT THAT NEVER COMES

Being eligible for a grant is one thing. But actually getting a grant is another. In some cases, you could find that while your restoration project is impressive and everybody loves your historic house, AND you are eligible for a grant...cash simply never comes. The regional fund to help people restore properties like yours could simply be empty!

A trip to a decent builder's merchant in France can show you an interesting range of building materials that will suddenly make your job a lot easier. In the next few pages, we look at building blocks for both partition walls and structural walls, and also take a look at stone. And we wrap up this section with a cocktail of termites, staircases, ventilation, and swimming pool security.

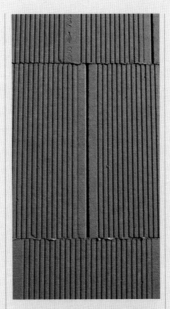

BRICKS AND BLOCKS

Partition wall materials

There is a wide choice in materials if you need to create partition walls. The most common is plasterboard on a metal frame, though block-based walls, which tend to cost more, have good performance in terms of insulation and noise reduction. The denser and heavier the wall material, the better its sound insulating qualities. However sound 'deadening' is important too – so mixes of plasterboard or block walls incorporating some kind of soft insulating material are also effective.

Honeycomb partition panels
Cloisons alvéolaires
The cheapest and simplest option, these are made of two sheets of plasterboard, with a honeycomb structure sandwiched in the middle. They are quick and cheap to put up, but are not strong on sound insulation and are around half the weight of some of the block-built walls described below.

Plasterboard
Plaques de plâtre, or 'placo'
Two sheets of plasterboard screwed to a rigid framework (*ossature*) which can be made of wood or metal (the latter is better for stability) and carrying a thick wad of insulation between the two boards. Pipework or power cables can also go in the space between the plasterboards. Boards are available in thicknesses between 1 cm and 1.8 cm, and sizes up to about 3 m by 1.25 m. For high performance sound insulation, you could install **two metal frameworks** next to each other, adding insulation to each, and for extra performance, use a double layer of plasterboard on each side. The plasterboard option is ideal for building partitions on wood floors, as the weight is spread evenly. A variant of this system is a different kind of board called *fibrociment* which is much more waterproof than plaster, and better for dry-lining a damp wall, or for creating new partitions around a bathroom. If you are going to create a partition wall that will be exposed to humidity, then check for the French norm markings: NF CTB-H for boards that can deal with humidity, and NF CTB-S for those that can't.

Plaster blocks
Carreaux de plâtre
Very popular in France, these measure around 66 cm by 50 cm, and give a solid wall with good acoustic qualities, and are a good support for shelving and fitments. Widths vary from 4 cm to 15 cm, and they come in a range of sizes, from about 40–50 cm wide right up to a full metre in width, and up to about 50 cm high. They are built using a plaster-based mortar which holds them together. They are available as a 'regular' block as well as special versions and are colour coded for easy recognition. These include two levels of waterproofing (green and blue blocks), an extra tough version, lightweight versions and even one with integrated insulation. If you need to integrate wiring into these blocks, you will need to cut in a channel – affecting your choice of block thickness. As they are relatively heavy once built up, they are better on a very solid floor that can bear the weight – ideally concrete.

Cellular concrete blocks
Béton cellulaire
Easy to saw into shape, these blocks mean easy bricklaying for a first time

Bricks & blocks: Exterior walls

DIY–er, and the resulting wall will have great acoustic qualities. The blocks are made of a mix of, among other ingredients, sand, lime and cement, and are between 5 cm and 12.5 cm thick. They are a fairly large format, at around 40 cm by 60cm or even longer, making them quick to put up. The surface can be left unfinished (though it will need sealing to avoid powder coming off) or it can be plastered or papered. Again, if you need to integrate wiring into these blocks, you will need to chase in a channel. This wall system works well on a solid floor.

Terracotta blocks and tiles
Briques et carreaux en terre cuite

Brick is a good material to use for interior walls, though it is heavy and more costly than some of the other options. However, it will give you good acoustic insulation, and help keep you warm in the winter and cool in the summer. Thicknesses vary from around 3 cm to 12 cm. The tile versions are fairly large – with the standard tile size being 66 cm by 50 cm. The bricks however come in a variety of sizes up to 25 cm by 50 cm, and are typically twice as long as they are wide. Whether you use bricks or tiles for internal walls, they are fixed together with plaster rather than cement. Some versions include an insulator sealed in the middle of the brick, which creates an excellent acoustic barrier. As terracotta is resistant to water, it is a good material for bathroom projects too. The bricks have a hollow structure – allowing you to insert ducts or electric wires into the fabric of the wall. However, their weight means they are best installed on a solid floor.

BUILDING EXTERIOR WALLS

French style bricks

If you drive past building sites in France, you will see a wide range of different materials used to build houses, depending on where you are. Walls are made of solid bricks in the north of the country, structures of concrete blocks more or less everywhere, and, in the warmer parts of France, walls are made of lightweight terracotta blocks. Both the terracotta and concrete blocks are designed to be covered with a render on the outside, and dry-lined on the inside.

Hollow brick
Brique creuse

Terracotta block is the building material that is least known to builders from the UK and some other northern European countries, but it is an effective and quick means of building a house. The typical block is known as 'hollow brick' or *brique creuse* and has horizontal perforations right through it, end to end. They are typically 40cm long, 25cm in width, and come in a range of heights from just 8cm to 30cm. Their size makes them quicker to build than ordinary solid bricks, while they have better thermal qualities than concrete blocks. The joints between the bricks are fine, making them quick to dry.

The outer face of the brick is rendered once the build is complete, with a cement or lime-based render. Inside, a layer of insulation is fitted, followed by the interior wall, built from one of the panel or blockwork materials described above.

Monomur

An even quicker technique is becoming popular – the so-called *Monomur* system, which as the name suggests, is a 'single wall'. This terracotta brick is also hollow, but much wider this time – up to 37cm. It has vertical, rather than horizontal, perforations, which are much finer than those of the hollow brick, and which act as insulation. This means that this single layer of brick does not need an additional layer of insulation inside the house. It has been designed to take a 'breathable' lime-based render on the outer face, and a coat of plaster on the interior – which is the finishing coat for your interior walls. The blocks have been developed as a system, incorporating special shapes to go round window openings, and U-shaped blocks that can be built in a line and then filled with concrete and reinforcement bars (*chainage*) to create a lintel. It's clever stuff.

Breeze blocks
Parpaings

Concrete blocks are a familiar material to many DIY builders, and in France they are similar to those throughout Europe. Some are now available with an inner filling of insulation, which enables them to behave a bit like the *Monomur* described above: the interior wall in such cases does not need extra insulation, but can simply be dry-lined with plasterboard, or plastered. Various types are available, allowing reinforcement bars to be inserted where necessary.

Cellular concrete blocks

These are bigger, tougher and heavier versions of the blocks described (see p205) for building interior partitions. Like breeze blocks, these are easy to cut and manipulate, but are heavier and have better thermal and acoustic insulating qualities. Again, special shapes are widely available.

BUYING STONE

A wealth of choice

If you are renovating or repairing traditional stone walls, you may need to get hold of some extra stone. If you are lucky, you might be able to salvage some on your own property, free of charge, from a derelict outbuilding, or use the stone you recover from demolishing a wall or opening up a new window. This kind of stone, known as rubble stone, (*moëllons*) is the cheapest and easiest to find. Your local masons may be able to get hold of it for you, or alternatively you could ask local farmers, or put an ad in the local café in your village. Sometimes it will be free of charge to whoever can take it away, but regional scarcity may make it rare, and pricey.

Local quarries will also be an

obvious source – but remember that the stuff could arrive in a 20-tonne articulated tipper lorry, which will need easy and safe access to your property and somewhere convenient to drop the stone. If you can look further afield, there are major stone suppliers in France that will supply any kind of stone anywhere in France. Some people also import Cotswold stone into France from the UK, to the areas where it appears to match the local stone. Some French stone is even exported to the USA.

New walls in old stone

Your project may require a new external wall which you want built in traditional stone. A modern variant on the techniques employed a hundred or so years ago is to build the supporting structural wall from concrete blocks (see p206) which will support the roof and upper floors. This blockwork wall is then clad in traditional stone. This is not a question of stick-on stone facings, as you actually build a proper stone wall right next to the blockwork wall, usually leaving a small air gap for insulation and as a barrier against damp. (Sometimes, builders will recommend clipping a damp-proof barrier against the blockwork wall too, or painting on a bituminous paint, if damp is a big potential problem. This can also depend on what you want to use the building for.)

The stone wall is then built up with a traditional lime or cement based mortar, ideally with the joints pointed up generously to create a flattish 'buttered' surface, often brushed or sponged over when starting to set. Local practice may of course dictate joints that highlight every stone, but an advantage of this former technique is that it is quicker to finish, while still looking authentic.

Dressed stone

If you are renovating or repairing a rubble-stone wall, then in some rural settings, rough stone around the windows and doorways will look perfectly OK. However, you may need to get hold of stone which has been cut (*taillée*) on one or several faces to create a cleaner

look. There are two options here. One is to get stone cut to size using a building firm that offers *maçonnerie en pierre* or *taille de pierre,* which both imply the firm has stone-cutting skills and the right equipment and suppliers. Some firms will even be able to 'distress' the stone so that it looks more weathered.

The alternative is to try to find window or door surrounds at a salvage yard or by just asking around. This approach is better suited to creating a new window or door opening (where the opening is made to exactly fit the stone facings that you have found).

The prices of new stone versus reclaimed stone are not that far apart. A big window surround, measuring about 1 m by 1.8 m, with a bit of carved detailing on it, could cost around €1,500 at a salvage yard. And it could set you back a similar amount if cut from new stone too.

Finding the right people

Most French masons will tell you they can build a good stone wall using rubble stone, though some will be better and quicker at this than others.

If a building company carries out renovation or restoration as part of its bread-and-butter work, it is likely they will have a team that can do decent stonework effectively.

Basics: Stone, termites, and ventilation

If the company's focus is more on new build, they may be less keen to take the job on.

When it comes to dressed stone, you will find that the services of a company offering *taille de pierre* (as described above) will do the job. However, the top-notch craftsman, who can cut stone and also carve it, is known as a *tailleur de pierre* (see box, left).

A worthwhile investment?
Adding a stonework feature to your renovation project – such as a carved lintel or door surround – could cost a few thousand euros, but can be a valuable addition to your property if it forms part of a good quality renovation. When you come to sell, it will make your house stand out from the crowd.

Alternatively, if you are planning to rent your property and you have space, say, for just a few photos on a website or brochure, a good close-up shot of a carved stone feature will add instant appeal.

However, don't go overboard. You won't have to be completely historically correct, but try to get the stonework to feel like it really is part of the house. And make sure it is visible enough if it is meant to be a selling point, not hidden away somewhere in a downstairs loo.

NOT QUITE THE OLDEST PROFESSION

Given half a chance, a tailleur de pierre would carve small gothic creatures into your stone lintel. These craftsmen can make replicas of anything you might spot on an ancient chateau or cathedral, and have continued a traditional skill that is a thousand years old. It is a sad fact that despite the rarity and skill of these people, they often earn little more than the general building labourers working alongside them.

TERMITES, ASBESTOS AND LEAD

A clean bill of health
Termites are a problem in France, especially in the south. Thanks to French law, areas where buildings are prone to contamination have been identified and documented. This is supposed to protect home buyers, as it obliges vendors to produce a certificate to prove the property is termite-free. Only if the house has been certified with an *état des lieux* by a recognised termite expert can you rest assured that, at the time of the test, the house was indeed termite-free. Similar legislation has been designed for other health hazards: asbestos and lead.

Termite avoidance

To make sure your house, once you have bought it, is not invaded by termites, you need to take some simple precautions. First of all, make sure the house is well ventilated and dry. Second, avoid stocking firewood against an external wall, or near kitchen waste or a rubbish sack. And third, treat the house itself with insecticide – especially floors and the base of the walls. Treat any exposed wood both on the surface, and through its interior, via an injection until it is saturated.

Detection
Termites avoid light, so they are difficult to detect. Often, it is only because of the damage they cause that their presence is known.

Here are three tests that will help to find them:

1) Probe wooden surfaces to find out if they are flaking or cracking.

2) Scratch off any filler that has been applied, to see if it hides worm holes.

3) Take a close look at plaster, especially ceilings. If you find small circles – around 2 mm in diameter – these are likely to be 'ventilation ducts' of the termites' network of tunnels.

If any of the above tests are positive, you will need to call in an expert, as this is the only way you will get the all-important certification once the bugs have been eradicated.

VENTILATION AND HUMIDITY

Mechanical systems
Holiday homes have a difficult life. One moment they are being opened up for occupation, heated and ventilated to create a warm welcoming environment.

And the next they are shut down for weeks or even months on end. These periods of inoccupation can cause trouble: damp and mould, peeling wallpaper, black spots on the walls in the corners.

So how can you avoid this? Obviously, if the heating was left on all the time, you would go some way to drying the walls and cold spots. But this is hardly feasible if you don't live there, and in any case, it may not even solve the problem.

The priority is to get rid of water vapour that is hanging around in your house. If you are carrying out a renovation of the entire house, it is worth considering some kind of ventilation system. There are two kinds.

Ventilation Mécanique Controlée (VMC) consists of a system of entry and exit points for air to circulate, with a fan system that switches on automatically at a given level of humidity. A more complex system is *Ventilation Mécanique Ponctuelle (VMP)*, which works on a room by room basis, rather than across the whole house, again with the airflow taken care of automatically.

Dehumidifiers

Of course, if you don't want to get involved with ducts, extractors and so on, the simpler solution is to buy a dehumidifier. A wide range are available.

The cheapest use chemical salt in a plastic container, collecting water which needs emptying from time to time, while the high performance electric versions dry and circulate the air. However, the smaller salt-based systems are not sufficient on their own to deal with serious humidity problems.

RENOVATING A STAIRCASE

An ancient staircase may be full of charm, but it can also be risky or inconvenient, especially a wooden one that creaks at night and wakes your guests.

Nevertheless that staircase, full of character and as old as the house itself should be retained, if you possibly can.

Worn, cracked and creaking

If a staircase is too worn out for safety, whether it's made of timber or stone (or even a hybrid in wood, plaster & terracotta tile), get some quotes from the specialists.

This could be for major repairs, with the complete removal and re-fitting of some sections.

Or you may prefer to get a replica made, to bring it in line with better safety standards. After all, just because

a new industrially made staircase may prove cheaper, that's no reason for scrapping original features. If your stairs are beyond repair, or you want to completely reorganise the layout of your house, then this may mean you have to put the stairs in a new location, or redesign it entirely. Think through the logic of your overall scheme.

If your project theme emphasises restoration, look at designs, perhaps very locally, that will be more authentic.

If your renovation has some bold use of space but without really becoming something 'contemporary', then there are many different materials and configurations available.

Choices, choices

A well-designed bespoke staircase will usually appear simple when finished, but the choices are vast. You could use pine, oak, elm or a number of other woods in straight, 90° and 180° turns, and even spiral.

Reinforced concrete is another option, as is cladding with new or antique stone (such as limestone or slate), terracotta, modern tiles, or a painted mortar. You could even go for solid blocks of slate or limestone for both interior and exterior use.

There is also a wide choice for hand-rails, which could be made from painted natural plaster over blockwork, or wrought iron or steel in waxed rust finish, or stainless steel, or wood.

A new staircase

A 'standard' staircase is generally between 2.72 m and 2.81 m, and has 13 to 15 steps. In all cases, unless it incorporates some kind of landing, it should have no more than 20 steps in total. Depending on your budget, you can buy a pre-fabricated staircase or have one made to measure – though in most older houses, a ready–made staircase may need a bit of work to fit securely, probably requiring a plinth below it.

As for which wood to choose, this again depends on budget. Oak is by far the most hard-wearing, and offers a wide choice of finishes (waxed, oiled and so on), but will probably cost up to €15,000 for a bespoke version.

A ready-made standard staircase in oak could be €5,000, while something similar in beech or ash, which will give a slightly more contemporary feel, could cost between €2,000 and €4,000.

Finally, if you are looking for a cheap staircase to a mezzanine or attic room, a basic ready–made pine model could be the perfect option. They can cost as little as €400 or €500 from a building supplies centre.

THE TOP STAIR

This may sound obvious, but sometimes people forget: when calculating how many stairs you need in a new staircase, don't forget that the top stair is actually the floor of the upper level of your house. So you may count 14 steps going upstairs, but the staircase itself only has 13.

Basics: Swimming pool safety

With swimming pools becoming ever more widespread in France, so too, tragically, have drowning accidents. This prompted the French government to bring in, effective from 2004, a new law governing pool safety.

Safety systems, by law
The law relates only to pools built into the ground (*piscines enterrées*). It states that all pools, for private use or for use in holiday accommodation, must have a security system built in. From May 2004, a pool builder is required to indicate, in writing, what kind of security system will be used. The four types are explained below.

Timescale for action
If you have a pool on your property which was completed before 1 January 2004, you will need to install one of the approved security systems by 1 January 2006, provided there is a system that can be adapted for use for the kind of pool which you have installed.
For properties which are to be rented, security systems need to be in place by May 2004. The fine for failing to comply is a hefty €45,000.

Four techniques
There are four main options for security, each covered by a lengthy document available (for a fee) from the French technical standards agency, AFNOR. These are really guidelines for the manufacturers and suppliers of the various systems. The main question you should have if you are getting a security system installed is: does it meet the relevant norms? If the security system does not meet the standards, your insurance company will not insure the pool.

1) Enclosures and fences
Gates, fences and other barriers need a height between foot-holds of at least 1.1 m, with railings less than 102 mm apart. Child-proof safety locks must be fitted to the gates, and the fences made of a material that makes them impossible for children under five to climb over. Spikes are not allowed, as these could also cause injury. Expect to pay less than €100 per linear metre for this kind of fencing.

2) Alarm systems
These will either cover the perimeter area of the pool (and so will be set off if someone approaches the edge) or they will be activated when someone falls into the water. Obviously, alarms do not prevent children falling into the water, and will serve no purpose unless the pool is being supervised by someone very close by at all times. This will be a factor that the insurance companies (and the law, should an accident ever happen) will be careful to examine. You could probably buy and fit such an alarm from €700.

3) Security pool covers
These are completely different from a floating cover designed to keep the sun off the water in the summer. Security covers have special fixings all round the pool, and are rigid enough to support the weight of an adult. Typical examples are PVC slatted covers that roll up at one end of the pool, or others that are strengthened with aluminium bars. These could cost from around €5,000 to supply and install.

4) Pool shelters
These can be big enough to create an 'indoor pool' atmosphere when closed, and can be fixed or removable, telescopic or even inflatable. Again, they must be strong enough to prevent anyone falling through the structure, and secure enough not to be opened.

Can't beat adult supervision
All these techniques can prevent accidents, but will still demand a high level of vigilance and discipline in utilising them. Opening and closing a pool cover or shelter is not difficult, but doing so several times a day could become an unwelcome chore that is eventually overlooked. A security gate could be left open or an alarm may sound when no-one is around to hear it. In effect, these security measures can only help to prevent accidents, but will not guarantee against them happening. When it comes to swimming pools, supervision of young children, by adults who can swim, is essential.

THE DEADLINES

There are two important deadlines for getting your pool safety sorted out.

May 2004: The date by which owners of properties being rented out to the public must put in place safety measures conforming to the new AFNOR norms, if the pool was completed before January 1st 2004.

January 2006: This is the deadline for private householders to get their pool safety in line with the new norms (again, this is for pools built before January 1st 2004).

Pools built after January 1st 2004 must be designed to comply with the new safety laws, whether they are for public or private use.

Getting to grips with the French language while running a renovation project is a tall order. So here are a few words that relate to some of the things we have been talking about in this book. This short selection is taken from AS Lindsey's useful **Concise Dictionary of House Building Terms**, which has more than 10,000 words or phrases, arranged by trades, in both languages. (For order details see p220). But if this is all getting a bit too technical, we have also added a few tips on **how to make friends** with your new French neighbours!

ENGLISH TO FRENCH

Acrow prop
étrésillon m à vis ; étrésillon m à verin
air gap
couche f d'air
angle bead
baguette f d'angle
architrave
chambranle m; architrave f
asbestos
amiante m
ballcock
robinet m à flotteur
band of foam rubber
bande f de mousse
banisters
rampe f d'escalier
barrow
brouette f
base
fondation f;soubassement m
basic area of the house
surface f hors oeuvre nette
batten
liteau m ;tasseau m
be out of true (to)
porter v à faux
beam, exposed
poutre f apparente
bed of concrete
lit m de béton
blade
lame f
bleed-tap (of radiator)
purgeur m
block, breeze
parpaing m aggloméré; aggloméré m
block, cellular concrete
bloc m de béton cellulaire
block, concrete, with air channels
parpaing m
board, warped
planche f voilée
boarded ceiling
plafond m en lambris
bolt
boulon m
boring
percement m; perçage m
botch (to)
bâcler v
boundary fence
clôture f de bornage
boundary limit
borne f
box-spanner
clé f à douille
bracket (for shelf)
liteau m (d'étagère)
brick (to)
maçonner v
brick, hollow
brique f creuse

brick, solid
brique f pleine
building permit
permis m de construire
building site
chantier m de construction
building (with doors and windows completed)
mise hors d'air (la)
building stage (with roof completed)
mise hors d'eau (la)
building surveyor
géomètre m du cadastre
bulge (to) (eg wall)
bomber v
burning off (eg paint)
décapage m
cable duct
conduit m gaine f
carpentry
menuiserie f
casement-fastener (in wall)
agrafe f; attache f
casing (of door or window)
dormant m
ceiling, false or suspended
faux-plafond m
cement rough render
crépi m
central heating
chauffage m central
chasing
rainurage m
chimney cowl with rain protector
aspirateur m statique
chimney stack
souche f
chipboard
aggloméré m; panneau m de particules
chippings
gravillons mpl
coat, skimming
couche f de finition
coating, exterior
enduit m de façade
coating, waterproof
revêtement m impermeable
coffered ceiling
plafond m à caissons
concrete cast in situ
béton m banché
concrete mixer
bétonnière f
concrete, precast
béton m precoulé
concrete, reinforced
béton armé m ; B.A. abb
connecting the telephone
raccordement m au réseau
connecting to the drains
raccordement aux égouts
conservatory
jardin m d'hiver

construction fault/damage
vice m de construction
convert (to)
aménager v
coping
chaperon m; crête f; couronnement m
cornice
corniche f
course, damp-proof
couche f d'étanchéité; couche f isolant imperméable
covering for underside of a roof
sous-toiture f
crack
lézarde f ; fente f ; fissure f
crushed rock/stone
roche f concassée
dado (wall)
lambris d'appui m
damp-proofing
isolation f contre l'humidité
deadline
délai m (d'exécution)
debris
décombres mpl
delay
délai m
delivery date
délai m de livraison
detailed specification
cahier m des charges dtaill
details of implementation
modalités fpl de mise en oeuvre
distemper
badigeon m
district
commune f
double door or gate
porte f à deux battants
double glazing
double vitrage m
downpipe
chute f; descente f
downpipe, cast iron
chute f en fonte
dry rot
pourriture f sèche
earth (elect)
terre f ; sol m
earthenware drainpipe
conduit m en grés
estimate
devis m
excavator
pelleteuse f
expansion joint
joint de dilatation m; joint glissant
extension of time
prolongation de temps f
face of wall
parement m d'un mur

facing south, north etc
expos au sud/nord etc
fault (due to bad workmanship)
malfaçon f
felt, roofing
carton m bitumé
fibrocement
fibrociment m
fire-proofing agent
ignifuge m
fitting-out
aménagement m
flagstone
dalle f
floor covering
revêtement m du sol
floor joist
solive f de plancher
floor, heated
plancher m chauffant
flue
conduit m de cheminée
foreman
chef m d'équipe
foul water piping/sewer
tuyauterie f des eaux usées
foundation trench
tranchée f de fondation
foundations and walls
gros oeuvre f
french window
porte-fenêtre f
gable
pignon m
G-clamp
bride f à capote ; serre-joint m de maçon
get-out clauses (buying a house)
conditions suspensives
glass fibre
fibre f de verre
glazing
vitrerie f; vitrage m
glue gun
pistolet m à colle
grout
coulis m
habitable floor area
surface hors oeuvre nette f; surface habitable f
half-timbered
colombage m
hand-rail
lisse f ; garde-corps m
hardening interval
délai m de durcissement
hinge
charnière f
hook (to)
agrafer v
hot water tank
ballon m d'eau chaude
house survey
visite d'expert f

imperviousness
étanchéité f
instructions
prescriptions fpl
insulating plasterboard
plaque de plâtre f
placoplâtre m (marque commerciale)
insulation, sound
isolation f acoustique; isolation f phonique
insulation, thermal
isolation thermique f
insurance against building faults
assurance f dommage-ouvrage
invoice
facture f
ironmongery
quincaillerie f
joinery
menuiserie f
kitchen unit
élément m de cuisine
labour
main-d'oeuvre f
lag (to)
calorifuger v ; garnir v
land on which one can build
terrain constructible m
land registry
cadastre m
landscaping
aménagements mpl paysagers
lawn (smooth, well kept)
gazon m anglais
lead flashing (roof)
revêtement m de plomb
lean-to
appentis m
lime, hydraulic
chaux f hydraulique
lime, non-hydraulic
chaux f aérienne
lining for flue (metal liner)
tubage m
loadbearing element
élément m porteur
main drain (sewage)
grand collecteur m; égout m collecteur ; collecteur m à l'égout
mains drainage
tout-à-l'égout m
manhole cover
plaque f d'égout
mansard roof
comble m mansardé ; mansarde f; toit m à la mansarde
marble slab
plaque f de marbre
measuring tape
mètre m à ruban

membrane, damp-proof
membrane f d'étanchéité
mesh framework (for concrete reinforcement)
ferraillage m
methods of payment
modalités fpl de paiement
mildew
moisissure f
mineral fibre
fibre f minérale
mixing tray (eg for mortar)
bac m à gâcher
mortar
mortier m
mortar, bonding
mortier m de liaison
mortar, masonry
mortier m normal
moulding
moulure f
noise reduction
réduction f de bruit
nozzle, nose-piece
buse f
out of square
hors d'équerre
outline specification
devis m préliminaire
overmantel (fireplace)
trumeau m
owner (commissioning building work)
maître m d'ouvrage
paint, masonry
peinture f crépie
panel, insulation, faced both sides
panneau 'sandwich' m
panelling
lambrissage m ; boiserie f
partition
cloison f
paving
dallage m; pavage m
penalty clause
clause f pénale
piling
pilotage m; pilotis m
pipe, overflow
tuyau m de trop-plein
pipework
canalisation f ; tuyauterie f
pipework installation
travaux mpl de canalisation
pitch
bitume m
pitch of roof
chute f de comble ; pente f
planing machine
raboteuse f
plaster filling between ceiling joists
auget m
plywood
bois m contreplaqué

HOW TO CONVERT NEIGHBOURS INTO FRIENDS.

You don't have to be brilliant at French to get on well with your new neighbours in France. When the building work on your house is coming along nicely, here are some ideas for building up your links with the local community too.

1 Language This needs patience on both sides. Throughout this book we have recommended that for important technical stuff, you need to get a good French and English speaker to help you. Socially, though, don't worry about feeling awkward or completely failing to understand what someone is saying to you. A smile will usually help things along. When talking to a French person who understands English, give them a break by speaking just a little more slowly and clearly. Avoid cockney rhyming slang, too.

2 Mingle One of your first duties when settling in your new area is to introduce yourself to your new neighbours (and eventually the *maire*). French people can be particularly friendly and helpful if you know how to get on the right side of them.

3 Be polite This simply comes down to saying 'Bonjour Monsieur' or 'Madame' when you meet people. It's best to avoid speaking to people abruptly in a language they do not understand, even if you are just remarking on the nice weather. You will make friends quickly if you show your efforts to learn French and talk with your French neighbours. You may know that in

France there is the polite form of you (*vous*) and the more informal version (*tu*) which is also used with children. For an adult, use the *vous* form until you get to know each other better, and don't insist on being called by your first name. It might sound pushy. Be prepared to shake hands on greeting or on leaving: it is seen as a much more informal gesture than in Britain.

4 Kiss people! The first time you meet people, you will probably shake hands. With many French people, you will always keep this habit. However, in some regions, you may find you are encouraged to start kissing the second time you meet. So to be ready for it, see our tips on p215.

5 Be generous Come back from your home country with presents (such as whisky or other such specialities like shortbread, but perhaps not baked beans). Offer flowers (but not wine, usually) to your hostess when invited to a meal, and be generous with your time too, when it comes to aperitifs or meals with neighbours.

6 Inviting neighbours for a meal Be ready to give away all your recipes and to speak about food for hours, especially specialities

pneumatic drill
marteau m piqueur
pointing
jointoiement m
pointing tool, flat
fer m à joint plat
postponement
remise f
power point (plug/socket)
prise f de courant
prior notice
préavis m
progress of building work
déroulement m des travaux
progress report
compte-rendu m
project manager
maître m d'oeuvre
propping
étayage m; étayement m
put in a window pane (to)
poser v une vitre

putty (to)
mastiquer v
rafter
chevron m
ready-mix concrete
béton prêt à l'emploi m
reconditioning
remise f en état
refilling (eg cracks)
rebouchage m
reinforced concrete beam
poutre en béton armé f
reinforced concrete slab
dalle en béton armé f
reinforcement (concrete)
armature f
removal of formwork
décoffrage m
render, rough (to)
hourder v
rendering of facade
enduit de façade m

resurface (to)
refaire la surface v
ridge beam
madrier m de faîtage
ridge tile
faîtière f ; tuile f faîtière
right to pump water
droit m de puisage
risk of sinking
risque d'enfoncement m
Rockwool (TM)
laine f minérale de roche
roof board, roof sheathing
volige f
roof space
comble m
roof truss/trussing
ferme f ; armature f à toit
roof-light
vélux m (TM); vasistas m
rough sketch
ébauche f ; esquisse f

...IN TEN EASY STEPS!

from your region where you come from. (OK, make them up if you don't think you have any).

7 For men in the countryside Never refuse to follow the French menfolk into the wine cellar for a traditional chat and taste of the maturing wine, and don't forget to take your coat: you could be there for hours and it will be chilly. Sometimes, the custom is to have just one small glass, which is filled and handed to one man, who drains it and hands it back to the '*patron*'. When you have the glass, it's your cue to be in the conversation spotlight, so if you speak a bit of French, have something to say about Royal family gossip. The French expect Brits to know about this. Talk about your planned renovation works, but don't flaunt

the money you're spending on it: you will bore them to death and they might think you are a rich show-off. Much better to ask them about projects they have done, or for advice, or about good builders they know.

8 Little and often Regular short visits to see neighbours are good, such as popping around to drop off a basket of home-grown beans. This is better than ringing in advance to plan some kind of 'official' visit.

9 The right aperitifs Find out what your neighbours have on offer, and get something similar, so they can feel at home when they visit. Whisky and port are both served as aperitifs, rather than after a meal. Don't forget the tasty crackers to pass around. The trick is to circulate them, rather than parking them in front of you and wolfing down the whole lot.

10 How to say goodbye There are many, many ways to say goodbye in French, and it can become fairly long and drawn out. Don't consider that saying a simple '*A bientôt*' (See you soon!) will be enough. The ritual will last for a few minutes, which will seem to be hours if you have run out of inspiration.
The box on the right has a few examples. In the meantime, we are sure you will forge many close and fruitful friendships with your new French community. *A bientôt!*

---

rub down (to)
poncer v
rubble
blocaille
rustproofing
traitement m antirouille
sagging
flexion f
sander
ponceuse f
sandstone
grès m
sash window
fenêtre f à guillotine
saw-blade
feuille f de scie
scafflod boards
platelage m d'échafaud
scaffolding
échafaud m; échafaudage m
screed
chape f

screed, floating
chape f flottante
screed, levelling layer of
chape f d'arase
scrim
bande f à joint
settlement (eg of ground)
tassement m
settlement of account
arrêté m de compte
settlement of an invoice)
règlement m
sewage disposal
assainissement m
sheet, corrugated metal
tôle f ondulée
shingle
bardeau m
shoring up
blindage m
shower tray
bac m de douche

silicone sealant pistol
pistolet m pour mastic
sill
appui m
site with services laid on
terrain m viabilisé
size (of land area)
contenance f
skip
benne f
skirting
plinthe f
slab, concrete
dalle f
space between joists
solin m
spanner
clef f; clé f
stair cavity, stair well
jour m
stake
piquet m

start of building work
ouverture f de chantier
steel joist
solive f en acier
steel wool
laine f d'acier
stopcock
robinet m d'arrêt
structure
construction f
supply (eg of gas, water)
alimentation f (en gaz, eau)
survey report
levé m de géomètre
surveyor
géomètre m
tank
citerne f
taps and fittings
robinetterie f
tarpaulin
bâche f
tenure
jouissance f
tie-beam
entrait m
tile adhesive
ciment m colle
time for consideration
délai m de réflexion
to draw up a contract (to)
rédiger v un contrat
tread width (stairs)
emmarchement m
trowel
truelle f
truss
ferme f
turf (to)
gazoner
under-floor space
vide sanitaire m
underpinning
sous-oeuvre m
valley (roof)
noue f
vaulted/arched ceiling
plafond voûté m
veneer
placage m
wall, partition
cloison f
wall, retaining
mur m de retenue
wallplug
cheville f
washer
rondelle f
water-tightness
étanchéité f
wire brush
brosse f métallique
woodworm holes
vermoulure f
zinc flashing (roof)
revêtement m de zinc

FRENCH TO ENGLISH

aggloméré m; panneau m de particules
chipboard
agrafe f; attache f
casement-fastener (in wall)
agrafer v
hook (to)
alimentation f (en gaz, en eau)
supply (eg of gas, water)
aménagement m
fitting-out
aménagements mpl paysagers
landscaping
aménager v
convert (to)
amiante m
asbestos
appentis m
lean-to
appui m
sill
armature f
reinforcement (for concrete)
arrêté m de compte
settlement of account
aspirateur m statique pare-pluie
chimney cowl with rain protector
assainissement m
sewage disposal
assurance f dommage-ouvrage
insurance against building faults
auget m
filling between ceiling joists
bac m à gâcher
mixing tray (eg for mortar)
bac m de douche
shower tray
bâche f
tarpaulin
bâcler v
botch (to)
badigeon m
lime-based distemper
baguette f d'angle
angle bead
ballon m d'eau chaude
hot water tank
bande f à joint
scrim
bande f de mousse
band of foam rubber
bardeau m
shingle
benne f
skip
béton armé m
concrete, reinforced
béton m banché
concrete cast in situ

BEST 'BYES

If you want to add a bit of variety when you say **goodbye** to people, here are some you can try out.

Bon courage!
(Good luck)
Bon week-end!
(You can guess this one)
A plus tard!
(See you soon)
Bonne fin d'après-midi!
(Have a good rest of the afternoon)
Bonne rentrée!
(All the best for the return to work after the holidays)
Bonne baignade!
(Enjoy the swim)
Bonne promenade!
(Enjoy your walk)
Bon retour!
(Have a good journey back)
Bonne sieste!
(Have a good nap)
Bon bricolage!
(Good luck with your DIY!)

Language Lab: Glossary: French to English

béton m precoulé
concrete, precast
béton prêt à l'emploi m
ready-mix concrete
bétonnière f
concrete mixer
bitume m
pitch
blindage m
shoring up
bloc m de/en béton cellulaire
block, cellular concrete
blocaille
rubble
bois m contreplaqué
plywood
bomber v
bulge (to) (eg wall)
borne f
boundary limit
boulon m
bolt
bride f à capote ; serre-joint m de maçon
G-clamp
brique f creuse
brick, hollow
brique f pleine
brick, solid
brosse f métallique
wire brush
brouette f
barrow
buse f
nozzle, nose-piece
cadastre m
land registry
cahier m des charges
detailed specification
calorifuger v ; garnir v
lag (to)
canalisation f ; tuyauterie f
pipework
carton m bitumé
felt, roofing
chambranle m; architrave f
architrave
chantier m de construction
building site
chape f
screed
chape f d'arase
screed, levelling layer of
chape f flottante
screed, floating
chaperon m; crête f;
couronnement m
coping
charnière f
hinge
chauffage m central
central heating
chaux f aérienne
lime, non-hydraulic

chaux f hydraulique
lime, hydraulic
chef m d'équipe
foreman
cheville f
wallplug
chevron m
rafter
chute f de comble ; pente f
pitch of roof
chute f en fonte
downpipe, cast iron
chute f; descente f
downpipe
ciment m colle
tile adhesive
citerne f
tank
clause f pénale
penalty clause
clé f à douille
box-spanner
clef f; clé f
spanner
cloison f
partition
clôture f de bornage
boundary fence
colombage m
half-timbered
comble m
roof space
comble m mansardé; toit m à la mansarde
mansard roof
commune f
district
compte-rendu m
progress report
conduit m
cable duct
conduit m de cheminée
flue
conduit m en grés
earthenware drainpipe
constat m parasitaire
report on whether property is free of parasites (eg termites etc)
construction f
structure
contenance f
size (of land area)
corniche f
cornice
couche f d'air
air gap
couche f de finition
coat, skimming
couche f d'étanchéité;
couche f isolante imper-méable
course, damp-proof
coulis m
grout
crépi m
rough rendering

dallage m; pavage m
paving
dalle en béton armé f
reinforced slab floor (concrete)
dalle f
flagstone, flag, or concrete
décapage m
burning off (eg paint)
déclaration f d'achèvement des travaux
notification that permitted building work has been completed
décoffrage m
removal of formwork
décombres mpl
debris
délai m
delay
délai m (d'exécution)
deadline
délai m de durcissement
hardening interval
délai m de livraison
delivery date
délai m de réflexion
time for consideration
déroulement m des travaux
progress of building work
devis m
estimate
devis m préliminaire
outline specification
dormant m
casing (of door or window)
double vitrage m
double glazing
droit m de puisage
right to pump water (from the grounds)
ébauche f ; esquisse f
rough sketch
échafaudage m
scaffolding
élément m de cuisine
kitchen unit
élément m porteur
loadbearing element
emmarchement m
tread width (stairs)
enduit de façade m
rendering of facade
entrait m
tie-beam
étanchéité f
imperviousness
étayage m; étayement m
propping
étrésillon m à vis ; étrésil-lon m à verin
adjustable prop (Acrow type)
expos au sud/au nord/ l'est/ l'ouest
facing south/north/east/west
facture f
invoice

faîtière f ; tuile f faîtière
ridge tile
faux-plafond m
ceiling, false or suspended
fenêtre f à guillotine
sash window
fer m à joint plat
pointing tool, flat
ferme f
truss
ferme f ; armature f à toit
roof truss/trussing
ferraillage m
iron framework (for concrete reinforcement)
feuille f de scie
saw-blade
fibre f de verre
glass fibre
fibre f minérale
mineral fibre
fibrociment m
fibrocement
flexion f
sagging
fondation f;
soubassement m
base
gazon m anglais
smooth, well-kept lawn
gazonner v
turf (to)
géomètre m
surveyor
géomètre m du cadastre
building surveyor
grand collecteur m; égout m collecteur
main drain (sewage)
gravillons mpl
chippings
grès m
sandstone
gros oeuvre f
foundations and walls
hors d'équerre
out of square
hourder v
render, rough (to)
ignifuge m
fire-proofing agent
isolation f acoustique ;
isolation f phonique
insulation, sound
isolation f contre l'humidité
damp-proofing
isolation thermique f
insulation, thermal
jardin m d'hiver
conservatory
joint de dilatation m; joint glissant
expansion joint
jointoiement m
pointing
jouissance f
tenure

jour m
stair cavity, stair well
laine f d'acier
steel wool
laine f minérale de roche
rock wool
lambris d'appui m
dado (wall)
lambrissage m ; boiserie f
panelling
lame f
blade
levé m de géomètre
survey report
lézarde f ; fente f ; fissure f
crack
lisse f ; garde-corps m
hand-rail
lit m de béton
bed of concrete
liteau m (d'étagère)
bracket (for shelf)
liteau m ;tasseau m
batten
maçonner v
brick (to)
madrier m de faîtage
ridge beam
main-d'oeuvre f
labour
maître m d'oeuvre
project manager
maître m d'ouvrage
owner (commissioning building work)
malfaçon f
fault (due to bad workmanship)
marteau m piqueur
pneumatic drill
mastiquer v
putty (to)
membrane f d'étanchéité
membrane, damp-proof
menuiserie f
carpentry, joinery
mètre m à ruban
measuring tape
mise hors d'air (la)
building stage with doors and windows
mise hors d'eau (la)
building stage with roof completed
modalités fpl de mise en oeuvre
details of implementation
modalités fpl de paiement
methods/terms of payment
moisissure f
mildew
mortier m
mortar
mortier m de liaison
mortar, bonding
mortier m normal
mortar, masonry

TEN TOP KISSING TIPS:
A TONGUE-IN-CHEEK GUIDE

If you really want to feel at home in France, you'll need to get to grips with the customs of how to greet your new friends in the proper French style. So here's a quick guide to how the French kiss. Stiff upper lips not required.

Hands off Don't grab them by the shoulders, unless you want to come across like somebody's great aunt. Keep your arms by your sides, but not in your pockets. Bend forward from the waist, chin up. Make eye contact.

English style Don't say 'Mwah!'

No suction The kiss itself is fairly low-key. The corner of your mouth, or sometimes just your cheek, will make contact with the other person's cheek, often silently. Planting a 'big smacker' on the side of someone's face with a great 'PTCHUH!' noise is not really on, and will only slow your kiss down too much (see 'Speed'). This is not about suction.

Tongues It's not about tongues, either.

Lots of speed Kiss-me-quick. The younger people are, the quicker they will expect to do the kiss, bobbing backwards and forwards from the neck, calling to mind the complex mating ritual of an exotic wading bird. With older people it is sometimes more like a clash of the dinosaurs in a 1950s B-movie.

What to say It is OK to speak while doing this: *Bonne Année* is perfect, but only around New Year, though.

How many Find out in advance how many kisses people give in that region. It is generally two, but it can go up to four or six! You can check this at the mairie.

Which side to start To be an advanced kisser, anticipate which cheek people are offering to be kissed first. Watch the tip, or 'prow' of their nose first, as this will give the first hint of which way they are turning. If you get it wrong, there will be an embarrassing nose clash, and you will have to start again.

The glasses clash If you wear glasses, and your friend does too, remove yours first to avoid a tangle of twisted metal. Best to keep wire cutters handy in case something goes wrong.

Don't forget the kids Kiss kids. If you don't kiss them, they might even offer to shake your hand, English-style.

---

moulure f
moulding
mur m **de retenue**
wall, retaining
noue f
valley (roof)
ouverture f **de chantier**
start of building work
panneau m **composite**
panel, composite insulation
panneau 'sandwich' m
panel, insulation, faced both sides
parement m **d'un mur**
face of wall
parpaing m
block, concrete, with air channels
parpaing m **aggloméré ; aggloméré** m
block, breeze
peinture f **crépie**
paint, masonry
pelleteuse f
excavator
percement m; **perçage** m
boring
permis m **de construire**
building permit
pignon m
gable
pilotage m; **pilotis** m
piling
piquet m
stake
pistolet m **à colle**
glue gun
pistolet m **pour mastic au silicone**
silicone sealant pistol
placage m
veneer
placoplâtre m **(marque commerciale)**
insulating plasterboard
plafond m **à caissons**
coffered ceiling
plafond m **en lambris**
boarded ceiling
plafond voûté m
vaulted/arched ceiling
planche f **voilée**
board, warped
plancher m **chauffant**
floor, heated
plaque f **de marbre**
marble slab
plaque f **d'égout**
manhole cover
platelage m **d'échafaud**
scaflod boards
plinthe f
skirting
poncer v
rub down (to)
ponceuse f
sander

porte f **à deux battants**
double door or gate
porte-fenêtre f
french window
porter v **à faux**
be out of plumb/true (to)
poser v **une vitre**
put in a window pane (to)
pourriture f **sèche**
dry rot
poutre en béton armé f
reinforced concrete beam
poutre f **apparente**
beam, exposed
préavis m
prior notice
prescriptions fpl
instructions
prise f **de courant (mâle/femelle)**
power point (plug/socket)
prolongation de temps f
extension of time
purgeur m
bleed-tap (of radiator)
quincaillerie f
ironmongery
raboteuse f
planing machine
raccordement aux égouts
connecting to the drains
raccordement m **au réseau**
connecting the telephone
rainurage m
chasing
rampe f **d'escalier**
banisters
rebouchage m
refilling (eg cracks)
rédiger v **un contrat**
to draw up a contract (to)
réduction f **de bruit**
noise reduction
refaire la surface v
resurface (to)
règlement m
settlement/payment (eg of an invoice)
remise f
postponement
remise en état
reconditioning
réseau m **primaire en boucle**
ring-main (elect)
revêtement m **de plomb**
lead flashing (roof)
revêtement m **de zinc**
zinc flashing (roof)
revêtement m **du sol**
floor covering
revêtement m **imperméable**
coating, waterproof
rigole f ; **tranchée** f **de fondation**
foundation trench

risque d'enfoncement m
risk of sinking (eg foundation)
robinet m **à flotteur**
ballcock
robinet m **d'arrêt**
stopcock
robinetterie f
taps and fittings
roche f **concassée**
crushed rock/stone
rondelle f
washer
solin m
space between joists
solive f **de plancher**
floor joist
solive f **en acier**
steel joist
souche f
chimney stack
sous-toiture f
covering of the underside of a roof
surface f **hors oeuvre nette**
basic area of the house
tassement m
settlement (eg of ground)
terrain constructible m
land on which one can build technically and legally
terrain m **viabilisé**
site with services laid on
terre f ; **sol** m
earth (elect)
tôle f **ondulée**
sheet, corrugated metal
tout-à-l'égout m
mains drainage
traitement m **antirouille**
rustproofing
travaux mpl de canalisation
pipework installation
truelle f
trowel
trumeau m
overmantel (fireplace)
tubage m
l metal flue liner
tuyau m **de trop-plein**
pipe, overflow
tuyauterie f **des eaux usées**
foul water piping/sewer
vermoulure f
woodworm holes
vice m **de construction**
construction fault or damage
vide sanitaire m
under-floor space
visite d'expert f
house survey
vitrerie f; **vitrage** m
glazing
volige f
roof board, roof sheathing

Index

Index

Index

Index

Useful Contacts

This is not a list of every publication and organisation that is active in this field. However, it does list those which we found during the course of compiling this book, and which you may find useful too. Apologies in advance to anyone we have forgotten.

BOOKS

There is a growing collection of books on the subject of buying and **renovating** in France. One of the earliest to get to grips with the subject of renovation (first published in 1992), and with more recent updates in paperback, is *Buying & Restoring Old Property in France*, by David Everett, published by Robert Hale Ltd.
For specialist information on the **buying process**, we recommend *The Sunday Times – Buying a Property in France*, By Mark Igoe and John Howell. It is published by Cadogan Guides. Also useful is *Buying a Home in France*, by David Hampshire, and published by Survival Books.
For detailed information on **financial planning**, law and tax, the best source available currently is *The Blevins Franks Guide to Living in France*, by Bill Blevins and David Franks, and published by, you guessed it, BlevinsFranks.

There are also some excellent specialist **French-English-French dictionaries** available from Hadley Pager Information. We particularly like these:
Concise Dictionary of House Building Terms, by Alan Lindsey, which costs around £27. Also good, is the smaller *Glossary of House Purchase and Renovation Terms (French-English, English-French)*, which again is by Alan Lindsey.
You can order them from a bookshop, or from Hadley Pager Info at Fetcham Park House, Lower Road, Fetcham, Leatherhead, Surrey KT22 9HD. Tel: 01372 458550. Email: hpinfo@aol.com.

TECHNICAL GUIDE BOOK IN FRENCH

Armed with a good dictionary, and if you can handle reading a bit of French, we highly recommend Gedimat's annual guidebook with its great diagrams and step-by-step pictures.
Gedimat is a French building materials supplier.
The book is available from French newsagents, with the new version appearing each spring.

Gedimat: 2004-Le Guide: Des Fondations aux Finitions. Published by Gedex. (Available from newsagents from May 2004.)

FRENCH BUILDING RETAILERS' WEBSITES

Here are some website links for other major building materials suppliers in France – some of which have useful technical information. Again, it will be in French, but some of their data and pictures can be useful.
Big Mat (www.bigmat.be) Castorama (www.castorama.fr)
Gedimat (www.gedimat.fr) Jardiland (www.jardiland.fr)
Le Roy Merlin (www.leroymerlin.fr) Point P (www.pointp.fr)
M Bricolage (www.mr-bricolage.fr) Lapeyre (www.lapeyre.fr)

AN ALTERNATIVE APPROACH

A good approach is to find UK suppliers of building equipment, so that you can read up in depth about the technical properties of different kinds of say, insulated plasterboard. You will then find that similar materials are available in France, and you can refer to the technical details you have found in English.

INFORMATION IN ENGLISH

First you should visit our own website, **www.renovationfrance.net**, of which more on the next page.

However, another useful site is that of the **SPAB**, or the Society for the Protection of Ancient Buildings. There is a lot in common with the kind of buildings the SPAB talks about and the kind of buildings you will find in France. The SPAB publishes a range of technical leaflets. Their website: www.spab.org.uk

VOLUNTARY ORGANISATIONS IN FRANCE

VMF is Vieilles Maisons Françaises (www.vmf.org), which is aimed more at the bigger, historic buildings, and has an English language section on its site. Maisons Paysannes de France (www.maisons-paysannes.org) promotes the sensitive restoration of smaller, rural houses.

ELECTRICITY AND GAS

EDF, the electricity supplier, and GDF, which supplies gas, have good websites, but again most of the information is in French.
http://particuliers.edf.fr
www.gazdefrance.com/particuliers/index.htm

ELECTRICAL INSTALLATIONS

These sites are both in French, and are the quality standards and certification bodies you may need to contact:
www.promotelec.com and www.consuel.com (see page 179).

GENERAL BUILDING AND DIY SITES IN FRENCH

Some useful sites we have found, which are in French only:
www.batirenover.com
www.batitel.com
www.commeunpro.com (Comme un Pro – Like a pro!)
www.cyberbricoleur.com

Some useful contacts who have helped us with this book

SURVEYORS AND ARCHITECTS

Getting a property surveyed before you buy is a worthwhile investment, and we have been grateful to a team who have given this book the once-over too before we published. **Surveyors en France** is a group of four professional surveyors spread across France. You can visit their website www.surveyors-en-france.com or contact them individually:
James Latter (james.latter@wanadoo.fr)
Pierre Weingaertner (expert-surveyor@wanadoo.fr)
Andrew Burrows (burrowhutch@aol.com)
and Ian Morris (french-surveys@ianmorris.co.uk)
While not linked with the above group, British architect Oliver Cockell, based in Perpignan, also reviewed an early draft of this book, and added some useful corrections to our Basics section. Oliver can be contacted at oliverc@free.fr.
And the English ex-pat Tim Badgett, who managed the project on pp164-5 in Gascony, can be reached at tim.badgett@wanadoo.fr.

To find **French architects** working in France, you could try www.cyberarchi.com, or www.architecteurs.com.
To find quality-certified **French builders**, you could try the organisation Qualibat, at www.qualibat.com.

RECLAIMED MATERIALS

BCA Matériaux Anciens, based 40km north of Angers, supplied us with a number of photos of some of their stock, which appear in Chapter 4. They can be contacted at www.bcasa.com. www.salvoweb.com is a good international source.

BUYING PROPERTY: SOLICITORS AND NOTAIRES

Many of the UK-based solicitors active in this area also have very full accounts of the buying process – notably, Prettys Solicitors (www.prettys.co.uk). We are grateful to another firm, though, Blake Lapthorne Linnell (www.bllaw.co.uk), who fielded the head of their French team, Philippe Piédon-Lavaux to take a close look at our account of how to buy property. Philippe is possibly the only man in the UK who is both a solicitor and a qualified French notaire. He can be contacted on philippe.piedon@bllaw.co.uk.

ELECTRICITY

British electrician Craig Hutchinson took a look at our section on electrical installations. Craig has lived in France for nine years. He used to instruct French shop fitters on the electrical norms required in France, so knows his stuff. He can be contacted on craighutchinson@aol.com.

PLUMBING AND HEATING

Ray Fletton, another reader of earlier drafts, left the Royal Air Force and at the age of 49 went back to college to learn plumbing (with a bunch of teenagers as classmates) so that he would understand more about the subject when it came to renovating his house in France. Ray has since worked alongside French plumbers in Tarn, so understands the similarities and differences with the UK set-up. While not working as a plumber now (he runs a gîte) he is happy to discuss various pipe-related matters: He can be contacted on flettonav@aol.com.

GARDENS AND LANDSCAPING

We don't go into great detail about plants in this book, and give a brief overview of garden landscaping. Catherine Gamble, one of the people who sparked the idea for this book (and has renovated an old house near Nîmes) has since qualified in landscape gardening and has run garden projects in France. She recommends a couple of web resources: on terraces, there is www.pavingexpert.com. And the site of the Mediterranean Garden Society, www.mediterraneangardensociety.com is also good. Catherine can be contacted on cngdesign@homechoice.co.uk.

SWIMMING POOLS

We are grateful to Imogen Barneaud from CVP Piscines in La Destrousse, near Marseille in France, for reading through our pools chapter and helping us understand the latest safety laws. Imogen is English, and has lived in France for 25 years. She can be contacted on imogen.barneaud@cvp-piscines.com.

PROPERTY INSURANCE

Property insurance in France was another area where we needed some specialist help, especially with the complex business of insuring a semi-derelict property. Thanks to Marc-Henri Herrmann at Axa-Baud in Brittany for patiently talking it through with us – in English, too! M Herrmann can be contacted on agence.herrmann@axa.fr.

Websites, books and magazines from the publishers of How to Renovate a House in France

**TWO GREAT WEBSITES
FOR ANYONE BUYING AND RENOVATING IN FRANCE!**

www.PropertyFinderFrance.net

PropertyFinderFrance is designed for anyone thinking of buying a place in France. Working with more than 100 estate agents across all the most popular and beautiful regions of France, the site has well over 2,000 properties (including building plots) for sale on its listings, all of which are selected with UK or international buyers in mind. Prices start from as little as €20,000, making this the ideal place to start your search for that dream home in France. With so many properties on offer, you can manage your own selections with a favourites file, which you can return to each time you come back to the site. PropertyFinderFrance gives you direct links to the estate agents, so there are no middle-men involved, making your house-hunting as effective as possible.

www.RenovationFrance.net

A sister-site to PropertyFinder France, RenovationFrance is an online magazine for people renovating properties in France, and is the ideal place to share experiences and information. The 'Project Diaries' section gives you a chance to post pictures and updates about your own project on the site, while there is a growing collection of features on completed home renovations too. The site also has a range of advice and information on many different aspects of renovating in France, as well as a directory of products and services, including English-speaking builders, and a lively discussion forum.

WE ALSO HAVE A RANGE OF TITLES FOR THOSE PLANNING RENOVATION AND SELF-BUILD PROJECTS IN BRITAIN:

Homebuilding & Renovating magazine

Britain's best selling self-build and home renovation magazine is a must for anyone planning, just starting or in the middle of a self-build, renovation or conversion. Full of inspirational readers' homes, houseplan ideas, practical guides, expert advice and a complete Beginner's Guide section.

www.homebuilding.co.uk

Access vast amounts of self-build and home renovation information, including a huge directory of supplier contacts and hundreds of case history examples complete with pictures and costings. If you're new to self-build, start by taking a look at our Beginners Guide section.

www.plotfinder.net

Find your perfect plot of land with www.plotfinder.net. This site is a database which holds details on over 5,000 building plots and properties for renovation currently for sale in the UK.

The Homebuilder's Handbook (ISBN 0-9544669 1-8)

Featuring thousands of contact details, this is the ultimate sourcebook for anyone planning to renovate, convert, or build their own home. It contains great solutions to make your build happen faster and cheaper, and essential leads to choosing and buying materials.

Homebuilding & Renovating Shows

Whatever stage you are at in creating your perfect home, from planning to building, converting, extending or renovating; the Homebuilding and Renovating Show can provide you with the inspiration, solutions, products and services you need to help you achieve your dream.

Book of Great Value Self-Build Homes (ISBN 0-9544669-0-X)

A collection of 24 inspiring high quality, low budget self-built homes from £32,000 up to £150,000. They all show how it is possible for you to achieve a spacious family home in any style on a budget. How to maximise usable floorspace, and at the same time create a unique family home.

Book of Contemporary Homes (ISBN 0-9544669-2-6)

Nineteen unique contemporary style homes in full colour. An invaluable source of inspiration for anyone planning to build. Remarkable projects built from £60,000 to over £1m. If you dream of designing and building a contemporary style home, this book is for you.

**TO ORDER ANY OF OUR BOOKS,
CALL US ON: 01527 834406**

Photo Credits

Cover Pictures: Main image: 20, Serregio/Francedias.com; Inset pictures, left to right: J Nicolas/Francedias.com; Michael Dunne/www.elizabethwhiting.com; PJ Verger/MM-CM; Spine: Yves Robic;

3, Patrick Eoche; 4-5, (see first page of each chapter for credits); 6, David George/www.elizabethwhiting.com;

Chapter 1
8, Serregio/Francedias.com; 10, Patrick Eoche; 12, Philippe Saharoff; 13, (left) Ida Lyrthe/Francedias.com; 13, (right) F Lherpiniere/Francedias.com; 14-15, Anne See/Francedias.com; 15, John Ferro Sims; 16, JP Johannes/Francedias.com; 16-17, Ida Lyrthe/Francedias.com; 18, Vincent Gremillet /MM-CM; 19, PJ Verger/Sophie Maillot Juillet/Architect: Olivier Roy (address below) /MM-CM;

Chapter 2
20, Serregio/Francedias.com; 22, Chabanne/Francedias.com; 23, (all three) Architype/Bill Laws; 24, John Ferro Sims; 25, (bottom) Patrick Eoche; 25, (top) John Ferro Sims; 25, (three pictures in box) Yves Robic; 26, Michel Fernin /MM-CM; 27, Patrick Eoche; 27, (top) John Ferro Sims; 28, (both pictures) John Ferro Sims; 29, Yves Robic; 30, (top) Antoine Rozes; 30, (bottom) Yves Robic; 31, (top) Yves Robic; 32, (left) Talbot/Francedias.com; 32, (right) PJ Verger /MM-CM; 33, Yves Robic;

Chapter 3
35, J Nicolas/Francedias.com; 36, John Ferro Sims; 37, John Ferro Sims; 38, (both pictures) John Ferro Sims; 39, Philippe Saharoff; 40, John Ferro Sims; 40-41, John Ferro Sims; 43, Antoine Rozes; 44, Michael Dunne/www.elizabethwhiting.com; 45, (from the top): MJ Jarry & F Tripelon/Francedias.com; Philippe Saharoff; Gay Badgett;

Chapter 4
46, PJ Verger /MM-CM; 48-49, John Ferro Sims; 48, Yves Robic; 49, John Ferro Sims; 50, (all three) BCA Matériaux; 51, Gilles Lansard/Francedias.com; 52, (both) BCA Matériaux; 52-3, (main picture) PJ Verger /MM-CM; 54, (bottom) BCA Matériaux; 54-5, (main picture) PJ Verger /MM-CM; 56, (both) BCA Matériaux; 57, PJ Verger /MM-CM;

Chapter 5
59, Yves Robic; 60, (both) Yves Robic; 61, (top) Yves Robic; 61, (bottom) P Vaures; 62-63, (main picture) Yves Robic; 62, (left) BCA Matériaux; 63, (four pictures in box) Yves Robic; 64-65, (main pic-

ture) Boelle/Francedias.com; 65, Talbot/Francedias.com; 66, (top) Ida Lyrthe/Francedias.com; 66, (bottom) Serregio/Francedias.com; 66-67, Yves Robic; 68-69, (main picture) Serregio/Francedias.com; 69, (right) Yves Robic; 70, John Ferro Sims; 71, (three pictures in box) Patrick Eoche; 72-73, Boelle/Francedias.com; 73, John Ferro Sims;

Chapter 6
74, Yves Robic; 76-77, (all six) Yves Robic; 78-79, (all eight) Yves Robic; 80, (all four) Yves Robic; 81, Patrick Eoche; 82-83, (all six) Yves Robic; 84, (both pictures) Yves Robic; 85, (left) Patrick Eoche; 85, (bottom right) Philippe Saharoff; 85, (top right) Patrick Eoche; 86, Di Lewis/www.elizabethwhiting.com; 87, (top) Michael Dunne/www.elizabethwhiting.com; 87, (bottom) Yves Robic;

Chapter 7
88, David George/www.elizabethwhiting.com; 90, David George/www.elizabethwhiting.com; 91, Tommy Candler/www.elizabethwhiting.com; 92, (left) www.elizabethwhiting.com; 92, (main picture) www.elizabethwhiting.com; 94, (left) Marie O'Hara/www.elizabethwhiting.com; 94, (right) Yves Robic; 95, PJ Verger/Sophie Marty /MM-CM; 96-97, (main picture) Brian Harrison/www.elizabethwhiting.com; 97, (right) Di Lewis/www.elizabethwhiting.com; 99, (top right) John Ferro Sims; 99, (three pictures in box) Yves Robic;

Chapter 8
101, Yves Robic; 102, Philippe Saharoff; 104, (all four) Yves Robic; 104, (drawing) A Doutreligne /MM-CM; 105, (all four) Yves Robic; 105, (drawing) A Doutreligne /MM-CM; 106-107, Thersiquel/Francedias.com; 108, (top) John Ferro Sims; 108, (bottom) Architype/Bill Laws; 109, Patrick Eoche;

Chapter 9
111, Rodney Hyett/www.elizabethwhiting.com; 112, Jarry-Tripelon/Francedias.com; 113, Olivier/Francedias.com; 114-115, Ngo-Dinh-Phu/Francedias.com; 116, (both pictures) Yves Robic; 117, Pambour/Francedias.com;

Chapter 10
118, PJ Verger/Sophie Marty /MM-CM; 120, (left) Philippe Saharoff; 120-121, (main picture) www.elizabethwhiting.com; 122, PJ Verger/Le Thurel Gite (address below) /MM-CM; 123, Philippe Saharoff; 124-125, (main picture) Patrick Eoche; 125, Yves Robic; 126, Philippe Saharoff; 127, Philippe Saharoff;

Chapter 11

129, Philippe Saharoff; 130, (drawings) A Doutreligne /MM-CM; 130-31, PJ Verger/Sophie Marty /MM-CM; 133, Philippe Saharoff; 134, Patrick Eoche; 135, Yves Robic;

Chapter 12
137, Philippe Saharoff; 138-139, (main picture) Ida Lyrthe/Francedias.com; 139, David George/www.elizabethwhiting.com; 140, Michael Dunne/www.elizabethwhiting.com; 141, (drawings) A Doutreligne /MM-CM; 142-143, Michael Dunne/www.elizabethwhiting.com; 144-145, Yves Robic; 145, (right) www.elizabethwhiting.com; 146, (bottom) Philippe Saharoff; 146, (top) David George/www.elizabethwhiting.com; 147, Patrick Eoche;

Chapter 13
148, PJ Verger/Architect: Maurice Sauzet /MM-CM; 150, (left) Spike Powell/www.elizabethwhiting.com; 150-1, (main picture) PJ Verger/Sophie Marty/Architect: Axel Bretigniere (address below) /MM-CM; 152, (left) Yves Robic; 152, (pool, top right) PJ Verger/Sophie Marty/Architect: Rudy Ricciotti (address below) /MM-CM; 152, (pool, bottom) PJ Verger/Sophie Marty /MM-CM; 153, (pool, top) PJ Verger/Sophie Marty/Cabinet Marty Architecte (address below) /MM-CM; 153, (pool, bottom) PJ Verger/Architect: Christian Saulnier (address below) /MM-CM; 153, (drawings) A Doutreligne /MM-CM; 154-155, Patrick Eoche; 156-157, Patrick Eoche; 158-159, Patrick Eoche;

The Basics
160, Dumoulin/Pluriel/Francedias.com; 161, Serregio /Francedias.com; 163, (hand tools) C Soler /MM-CM; 166, David Ackers; 168, Architype/Bill Laws; 169, John Ferro Sims; 170, Architype/Bill Laws; 171, Architype/Bill Laws; 172, Architype /Bill Laws; 173, Architype/Bill Laws; 174, Architype/Bill Laws; 175, Anne See/Francedias.com; 177, Philippe Saharoff; 178, Paul Carslake; 179, Paul Carslake; 180, Yves Robic; 181, Yves Robic; 182, Patrick Eoche; 184, Philippe Saharoff; 185, Paul Carslake; 186, Yves Robic; 188, Architype/Bill Laws; 191, Yves Robic; 192, Yves Robic; 193, Dany Cartron; 194, Architype/Bill Laws; 197, John Ferro Sims; 198, Isabelle Carslake; 199, Dany Cartron; 200, Dany Cartron; 202, Ida Lyrthe/Francedias.com; 204, Architype/Bill Laws; 205, Paul Carslake; 207, Gilles Lansard /Francedias.com; 208, Yves Robic; 209, Christine Besson; 210, Patrick Eoche; 213, Architype/Bill Laws; 215, Illustrations: Ben Kirchner/Heart;

Back cover: (from the left) BCA Matériaux Anciens; Patrick Eoche; Yves Robic; Yves Robic.

Architects' credits for the following pictures:
Page 19: Olivier Roy, 6 Place du Mal Juin, 75017 Paris.
Page 152: Rudy Ricciotti, 'Tropismes', 83140 Bandol.
Page 153: Cabinet Marty architecte DPLG, 7 rue Laget, 83110 Sanary sur mer, tel: +33 (0)4 94 74 62 08.
Page 153: Christian Saulnier, 78110 Le Vesinet, tel +33 (0)1 30 15 13 88.
Page 150: Axel Bretigniere Architecte DPLG, 1 Traverse Lami, 83110 Sanary sur mer.
Additional credits:
Page 122: 'Le Thurel', Chambres, gîte et tables d'hôtes, 80120 Rue. Tel: +33 (0)3 22 25 04 44.

Note: MM/CM: These pictures courtesy of Maison Magazine/Coté Maison, Paris.

About the authors

 DAVID ACKERS graduated in 3D Design at Birmingham Polytechnic's School of Art & Design in 1979, before moving permanently to France four years later. Since then, as a certified *Architecte d'Interieur-Designer*, David has spent 20 years working with French, British and other international clients on residential projects across north western France. He is a fluent French speaker and regional president of the Union Nationale des Architectes d'Interieur-Designers. David lives in Barneville-Carteret, close to Cherbourg. Visit his website at www.dada-projects.com.

 JÉRÔME AUMONT is a French freelance journalist specialising in the practical side of building, renovating and DIY. Writing extensively for the major French magazines in this field over the last six years, Jérôme has built up an encyclopedic knowledge of the subject. He has practical experience too. Through his father's construction business, he learned the basics of building before starting his journalistic career, and is an expert DIY-er in his spare time. He lives in Caen, in Normandy.

 PAUL CARSLAKE is a journalist and editor with 15 years' experience in a range of fields including business, technology and motoring magazines. A fluent French speaker (who, like David Ackers, has a French wife), Paul has been closely following the British love affair with second-homes in France, and launched two new websites on this subject in 2003: www.propertyfinderfrance.net for house-hunters, and www.renovationfrance.net, an online magazine, advice site and forum for people renovating across the Channel.